LET MY PEOPLE LIVE

Urlo della difesa (Cry of Entreaty), 1979, by Jiménez Deredia, a native Costa Rican now living in Italy. Bronze, 34 cm. high, illustration courtesy of the artist.

"L E T | *Faith and*

M Y | *Struggle in*

P E O P L E | *Central*

L I V E | *America*

BY THE FELLOWS OF THE CALVIN CENTER FOR
CHRISTIAN SCHOLARSHIP, CALVIN COLLEGE

Gordon Spykman—Project Coordinator

Guillermo Cook • Michael Dodson
Lance Grahn • Sidney Rooy
John Stam

WILLIAM B. EERDMANS PUBLISHING COMPANY
GRAND RAPIDS, MICHIGAN

The cover art, *Cena Campesina* ("Peasant Meal"), is an oil-on-wood paint-ing done by Manuel García in 1978. García was born in Masaya, Nicaragua, in 1936, and still lives in his homeland today. He began to paint in 1959 under the direction of Rodrigo Peñalba. His works have been publicly exhibited in numerous countries outside Nicaragua, including the Federal Republic of Germany, Brazil, France, Italy, Cuba, and the Soviet Union. In 1983 García won the award for primitive painting in the National Competi-tion of the Plastic Arts in Managua, Nicaragua.

Copyright © 1988 by Wm. B. Eerdmans Publishing Co.
255 Jefferson Ave. S.E., Grand Rapids, Mich. 49503

Library of Congress Cataloging-in-Publication Data

Let my people live: faith and struggle in Central America /
Guillermo Cook . . . [et al.].
p.   cm.
Bibliography: p. 267
ISBN 0-8028-0373-3
1. Central America—Politics and government—1979–   . 2. Social conflict—
Central America—History—20th century.   3. Church and social problems—
Central America—History—20th century.   4. Church and social problems—
Reformed Church—History—20th century.   5. Reformed Church—Doctrines.
I. Cook, Guillermo.
F1439.5.L48   1988
277.28′082—dc19   88-11294
                                                          CIP

Contents

Acknowledgments

From beginning to end, without the generous cooperation of many people, our project would have been severely curtailed. Among those to whom we are deeply indebted for their valuable contributions, we take the liberty of mentioning the following: James Dekker and Richard Millett, who served as adjunct fellows; Laura O'Shaughnessy and Arie Van Eek, who accompanied us during segments of our Central American tour; the Latin American theologians Gustavo Gutiérrez, Pablo Richard, José Míguez Bonino, Jon Sobrino, and Emilio Núñez for their willingness to share their insights with us in personal interviews; Margarita Suarez, who coordinated our contacts in Washington, D.C.; the late Orlando Costas, who hosted our attendance at the Latin America Studies Association and Liberation Theology conferences in Boston; Rachel Smith, Mary Kalil, Jennifer Cosolo, Daniel Medina, Dick Junkin, Doris Stam, and Ines Fajardo for their helpfulness in working out the complex arrangements for our on-site research in Central America; Helen Bonzelaar for her expert services as art consultant for the book; Kirsten Dirksen (our student assistant) and Donna Quist and Esther Vander Tuig (Calvin College secretaries) for their work on the manuscripts. Also, to the numerous others who participated in our ongoing discussions and offered their input during our five-week mini-course, we express our sincere gratitude.

In the style of recent scholarship in Latin America, this book has been a joint effort extending beyond the members of the CCCS team. Before we sat down to finalize our chapters, we shared their general ideas with about one hundred North American Christians in two conferences, one at Calvin College and the other at the Institute for Christian Studies in Toronto. We are very grateful for the valuable contributions of those who served as respondents and all who attended these conferences. (For a resume of significant persons, places, offices, and agencies we contacted during our six- to eight-week study tour of Central America, we refer our readers to Appendix 2 at the back of the book.)

Finally, we acknowledge our indebtedness to the following institutions for granting leaves of absence to senior fellows on the CCCS team: Texas Christian University in the case of Michael Dodson, the Latin American Evangelical Center for Pastoral Studies in the case of Guillermo Cook and John Stam, and the Evangelical Institute for Advanced Theological Studies in the case of Sidney Rooy.

Personalia

Faculty Fellows

Guillermo Cook, 58, was born in Argentina to missionary parents; a lifelong resident of Latin America, he has worked in Guatemala and Honduras, and now resides in Costa Rica. He holds degrees from Bob Jones University (B.A., M.A.) and Fuller Theological Seminary (Ph.D.). A recognized expert on Latin American religious affairs, Cook is the author of numerous articles and books, including *The Expectation of the Poor* (Orbis Books, 1985). From 1982 to 1986 he was general director of CELEP (Latin American Evangelical Center for Pastoral Studies), which specializes in "grass-roots, nonformal theological education" through its thirty-three staff members in eight Latin American countries. He is now the director of CELEP's department of theological-pastoral training.

Michael Dodson, 43, is associate professor of political science at Texas Christian University. He holds degrees from the University of South Dakota (B.A.), the University of New Mexico (M.A.), and Indiana University (Ph.D.). A Danforth Associate (since 1977) and Fulbright Senior Lecturer (University of Nottingham, 1985), Dodson is noted for his analyses of religion and social change in Latin America. He has published extensively in both English and Spanish. Mr. Dodson served on the delegation of the Latin America Studies Association that observed the Nicaraguan elections in the fall of 1984.

Lance Grahn, 34, was recently appointed assistant professor of Latin American history at the University of Alabama at Birmingham. He earned degrees from Abilene Christian University (B.A.), Texas Tech University (M.A.), and Duke University (Ph.D.). Grahn has taught Latin American and Native American history at Radford University in Virginia. He has published in the fields of colonial Spanish-American economic and social history.

Sidney Rooy, 60, is professor of church history at the Instituto Superior Evangelico de Estudios Teologicos (ISEDET) in Buenos Aires, Argentina. He holds degrees from Calvin College (A.B.), Calvin Seminary (B.D.), Union Theological Seminary (S.T.M.), and the Free University of Amsterdam (Th.D.). He has been a pastor in the United States and the Netherlands and a missionary-teacher in Argentina (1965-1987). In his writing he has concentrated on Latin American church history, his English and Spanish publications including articles on that topic in Macmillan's 16-volume *Encyclopedia of Religion.*

Gordon Spykman, 61, is professor of religion and theology at Calvin College. He is a graduate of Calvin (A.B.), Calvin Seminary (Th.B.), and the Free University of Amsterdam (Th.D.). This is Spykman's second CCCS fellowship: he also served as coordinator for the study that produced *Society, State, and Schools* (Eerdmans, 1980). His work beyond academic circles includes service to the Reformed Ecumenical Synod (Theological Interchange, Church and Society, Human Rights), the World Evangelical Fellowship (Task Force on Roman Catholicism), and the Association for Public Justice in Washington, D.C.

John Stam, 58, is a professor at the National University of Costa Rica and the Baptist Theological Seminary of Managua, Nicaragua. His more than three decades of service in Central America includes extensive grass-roots theological education under the auspices of CELEP in the entire region. He has degrees from Wheaton College (B.A., M.A.), Fuller Theological Seminary (B.D.), and Basel University (D.Th.); he pursued postdoctoral studies in Tübingen, Germany. He has also served on faculties in Argentina, Bolivia, El Salvador, India, the Netherlands, and the United States.

Project Consultants

Xabier Gorostiaga (Managua, Nicaragua), a member of the Jesuit order, is a renowned Panamanian economist. He was economic advisor on the Panamanian negotiating team for the Torrijos-Carter Panama Canal treaties. From 1979 to 1981 he was director of the National Planning Institute of Nicaragua. He is currently director of CRIES (Regional Center for Economic and Social Research) and a member of the Inter-American Dialogue Group that is coordinated by Sol Linowitz and Galo Plaza.

Edelberto Torres-Rivas (San José, Costa Rica), born in Guatemala, is one of Central America's most distinguished intellectuals. He has written numerous books and articles, almost all of them in Spanish, that have decisively shaped contemporary Central American sociological and historical thought. He was formerly general director of CSUCA (Higher Council of Central American Universities) and now directs FLACSO (U.N.-sponsored Latin American Faculty for Social Sciences). He is also co-director of ICADIS (Central American Institute of Social Research and Documentation, Guatemala).

Student Fellows

James H. De Borst, Jr., 21, is a senior Calvin honors student with a political science major and a Spanish minor. He spent an interim term in Central America and a study semester in Seville, Spain.

Piet Koene, 23, is a senior Calvin honors student majoring in history and international studies. He has traveled throughout Central America, completed a study semester in Spain, and given one year of service to the Christian Reformed Church of Honduras.

Timothy J. Steigenga, 22, is a senior Calvin honors student with a major in political science. He has completed a study semester in Spain, an independent study on Central America, and an interim term in Central America.

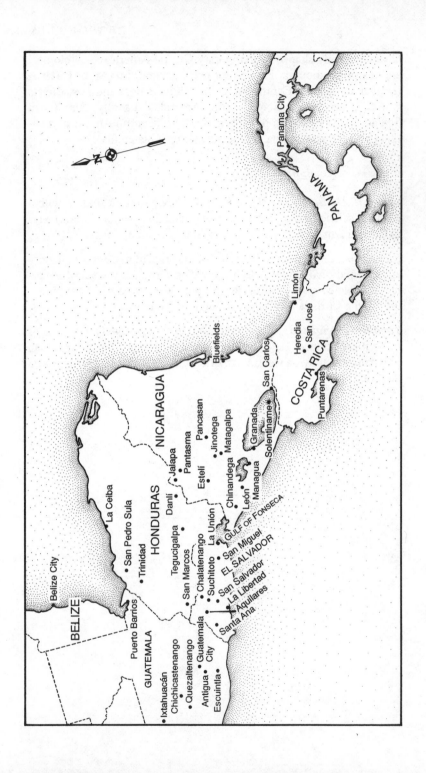

Preface

This book represents the end product of the joint research, reflection, and writing of a nine-member team that worked together during 1986-1987—a project carried out under the auspices of the Calvin Center for Christian Scholarship (CCCS). Through this text we hope to share with you the fruit of our year-long labors.

Our mandate was to elaborate "a Reformed approach to the crisis in Central America." As we developed this theme, our thinking was shaped by the guidelines of the CCCS constitution, which commit those involved in such projects (1) to engage in rigorous and creative scholarship that is articulately Christian, and in doing so, (2) to deal with fundamental issues of both practical and theoretical significance. Our ongoing research, conducted at the center as well as in the region under study, convinced us that our topic meets the latter criterion. We trust that our readers will conclude that this book also satisfies the former criterion.

Before proceeding, we wish to make clear our understanding of the terms of our research topic. Three key concepts call for definition.

First, we view "Central America" as embracing five countries: Guatemala, Honduras, El Salvador, Nicaragua, and Costa Rica. In our analysis we seek to respect the identity, integrity, and distinctive features of each of these countries in its own right. At the same time, we recognize that in many respects these five countries, taken together, share a common legacy that forms them into a regional unit. Members of our team also researched topics relating to the crisis that these five nations share with Panama and Belize, their neighbor countries.

Second, the concept "Reformed" calls for clarification. For purposes of this study, we understand "Reformed" not in an ecclesiastical sense (as referring to a cluster of churches) nor in a specifically confessional sense (as meaning adherence to a certain set of creeds that arose out of the Reformation era). These two ways of defining "Reformed" are certainly not wholly excluded, as our study makes clear. However, our basic working definition of "Reformed" points to a reformational, transformational, conversionist worldview. Accordingly, it stands for a cultural perspective that calls for the renewal of peoples and the reformation of society in keeping with biblical principles for our life together in God's world—a vision that Reformed Christians share with many Christians from other traditions.

Third, few knowledgeable people doubt that "the crisis in Central America" is real and urgent. But what is the nature of this crisis? What are its roots, its parameters, its manifestations? The preceding definition of "Reformed" already offers a clue to our understanding of its dimensions. The crisis touches life as a whole. The interdisciplinary composition of our team is a further indication of the scope of the crisis. It draws upon several branches of learning (history, political theory, theology, economics, sociology, missiology, hermeneutics), thus reflecting various aspects of reality. The crisis, then, as we understand it, encompasses the life relationships of Central American peoples in all their facets. Ultimately, as we have come to recognize, it is a crisis in which we all share—both North and Central American peoples.

How does one view the Central American crisis? It is a question of perspective. It has to do with basic presuppositions about our North American cultural identity, and how this affects our understanding and practice of the Christian faith as it relates to Central America. In this respect, perceptions are as different as looking down at a hazy panorama from the top of a mountain is from eking out a living at the base of the mountain. North Americans see the world from a position of power and privilege as opposed to actually living in a situation of poverty and powerlessness.

From the very start we asked ourselves, Which perspective should we choose? What should disciples of the One who descended from the mountaintop of heaven to the valley of our sinful humanity do? Insofar as it is possible for scholars who have grown up on the mountaintop of North American affluence to do so, this book attempts to see the Central American crisis "from below," "from the bottom up," from "the underside of history," from the "base" of the societal pyramid. We shall use these and similar shorthand terms to describe the reality faced every day by millions of impoverished and disenfranchised Central Americans.

For some of us, our brief but intense plunge into the reality of Central American life has been something like a second conversion. For those with longer experience in Central America, this study tour served to reaffirm earlier conversions. How can we communicate to our readers what this meant for us? Perhaps by using a parable we can help our readers understand the perspective from which we write.

It is as though a large number of people were huddled together under a large, food-laden table. They can smell the food, but all they see is the underside, the base of the table. All they receive are the few crumbs that fall beneath the table. Only a privileged few are seated around that table enjoying the fullness of nature's bounty. Some are totally unconscious of what is happening underneath the table. Others are dimly aware of it and occasionally pass down some crumbs to those below. But several banqueters know well enough who is under the table but are doing their best—and worst—to keep things as they are. They don't want anyone to spoil their meal.

Then a Person enters the room. He walks across to the table. But instead of taking his place in the seat of honor, he stoops down and gets under the table. He sits with the hopeless people down below and shows them his love and concern. With him as their Head, they begin to have hope. God loves them! He has something good in store for them! They join in small groups to sing, pray, and study his Word. In time they will be ready to come out from under the table, to join the privileged few in a common meal around the table.

There *is* sufficient food to go around. Perhaps not enough for everyone to gorge on, but certainly sufficient to satisfy the basic needs of everyone—if those who are abundantly blessed are only willing to share what they have. But if the banqueters resist, if they should resort to force to keep the others down, it might become necessary, as a last resort, for those who are under the table to turn it upside down—as Jesus upset the tables of the money-changers in the temple. Of his followers it is written, "These men who have turned the world upside down have come here also" (Acts 17:6)—actually, in the end, to turn things right side up.

To address the crisis in this comprehensive "from-the-bottom-up" sense is indeed an enormous undertaking. We make no pretense of providing an exhaustive treatment. We recognize that in recent years a veritable avalanche of literature has been unleashed by observers, journalists, commentators, and scholars of Latin American affairs, including those who keep a studious eye on the Central American countries. We cannot possibly duplicate their efforts, and we have no intention of trying to do so. We shall rather make grateful use of many of their labors. Accordingly, our aim is to assimilate our findings, gathered from a voluminous body of literature on Central America and experienced in a "hands on" way in Central America itself, and then to integrate and interpret them in keeping with the stated purpose of this project. Whatever modest though distinctive contribution this book can make to the cause of peace, justice, hope, and love in our broken world lies in its attempt to *move toward a reformational approach to the crisis in Central America.*

In pursuing this goal, we have tried very self-consciously to keep our target audience clearly in mind. To whom, then, is this book addressed? Not primarily to the peoples of Central America. Our neighbors to the South neither need nor seek yet another solution to their crisis imposed upon them from abroad. It is not our place to tell them how to set their house in order.

Our primary objective is rather to reach out to our fellow North Americans. We include among them, quite naturally, members of the Reformed Christian community who constitute most directly the supporting network for Calvin College and its Center for Christian Scholarship. But along with them we have in mind the larger Christian community and all others who share with us a deep concern for the life of our brothers and sisters in the South. Through this book we hope our North American churches will be led to a more profound sense of their full-orbed calling—in evangelism, social concern, and political advocacy—in relation to the peoples of Central America. We also hope that our work will offer helpful insights for mission, relief, and social-service personnel active in their various Christian ministries throughout the region. Finally, through the influence of a Christian citizenry, we cherish the hope that this publication may serve to shape the foreign policies of North American governments in the direction of promoting a greater measure of peace, justice, democracy, and prosperity among the peoples of Central America.

As a means to these ends, we dedicate this book to the ideal—which is at the same time a gospel imperative—of fostering a better climate of understanding, dialogue, and interaction between the North and the South in solidarity with our fellow believers in that crucial region of the world.

January 1987

1. THE GOD OF LIFE OR THE IDOLS OF DEATH

Like every human being, the church must confront the most basic option for its faith: being for life or for death.

Oscar Romero

This single sentence captures in concentrated form the agonizing crisis of Central America: the struggle for life in the midst of death. Death holds the entire region in its relentless grip. Night and day, across the countryside and in the cities, it stalks its countless victims. This stark reality is not an entirely new turn of events. A majority of the peoples who inhabit these five small nations have endured a living death from colonial times to the present. All the while, a minority of wealthy and powerful elites has lived off the deadly exploitations inflicted upon the poor and powerless masses of peasants and laborers.

Death, it seems, reigns supreme, enforced by what the Bible calls "principalities and powers." For these people, wracked by forces from both home and abroad, the haunting prospect of death remains a many-sided reality. The grim reaper appears in many forms: the strong arm of police states, henchmen hired by the oligarchies, the crossfire of battle between insurgents and counterinsurgents, paramilitary units, and right-wing death squads. These fearful powers strike down their targeted victims with swift and sudden force and with irreversible finality.

But equally painful is the slow death that millions are forced to endure all their lives. The poor are beset by hunger, malnutrition, starvation, high infant mortality rates, low life expectancy, and the numbing routine of unemployment and underemployment. Even the traditional church offers little relief. Its often lifeless rituals create only a momentary haven for the masses, while withholding from them the life-renewing power of the gospel.

Death is an all-encompassing reality. It reduces people to nonpersons. All Latin America exists in "a situation of sin."[1]

THE WAY OF THE CROSS

Yet somehow, amazingly, resurrection light still breaks through in the midst of this Egyptian darkness. The struggle for new life lives on. This crisis of life and death was driven home to the CCCS team in the following encounter.

"What is my role here in El Salvador?" This question was posed by Juan, a social worker with an evangelical church whom we talked to in January 1987. We were seated on the littered porch of a thatch-roofed peasant hut located in a remote mountain village. With us were several members of a local Christian base community, one of numerous small neighboring groups of worshiping believers.

On the way to this gathering place, traveling by jeep along bumpy roads and on foot up a mountain trail, we were told about the plight of one of the community members. Three nights before, soldiers had dragged him from this very hut where we were meeting. His wife and friends had been unable to locate him since then.

Reflecting on our obligation in this situation, we were keenly aware of the grave risks to anyone who tried to follow through on the case. What could we do? Eventually our conversation turned to biblical reflection on the implications of this fearful event for that little grass-roots community.

"I am committed to the gospel," Juan continued. "I accepted Jesus Christ as my personal Lord and Savior during an evangelistic crusade. But what does this mean for me now in these circumstances? Is it enough," he asked, "for me to worship God in the comparative safety of a church building? Is that the best way I can serve Him? No matter what others may say or do—and it is not for us to judge their motives—I have decided to follow the way of the cross. In defense of my countrymen who suffer injustice, I have renounced my life."

EL SALVADOR AS A PARADIGM

This testimony to the readiness of Christians to die in the quest for new life, even in the face of the worst that the idols of death can do, is not an isolated episode. It is repeated almost daily in the bloody annals of recent Salvadoran history. Neighboring countries also recall their martyrs of faith. For now, however, let us allow El Salvador to serve as an index to the life-and-death crisis of the region as a whole.

Often described as the "Tom Thumb" of the Americas, El Salvador is the smallest of the five major Central American nations, about the size of Massachusetts. With over five million inhabitants, it constitutes the most densely populated country in the region—a concentration point in the life-and-death struggle. A Salvadoran pastor has, with wry and poignant humor, described El Salvador as a paradigm of a larger reality:

> Official language: Spanish, although officials speak English quite well.
>
> Government: counter-revolutionary junta made up of military men and Christian Democrats. They give the orders in El Salvador, but they get their instructions from Washington.
>
> Currency: the colon, even though the money that rules the roost is the good old American dollar.
>
> The laws are made by the rich to be followed by the poor. When the poor make the laws, the rich class will disappear.
>
> History: too much like the rest of Latin America. Enough said.[2]

As El Salvador is "like the rest of Latin America," so it is also very much like the rest of Central America—a mirror of the desperate conditions of the entire region.

ARCHBISHOP ROMERO: PASTORAL EXEMPLAR

Within the context of the troubled story of contemporary El Salvador, our focus falls on the pastoral role of Archbishop Oscar Romero (1917-1980). His life and death exemplify dramatically both the noblest aspirations and the bitterest sorrows of Salvadoran Christians. These bittersweet experiences in turn incarnate the mixed sentiments of millions of other people throughout Central America. The key to Romero's memorable place in recent Salvadoran history was his "conversion to the poor"—his turning his full attention to the plight of his impoverished people. This in turn impelled him to lead the way toward a "conversion of the church to the world"—a focusing of the church's ministries on the crying needs of his nation.

Deeply moved by his exposure to the desperate needs of his people, he cast his lot with growing abandon on the side of the disinherited masses and their network of newly emerging popular organizations. His vision of the biblical idea of the kingdom of God led him to commit his ministry to the needs of the people of the kingdom. He devoted the resources of his office to defending the flock under his pastoral care from the life-threatening reign of terror unleashed upon them by the powers of greed, status, and privilege. Through his weekly homilies, his regular radio broadcasts, his printed messages, his personal appearances in crisis situations—by seizing every available avenue of communication, and by exerting a kind of cumulative pressure, Romero mustered the full strength of his official and personal persuasive powers to bring healing to his bleeding world. He called for life in the midst of death and liberation in the face of oppression. What Romero stood for also captures very concretely the basic point that we plan to develop throughout this book—namely, the urgency of addressing the crisis situation in Central America "from below," from the perspective of the poor and powerless.[3]

Times That Tried Men's Souls

Romero rose through the ranks of the Salvadoran clergy, from parish priest to secretary of the Episcopal Conference, first of El Salvador and then of all Central America; he then moved on to two posts as auxiliary and diocesan bishop. In February 1977 the pope appointed him archbishop of San Salvador. The Vatican seems later to have had second thoughts about this choice.

Throughout Central America, and certainly in El Salvador, the late seventies were times that severely tested the spiritual stamina of even the most stalwart Christian leaders. The prophetic witness of Archbishop Romero, compressed into the brief span of three very intense years, must be understood within the context of that frightening situation. It was a time of widespread violence, bombings, and slaughter as well as carefully targeted arrests, torture, exile, and assassination. The oligarchy, security forces, and right-wing death squads were out to crush every popular movement that arose to challenge their long-established claim of control over the nation. An entire generation of peasant leaders, union organizers, reform-minded teachers, base community workers, and catechists was being swept away in a massive wave of reprisals. This ruthless repression of the late seventies was reminiscent of the Great Massacre of 1932, when up to 30,000 Indian peasants were systematically murdered. In nearly half a century, it seemed, nothing had changed. The structures of oppression were still firmly in place. The reactionary forces of organized injustice and institutionalized violence were descending again upon a defenseless populace.

There was, however, one new factor in this life-and-death equation. The church was coming under attack as never before. Traditionally, in El Salvador as in other Central American countries, the church had allied itself closely with conservative causes. It had tended to defend the long-standing status quo, acting in concert with the elites of society in a joint effort to maintain the stability of the old order, or to regain that stability if it was lost. But now the winds of change were blowing fresh life into the church. The newly discovered spirit of pastoral concern for the pressing problems of a deeply troubled world, enunciated by the fathers of the Second Vatican Council (1962-65), was reaching into the church of Central America. Even more significant were the revolutionary changes signaled by the Second Conference of Latin American Bishops held at Medellín, Colombia, in 1968.

Medellín marked a dramatic turning point in the life of the Latin church. Things would never be the same again. For there the fathers of the church vigorously affirmed the church's calling to foster movements of liberation by demonstrating its "preferential option for the poor." As a corollary, Medellín also denounced the "institutionalized violence" and "systemic injustice" so deeply ingrained in Latin American societies. These ground-breaking conciliar actions in the late sixties began to assume concrete shape in El Salvador during the seventies. Not only lay leaders in the church but many members of the clergy as well were beginning to embody the post–Vatican II, post-Medellín emphasis upon the "conversion of the church to the world" in their daily ministries.

Even modest moves in this direction, however, were viewed with alarm by the elites. A popular church, carving out a place for itself within the orbit of the hierarchical church of the past, posed a serious threat to the vested interests of the ruling class. In the eyes of the establishment, this renewal process in the life of the church meant breaking the ancient coalition. In violent reaction, the power brokers of Salvadoran society declared Romero, their former partner, a subversive leaven in society. The church now became a primary target for brutal reprisals. Priests, nuns, members of religious orders, catechists, lay workers, and Delegates of the Word (lay evangelizers) were singled out for retribution. These voices of the voiceless had to be muzzled. Tension ran high; the situation was ominous. The future of the church, it seemed, was hanging in the balance—and with it, the future of a better El Salvador.

At that precarious moment in Salvadoran history, Oscar Romero assumed the office of archbishop.

An Unlikely Candidate

Romero was not the common people's choice. He seemed an unlikely candidate to take up the cause of the grass-roots communities and the popular organizations. Little in his past offered any real promise of the momentous impact he was about to make as archbishop. He had won a reputation as an intelligent, reflective, deeply spiritual, morally strict bishop, but he was also known to be cautious and conciliatory on the crucial issues of the day. He seemed more inclined toward traditional conservative causes. All signs pointed toward his acting in alignment with the rich and powerful rather than in solidarity with the poor and powerless. The other candidate, Arturo Rivera y Damas, the current archbishop, was regarded as more progressive.

The oligarchy and its allies therefore greeted Romero's appointment with jubilant expressions of satisfaction. To them it was a great victory. He seemed a safe choice. They foresaw the possibility of bringing the church back to pre-Medellín and pre–Vatican II conditions. Understandably, however, the popular church was disheartened. The nightmarish tragedy of El Salvador seemed destined to continue unabated. In fact, as Romero was assuming office, oppression intensified and atrocities increased. The agencies of congregations and the buildings of churches pressing for constructive change were profaned and destroyed. But in time these very acts of violent reprisal became clear indications that a radical change was taking place in the office of the archbishop.[4]

In the Crucible of Conversion

Before long, Romero began turning the tables on the expectations of the elite landowners, the government, the security forces, even the papal nuncio and the U.S. foreign policy makers—the very parties that had urged his appointment. Simultaneously, as a pleasant surprise, he began to win the confidence of those among the clergy and the laity who cherished a vision of reformation. This shift began with his very simple, private, and unceremonious rite of inauguration, to which no government representative was invited. In this way Romero was already beginning to put critical distance between his ecclesiastical office and the powers of the ruling class. To offer silent yet unmistakably clear and conspicuous witness to the prophetic role he was about to play, Romero also absented himself from the presidential inauguration of General Carlos Humberto Romero (no relative), who had been fraudulently elected. These actions were a source of double irritation to the ruling powers. Their candidate for archbishop was showing signs of betraying their support. Now, to add insult to injury, he was even refusing to give his blessing to their political stratagems. He was in fact becoming their chief critic. When later, on 20 January 1979, General Romero stated during a news conference in Mexico City that "there is no persecution of the church in my country," Archbishop Romero exposed this blatant lie by denouncing the brutal invasion of parish grounds that had occurred during the early morning hours of that very day.[5] The attack had been triggered by the spiritual retreat being held there. The military had snuffed out the lives of Father Octavio Ortiz and four young people, and had arrested and imprisoned thirty-three others attending the retreat.

During Romero's early weeks in office, an often halting but profoundly moving conversion was steadily reshaping the direction of his life. It was an agonizing struggle. He meditated on the Scriptures. He wrestled in prayer. He reflected on the meaning of Vatican II and Medellín. He grieved over the shocking reports of brutality that poured into his office. But he was hesitant to pursue the promising initiatives of his predecessor, Archbishop Chavez. Often he found himself looking in from the outside upon the new prophetic role that was beckoning him onward.

Placido Erdozain, a reform-minded member of Romero's pastoral team, recalled later that "our relations with Bishop Romero were a bit prickly in the beginning."[6] Romero shied away from their meetings. He tended to avoid the more radical priests. He thought they were infected with dangerous ideas—misreading Scripture, departing from orthodoxy, politicizing the clergy, agitating the people, promoting liberation theology. He suspected them of being subversives, even communists. Preserving the peace and stability of the church was uppermost in his mind. Accordingly, he reasoned that the clergy should not get too involved in the revolutionary ferment of the day. The authorities, he believed, were not as bad as they seemed. In short, Romero preferred quiet diplomacy. Only later did it dawn upon him, to his deep regret, that he was being used by the elites to serve their own ends. At the time, however, he failed to realize that his passivity—or what at best could be called his moderately reformist attitude—was as much a political act as that of his more radical colleagues. It meant a tacit acceptance of an intolerable situation.

Throughout these weeks of soul-searching, Romero gradually learned to draw out more fully the conclusions implicit in the teachings of Vatican II and Medellín. But it was not easy for him to relinquish the relatively "cheap grace" of a sacerdotal church, with its clerical officialdom, and opt for the "costly discipleship" that awaited him. Finally, however, he was able to confide in his fellow pastors, to share their sorrow and indignation over mounting atrocities, and to participate in the hard decisions that had to be made. Most of all, however, Romero's eyes were opened to the plight of his people. He heard their cries for help. His resistance was broken. Conversion was running its full course. And with it came a new agenda. Romero took up the cause of the oppressed. He became the voice of the voiceless, the defender of the defenseless, the helper of the helpless. And so he won the hearts of his people. His fellow pastors, whom he had formerly suspected of radical politics, became his most trusted co-workers. But other priests and bishops actively resisted Romero's new vision for El Salvador. As a consequence, a sharp division arose within the ranks of the clergy.

In the end, few people disliked their archbishop. But those few who did were the powerful. Accordingly, for Romero the pathway of ongoing conversion and perseverance was besieged by persecution and bespattered with blood. The murder of his close colleague, Father Rutilio Grande, was a turning point.[7] It became clear that the opposition would stop at nothing. Then came the massacre of Fathers Navarro, Barrera, Ortiz, Palacios, Macías, and Reyes, together with countless other Christian advocates of liberation.[8] For Romero there was no turning back. His home became a haven for the desperate, his office a center for daily consultations, and innumerable grave sites the scene for his words of comfort. In the life-and-death struggles of his day he was always there as the sign of light in the midst of darkness, of hope in the midst of suffering.

This made Romero a marked man. He was willing to open up dialogue and engage in negotiations with the reigning coalition of political, military, and oligarchical powers, but only on the clear and firm condition of a demonstrated commitment to peaceful resolutions based on justice. His resolute stand was answered, however, with vicious smear campaigns against him and his office. He was labeled a "subversive," a "troublemaker," a "traitor." Perhaps most telling, he was charged with hatching a "communist conspiracy." Romero's opponents found the liberation movement he was leading too formidable to be ignored. In violent reaction the ruling classes consolidated their power in the national security state. It was in the name of this ideology of governmental supremacy that the memory of Archbishop Oscar Romero became inscribed in blood in the annals of contemporary history as "the martyr of El Salvador."

Murder during Mass

The Divine Providence Hospital in Salvador provided Romero's lodging and meals. He in turn provided its cancer patients with pastoral care. On Monday, 24 March 1980, while Romero was celebrating mass with the hospital nurses in their chapel, a shot rang out. Romero fell to the floor, mortally wounded by an assassin's bullet to the heart. The day before, he had preached a sermon entitled "The Church: Defender of Human Dignity." In a passionate appeal for life in the face of ever-haunting death, Romero had issued a climactic imperative:

> The church, defender of the rights of God, of God's law, of the dignity of the human being, of the person, cannot keep quiet before such abhorrent action. We want the government to take seriously the fact that its reforms are of no service if they continue to leave the people so bloodied. Why, in the name of God, and in the name of this suffering people whose cries rise up to the heavens every day in greater tumult, I implore them, I beg them, I order them in the name of God: Cease the repression![9]

For some time already, officials of both church and state—papal emissaries and U.S. diplomats—had been urging Romero to temper his stance. But Romero held firmly to his convictions: When the two wills clash, the Word of God must be obeyed rather than the will of men.

And so the die was cast. Those in power decided to get rid of Romero. This indomitable voice of the voiceless had to be silenced. And so the shot was fired.

Romero had certain premonitions that he would meet such an end. "I have frequently been threatened with death," he said, but added, "I do not believe in death but in resurrection." Then, in a very mystical vein, he went on to say, "If they manage to carry out their threats, I shall be offering my blood for the redemption and resurrection of El Salvador. . . . I will rise again in the people of El Salvador." Dubious words—but clearly, Romero anticipated his martyrdom. According to the Spanish-born theologian Jon Sobrino, who himself suffered many reprisals during his years as professor at the Catholic University in San Salvador, Romero looked upon his impending death as "the final service he could render to his church and to his country." In an interview he gave just two weeks before his final mass, Romero concluded with these parting words for his assassins: "I wish that they could realize that they are wasting their time. A bishop will die, but the church of God—the people—will never die."[10]

Among the church of the poor are many who cherish the memory of their beloved archbishop. One Salvadoran expressed it this way some seven years after Romero's death:

> Monsignor Romero brought hope. Through him God was bringing his message. People were sleeping, but he brought light to wake them up. He was a bridge between the Church and the people. He attracted people to the Church with 'furvor.' People like me! He was a voice for those who couldn't speak. He gave us permission to be ourselves. In El Salvador, the popular media tells you one thing—reality tells you something else. Archbishop Romero spoke of the reality we lived. The death squads, for example, he wanted to stop them. Archbishop Romero is today a reality in our hearts.[11]

THE LEGACY LIVES ON

The legacy of Romero, sustained by such shared memories, lives on in numerous publications.[12] Drawing upon these resources, we turn now to some of the fundamental themes from Romero's ministry as a way of addressing the crisis in Central America from the viewpoint of those who live on the underside of this tortured history.

Church of the Poor

In crisis-ridden Central America, the credibility of the church stands or falls with its commitment to the poor. As Romero put it, "In this world the poor are the key to understanding the Christian faith, the political dimension of it, and the church's action" (*Message,* p. 81). According to Jon Sobrino, Romero succeeded in "institutionalizing" the church's preferential option for the poor. This is a supreme test facing the churches in Central America—and facing the Christian communities of North America as well. Says Sobrino, "Not only should Christians as individuals make this option for the poor, but so should the church as such, placing at the disposal of the poor the resources that the church, as an institution, has at its disposal" (*Voice,* p. 31).

In siding with the poor, Romero was summoning the nation as well as the church to a radical and sweeping conversion, a conversion reminiscent of his own: "I am speaking of an incarnation that is preferential and partial: incarnation in the world of the poor. From that perspective the church will become a church for everybody. It will offer a service to the powerful, too, through the apostolate of conversion— but not the other way around, as has so often been the case in the past"

(*Voice*, p. 184). Sobrino explains that in embracing the poor, Romero was in that very act also reaching out to the rich. For "through his partiality for the poor, Romero could be impartial—and find God everywhere" (*Voice*, p. 28). He refused to make the gospel a victim of class conflict. He reached out above this conflict, appealing to a kingdom norm that holds for the states of wealth and poverty alike. Christ Jesus, he said, "will judge the consciences of political leaders and of the rich (and of the poor also), judging them from the eschatological and transcendent perspective of God's reign" (*Church*, p. 58). From this vantage point he issued a challenge: "[The poor] also have good news to proclaim to the rich: that they too may become poor in order to share the benefits of the Kingdom with the poor" (*Voice*, p. 186).

These are troubling words for those who revel in their riches and spiritualize the Bible's benedictions of the poor. Developing his ideas more fully, Romero argued that

> all of us, if we really want to know the meaning of conversion and of faith and of confidence in another, must become poor, or at least make the cause of the poor our own inner motivation. That is when one begins to experience faith and conversion: when one has the heart of the poor, when one knows that financial capital, political influence, and power are useless, and that without God we are nothing. To feel the need of God is faith and conversion. (*Church*, p. 61)

Such gospel proclamation is the task of the church. Therefore, Romero said, "it is not a mark of prestige for the church to be in good standing with the powerful." It is rather "to know that the church has a mission in the world to call all—even the rich—to repent and be saved as part of the world of the poor, who alone are the blessed" (*Message*, p. 89). This may sound offensive to some; nevertheless, instead of mincing his words, Romero held his ground. "When we speak of the church of the poor," he explained, "we are simply telling the rich also: Turn your eyes to this church and concern yourselves for the poor as for yourselves" (*Church*, p. 64). The crucial hermeneutical test is clear: the way we deal with the poor is an index to true Christian faith.

In thus siding with the millions of poor all around him, Romero appealed to the jubilee message of Jesus (Luke 4:18-19). "This preference of Jesus for the poor," Romero said, "stands out throughout the gospel. . . . This closeness of Jesus to those who were marginalized is a sign that He gives to confirm the content of what He preaches: the Kingdom of God is at hand" (*Voice*, p. 71). To console his poverty-stricken parishioners, Romero said, "You are better able to understand this than those who kneel in front of false idols and trust in them. You do not have these idols; you do not trust them because you have no money or power, but are the most helpless and poorest of all" (*Message*, p. 85). Understanding the life-and-death crisis of Central America from below is also the hermeneutical key to true prayer:

> The guarantee of one's petition is very easy to know: How do I treat the poor?—because that is where God is. The degree to which you approach them, and the love with which you approach them, or the scorn with which you approach them—that is how you approach God. What you do to them, you do to God. The way you look at them is the way you look at God. (*Church*, p. 35)

Romero offered courageous pastoral leadership to a sharply divided church in a badly broken nation. More than half of his Salvadoran bishops declined to walk in his footsteps. Yet it was his voice that won the hearts of the oppressed masses. He refused to disguise his identity. He was a Salvadoran among fellow Salvadorans, and his ministry was an unambiguous sign of solidarity with the plight of his nation—which he recognized as an index to the crisis that holds all of Central America in its grip.[13]

In siding with the poor, the church under Romero was suffering horrendous persecution. That was bad enough. But equally crucial is the question, Why? For, as Romero explained, "Not any and every priest has been persecuted, and not any and every institution has been attacked." At work in Salvadoran society was a vicious principle of selective atrocity: "That part of the church has been attacked and persecuted that placed itself on the side of the people and went to the people's defense. Here again we find the same key to understanding the persecution of the church: people's defense. Here again we find the same key to understanding the persecution of the church: the poor" (*Voice*, p. 182).

Since Romero's prophetic stance was not shared by all in the church, he was impelled to set forth in unmistakable terms the marks of a true church. In his words, "A church which sets itself up only to be well off, to have lots of money and comfort, but that forgets to protest injustices, would not be the true church of our divine Redeemer" (*Church*, p. 10). And again, "A church which does not unite itself to the poor in order to denounce from the place of the poor the injustices committed against them is not truly the church of Christ" (*Message*, p. 81). In thus defining the calling of the true church, Romero was setting himself on a collision course with a corrupt government and its armed allies. The conflict came to a head when the assassin's bullet found its mark.

Mortal Sin

Historically all of Latin America exists, to use an apt expression, in a "state of mortal sin." Central America is no exception. And perhaps no country embodies this very profound indictment more than El Salvador. But let us be clear: this highly charged theological phrase should not be taken as a subjective judgment, as though Salvadorans exceed all other sinners in their fall from "the state of grace." It is rather to be understood as an objective statement of reality: the outrageous evils long perpetrated against the Salvadoran population have imposed upon them this "state of mortal sin." This was Romero's burden. According to Sobrino, Romero saw sin as "an offense against God because it is an offense against his people. Sin is indeed something that causes death—that is why it is called mortal" (*Voice*, p. 24).

Is sin personal or structural? Romero rejected this either/or statement of the issue as a false dilemma. In an intimately interconnected way, sin is both. Both personal lives and societal structures therefore need conversion. Accordingly, Sobrino goes on to say that Romero "recognized that structures do not change merely out of a people's goodness of heart, but neither will hearts change simply because of better structures" (*Voice*, p. 49). Conversion calls for radical and comprehensive change. Citing Medellín, Romero held that "for our authentic liberation, all of us need a profound conversion" (*Voice*, p. 68).

Throughout Central America the awesome reality of sin requires no argumentation. It is the common people's daily food and drink. Its impact is ever with them, sleeping and waking. They live with it all their days, and then in the end they die by it too. Sin is "a fundamental datum of our Christian faith," said Romero. It "killed the son of God, and sin is what goes on killing the children of God" (*Voice*, p. 183). Thus there is no need to convince the peoples of Central America of the existential horrors of sin and evil. "In the light of the sins of El Salvador and her institutions," Romero says, the mission of the church is "to destroy sin and to forge the Kingdom of God in its stead" (*Message*, p. 12).

Romero believed that sin infects every dimension of life. It is a full-scale reality. He avoided the evangelical tendency to limit evil to personal sins as well as the liberal tendency to blame evil structures for sinful behavior. The root of all iniquity lies in the human heart. In his own words, "Personal sin is the root of great sins. . . . How easy it is to denounce structural injustice, institutionalized violence, social sin! All that is a reality, but where are the roots of that social sin? In the heart of every human being. . . . For that reason, salvation begins

13

with the human person, with human dignity, with freeing every person from sin" (*Message*, pp. 122-23). Romero did not minimize "the seriousness of individual sins," did not gloss over "the act of one who, in the depths of his or her will, denies or offends God." But to this he added that "the church today, more than before, stresses the seriousness of sin in its social consequences. The evil of interior sin crystallizes in the evil of exterior, historical situations" (*Voice*, p. 68).

Romero emphasized the structural dimension of sin because in it especially the conflict between death and life expresses itself with full force. "Certain structures are sinful," he said, "because they produce the fruits of sin, the death of Salvadorans—the rapid death caused by repression or the slow death of institutional oppression" (*Message*, p. 83).

The opposition often accused Romero of political preaching. He responded to such charges by affirming that his only aim was "conversion to God." But conversion—like salvation, evangelization, and liberation—is a concept that covers the whole of life. "If I point to political affairs," he could therefore argue, "it is often because of the corruption of political affairs, so that those whom God loves, even when they are mired in sin, may be converted too" (*Church*, p. 67). The call to conversion is a call to life in the midst of death and liberation in the face of bondage. "This is simply obedience to the command of Jesus to be light, salt, and ferment in society, incarnating itself more deeply in the people's own history, in its anguishes and in its hopes" (*Voice*, p. 174).

Neither "Left" nor "Right"

It was such obedient response to the gospel, as he understood it, that defined Romero's political position amid the ideological crosscurrents of his day. He was forced to face up to the widely held notion that all views of society fall into either the "leftist" or the "rightist" camp. He refused to be squeezed into this mold. The exploitations of colonial and modern capitalist policies were written deep on the faces of the poor. At the same time, one need not be a Marxist to stand where Romero stood. His legacy defies such easy categorization. In his weekly homilies he held out for a biblical alternative. "It's amusing," he noted once, ". . . this week I received accusations from both extremes—from the extreme right, that I am a Communist; from the extreme left, that I am joining the right. I am not with the right or with the left. I am trying to be faithful to the Word that the Lord bids me preach, to the message that cannot change, which tells both sides the good they do and the injustices they commit" (*Church*, p. 84).

Responding to his critics, Romero appealed consistently to the urgency of the gospel message that addresses the full range of historical reality. "If by the necessity of the moment I am throwing light on the politics of my motherland," he explained, "I do so only as a pastor, shedding the light of the gospel" (*Message*, p. 76). Romero sided with the integrity of the biblical message, which transcends the cruel choice between "rightist" and "leftist" ideologies. He refused to get stuck on the horns of this false dilemma. His position gained substance from the sharp critiques that he leveled against both capitalism and Marxism. Since postcolonial capitalism had left El Salvador with sinful social structures that breed death, Romero denounced "what in our country has become the idolatry of wealth, of absolute right, within the capitalist system, of private property, of political power in national security regimes, in the name of which personal security is itself institutionalized" (*Voice*, p. 183). In passing severe judgment on the sin of "the absolutizing of wealth," Romero was keenly aware of exposing himself to brutal retaliation. Yet he did not hesitate to expose "the great evil in El Salvador," which he identified as "wealth, private property, as an untouchable absolute. Woe to one who touches that high-tension wire! It burns" (*Church*, p. 96).

While thus distancing himself from the "rightist" power brokers who had long dominated Salvadoran society, Romero at the same time avoided a reactionary leap toward the more recently emergent "leftist" mentality. Exercising a preferential option for the poor in the Salvadoran situation does not mean embracing Marxism. Rather, "the Christian must work to exclude sin and establish God's reign. To struggle for this is not Communism" (*Church*, p. 4). He expanded on this gospel alternative, stating that "when we speak of the church of the poor, we are not using a Marxist dialectic, as though there were another church of the rich. What we are saying is that Christ, inspired by the Spirit of God, declared, 'The Lord has sent me to preach good news to the poor' (Luke 4:18)" (*Church*, p. 40).

Romero faced up squarely to those who seek to discredit the church by labeling it a leftist-leaning institution in view of its conversion to the world of the poor. This is yet "another way of accusing the church of infidelity," he said—namely, "to call it Marxist." He recognized that Marxism is "a complex phenomenon." Therefore, "it has to be studied from various points of view: economic, scientific, political, philosophical, and religious." What the church asserts, however, is that "insofar as Marxism is an atheistic ideology it is incompatible with the Christian faith. That conviction has never changed in the church's history. In that sense, the church cannot be Marxist" (*Voice*, p. 77).

Romero then went on to offer a counterpoint: "The real problem, however, arises from the fact that, alongside the traditional condemnation of Marxism, the church now lays down a condemnation of the capitalist system as well" (*Voice*, p. 77).

In reflecting on Romero's tenacious attempts to carve out a more distinctively Christian approach to the crisis of El Salvador—which is basically also the crisis of all of Central America—Jon Sobrino offers the following analysis:

> It would be a mistake to present Archbishop Romero as a man of the center, keeping himself equidistant from the left and the right. It would be a mistake because it would imply that he acted on the *negative* principle of avoiding extremes. In fact he acted out of *positive* principles, asking himself what would lead to deeper truth, greater justice, stronger possibilities for peace. . . . He wanted to avoid the trap that the very terminology "right," "left," and "center" offers, as if it were the job of an archbishop to choose the center *ex officio*. (*Voice*, p. 77)

According to Romero, therefore, capitalism and communism do not exhaust the viable options. A more authentically biblical view of society is possible. Romero was able to find support for this position in the declarations of the Medellín Conference. There the bishops declared that "both systems militate against the dignity of the human person":

> One takes for granted the primacy of capital, its power and its discriminatory utilization in the function of profit-making. The other, although it ideologically supports a kind of humanism, is more concerned with collective man, and in practice becomes a totalitarian concentration of state power. We must denounce the fact that Latin America sees itself caught between these two options and remains dependent on one or other of the centers of power which control its economy.[14]

But what would an alternative view of society look like? As a step in this direction, Medellín held that "intermediary structures—between the person and the state—should be freely organized, without unwarranted interference from authority or from dominant groups." Such "free functioning of intermediary structures" should include "the organization of peasants into effective intermediary structures, principally in the form of cooperatives."[15] More specifically still, the council encouraged the continued growth of what was then a fledgling movement, the formation of Christian base communities. "It is necessary," the council declared, "that small basic communities be developed in order to establish a balance with minority groups, which are the groups in power."[16] Reinforcing this point, the bishops decided "to encourage and favor the efforts of the people to create and develop their own grass-roots organizations for the redress and consolidation of their rights and the search for true justice."[17] Romero stood in this tradition.

Hope of Liberation

Across the pages of the Old and New Testaments, the biblical message of liberation has a clear and consistent Messianic focus. Therefore, among the people of God, today as well as in Bible times, this motif stands as a distinctively Christian mandate, hope, and goal. Accordingly, "we must not reject Christ," said Romero, "for He is the way and the goal of true liberation" (*Message*, p. 133). We must not "put our trust in earthly liberation movements. Yes, they are providential," Romero added, "but only if they do not forget that all the liberating force in the world comes from Christ" (*Church*, p. 87). There is nothing here of otherworldly escapism or societal quietism. At the same time Romero repudiated the pretended human autonomy that fuels many secularist movements for liberation. Sin and death are terrible realities. Only the power of Christ can subdue them. As Romero put it, "People are not fulfilled until they are able to free from sin those who are sinners, and from death those who are dead: this is what the great Liberator offers. Blessed are those who work for the political liberation of the world, keeping in mind the redemption wrought by Him who saves from sin and saves from death" (*Message*, p. 92).

In the struggle for liberation, Christians must not forget their identity. For "even though working for liberation along with those who hold other ideologies, Christians must cling to their original liberation" (*Church*, p. 2). Liberation means "total salvation." This means that "the liberation which Christ has bought is of the whole human being. The whole person must be saved, body and soul, individual and society. God's reign must be established now on earth" (*Church*, p. 56). This was the great expectation that sustained Romero's vision. Authentic Christian liberation is "from above": it is inaugurated by Christ the Liberator of the world. But this liberation insinuates itself into world history "from below": Christ enlists the poor as his agents of justice and peace.

In El Salvador as elsewhere, liberation remains a lively though trembling hope—hope for today or for tomorrow, hope for this generation, and if not, then for the next, or the next. Often, as the struggle goes on, hope gets reduced to hoping against hope. Yet, noted Romero, "we are a community of hope, and like the Israelites in Babylon, let us hope for the hour of liberation. It will come. It will come because 'God is faithful,' says St. Paul. This joy must be like a prayer. He who called you is faithful and will keep his promises" (*Church,* p. 45).

Romero was pressing the church to put into practice the principle of holistic evangelization in keeping with Scripture's all-encompassing view of kingdom living. In so doing, he was breaking with the ancient dualisms, so deeply entrenched in the life of the church, that drove wedges between allegedly sacred and secular parts of life. Romero endorsed the declaration by Medellín that "in the search for salvation we must avoid the dualism which separates temporal tasks from the work of sanctification."[18] Commenting on this shift toward a more unified worldview, Romero said, "Medellín put an end to the secular dualisms we had subscribed to, the dichotomy between the temporal and the eternal, between the secular and the religious, between the world and God, between history and the church."[19]

Life-and-Death Struggle

The single idea which best captures Romero's place in history is that of "prophetic ministry in time of crisis." At the heart of that crisis is the struggle for life in the midst of death. With that, we have now come full circle, back to the central theme of this opening chapter and of the chapters that follow.

This life-and-death struggle was Romero's reality and that of his people. Death was an everyday occurrence. "In El Salvador," said Romero, "we know beforehand the destiny of the poor: to disappear, to be captured, to be tortured, to reappear as corpses" (*Message,* p. 91). Nevertheless, death remains an alien intruder, for "death is the sign of sin, and sin produces it so directly among us: violence, murder, torture (which leaves so many dead), hacking with machetes, throwing into the sea—people discarded! All this is the reign of hell" (*Church,* p. 88).

In the face of this hellish reality, Romero appealed to the resurrection analogy in Paul's First Epistle to the Corinthians, which proclaims the hope of new life even in the pervasive presence of death. For "those who surrender in the service of the people through the love of Christ will live like the grain of wheat that dies" (*Message,* p. 163). Romero made these words his own, embodying this promise in his own life-and-death experience. He was convinced, says Jon Sobrino, that "he must not abandon his people, he must travel along with them, and, like a good shepherd, be ready to lay down his life for them" (*Voice,*

p. 33). This commitment was clearly expressed in Romero's prayerful pledge to his people: "I want to assure you—and I ask your prayers to be faithful to this promise—that I will not abandon my people, but that together with them I will run all the risks that my ministry demands" (*Church,* p. 100).

Romero left us with a profoundly crucial life-and-death decision, one that lays its claim upon us all. He spoke about it with the utmost force and clarity in an address he delivered at the University of Louvain in Belgium about one month before his assassination. Calling attention to the political dimension of the faith from the perspective of an option for the poor, Romero challenged his audience and us his readers with these words:

> We believe in Jesus who came to bring the fullness of life, and we believe in a living God who gives life to men and women and wants them truly to live. These radical truths of the faith become really true and truly radical when the church enters into the heart of the life and death of its people. Then there is put before the faith of the church, as it is put before the faith of every individual, the most fundamental choice: to be in favor of life or to be in favor of death. We see, with great clarity, that here neutrality is impossible. Either we serve the life of Salvadorans, or we are accomplices in their death. And here what is most fundamental about the faith is given expression in history: either we believe in a God of life, or we serve the idols of death. (*Voice,* p. 185)

THE BIBLE REVISITED

The life-and-death struggle going on in Central America raises this question: Is "the blood of the martyrs [still] the seed of the church"— its lifeblood? As one answer, consider the congregation of "Cristo Salvador," a parish located in Zacamil, a working-class neighborhood in San Salvador. Over the past several years—during Romero's time as archbishop and since then—this community has suffered staggering losses. Their original church building was destroyed by a blast of dynamite planted by the opposition. A rustic, makeshift, almost barn-like cinder-block structure now serves as their place of worship. Up front, behind the pulpit and communion table, in full view of the congregation, is a large mural, stretching nearly from the ceiling to the floor. On this tapestry are the faces of three of their beloved leaders. There is Father Octavio, gunned down and crushed by a military vehicle while conducting a retreat for young people. There is Sister Silvia, a founder of the grass-roots communities that form the backbone of the congregation, also murdered. And there is Father Rogelio, a founder of the congregation, so harassed by a cruel regime that he was forced to flee to the mountains and join the guerrillas.

But that's not all. This trio of faces also mirrors the congregation's shared memory of the more than six hundred fellow parishioners who have suffered a similar fate. They have witnessed over six hundred disappearances and assassinations within their ranks over the past decade. Along the way they also lost their strongest advocate, Archbishop Romero. If only we could write a happy ending to this tale of horrors. But no—only a week after our visit, yet another kidnapping took place.

Still, there they were, on this Sunday morning in January 1987, a vibrant congregation welcoming us into their fellowship for a celebration of the Word and sacrament. There was strong lay leadership in the liturgy, vigorous vocal participation by members of the congregation, and the robust singing of evangelical hymns centering on themes of Christian solidarity and liberation. The Scripture readings came from Isaiah, the Gospels, and the Epistles. The sermon by a guest priest focused on the doubts and fears that get in the way of Christian commitment. Prayers were offered for political prisoners in government jails and for a living faith to overcome the ever-present threat of death.

How are we to account for such resilient faith? What is the source of strength and perseverance in such battered communities, even when their pilgrimage leads them through "the valley of the shadow of death"? Only one answer will do: the life-sustaining power of the Word of God. For generations on end, the Bible had been for them a closed book, or no book at all. But Vatican II and Medellín in the sixties had introduced dramatic changes. For the first time, the Bible found its way into the hands of common people. Through the diligent labors of dedicated pastors and of laypeople serving as Delegates of the Word, the church of the poor discovered a new way of reading the Bible. They began learning how to interpret their reality in the light of the Scriptures, and to read the Scriptures in the light of their reality. Armed with such biblical reflection, courageous Christians in El Salvador and throughout Central America are managing to offset the ever-present threat of death by clinging tenaciously to the promises of life. By an active faith, newly discovered, they are being radicalized—driven back to the very roots of their faith—by the leaven of biblical revelation. A new three-step hermeneutic is taking over: *seeing* oppression for what it is, *judging* it by the light of the Word as read in the context of their times, and then *acting* upon the biblical guidelines for pastoral action. In the past, simple believers fatalistically resigned themselves to their plight; now they are being sensitized to the systemic injustice and institutionalized violence that bedevils their lives. Like believers in the sixteenth century, they are now emerging as "heralds of a new reformation."[20]

With Bible in hand, Christians in Central America, often at the price of their life's blood, are coming to recognize that their lot is not God's will. Scripture opens up new possibilities for them. Its crucial motifs such as justice, liberation, and peace, often overlooked, now speak to them in surprising ways. Let us review a few of these basic themes of life and death. In doing so, we shall follow the unfolding drama in the biblical story-line from creation, through the Fall, and on to the present reality of redemption, looking forward with hope to the final consummation of all things. This is the biblical setting for reflecting on our life together in God's world, for Christians in North America as well as for Christians in Central America.

SIGNPOSTS ALONG THE WAY

The Tree of Life (Gen. 1–2)

Seven times in the Genesis account of creation God pronounces his benediction upon the works of his hand: "And God saw that it was good." Daring to hope for a better life means starting where the Bible starts, with the blessings of a good creation. Human beings were given a place in the sun, with all its attendant rights and responsibilities. As the family of God, they were blessed with space to catch their breath and room to live out their lives fully and freely in God's world. Everything was in order, in its rightful place—shalom everywhere. Reality was friendly and meaningful. Life made perfect sense.

That is the picture that emerges from the Genesis story. It is told in vivid and concrete agrarian language, close to the daily experience of campesinos, the peasant farmers of Central America. Till the soil. Tend the garden. Give the earth tender, loving care. Reap the harvest of the land. Enjoy a Sabbath rest. Live under God and with each other in communal peace. And at the heart of it all was the Tree of Life (2:9), centrally located as an abiding symbol, a sacramental sign and seal of all that life was meant to be.

In the beginning the stakes were indeed high and the risks great. Yet rebellion did not have to happen. But it did, and with it came alienation, greed, and murder. The Tree of Life was eclipsed by sin and evil and death; it will reappear at last in the paradise regained (Rev. 2:7). Yet now, along the way, in the unfolding drama of sin and grace, the remembrance of that tree past and the anticipation of its full and final restoration stand as a sign of hope to people whose hopes have been so incessantly crushed. God does not create junk, and he does not junk what he created. The original good creation is a standing promise that things can and will be good again. Since evil is not built into creation, creation is redeemable. Liberation is possible—indeed, imperative. And given the joyous reality of Christmas and Easter, the outcome of history is no longer in doubt. The return of shalom is assured.

That is the sure hope of oppressed peoples, even as the awesome potentials of history still await their final consummation. The Tree of Life is neither a lost memory nor a mirage. It is firmly rooted in God's plan for all his people, who will one day sit down together, shading themselves beneath its outstretched branches. No more cruel dominance "from above" or abject dependence for those who live "from below." Why can we not begin to pluck some of the enticing fruit of the Tree of Life here and now? That is the passionate question of our brothers and sisters in Central America.

Choosing Life (Deut. 30:15-20)

At the time discussed in the closing chapters of Deuteronomy, the people of Israel had reached an either/or crossroads in their history. The Exodus had run its course. The forty years of wilderness wanderings were over. Before them lay the promised land. At that crucial juncture in their pilgrimage, Moses in his farewell address confronted his people with the most radical of all choices. At stake was the covenant: Israel had to decide between covenant-keeping and covenant-breaking, between blessings and cursings, between doing good and doing evil—in short, between life and death.

Then as now, choosing for obedience means "walking in God's ways" and "keeping his commandments." Its outcome, repeatedly affirmed, is "life to you" and "length of days" so that you may "dwell in the land." The way of disobedience, however, leads to death. The full weight of divine judgment rests heavily upon death-dealing covenant-breakers: "Cursed be he who removes his neighbor's landmark. . . . Cursed be he who perverts the justice due to the sojourner, the fatherless, and the widow. . . . Cursed be he who slays his neighbor in secret. . . . Cursed be he who takes a bribe to slay an innocent person" (27:17, 19, 24, 25). The call to life also resounds with a similar down-to-earth concreteness: it involves prosperity "in all the work of your hand, in the fruit of your body, and in the fruit of your cattle, and in the fruit of your ground" (30:9).

For Central American peasants and laborers, these lines from the "Second Law" of Moses bristle with meaning. As believers reflect on these injunctions in their grass-roots communities, they find themselves standing with Israel at the crossroads of decision. They too are enmeshed in a deeply spiritual and cultural situation of conflict. Are they to serve the God of life or those "other gods" (30:17), the idols of death, who practice the way of cursing instead of the way of blessing to which God calls all his people? And what about the landlessness so prevalent among the poor? Since "the earth is the Lord's," why should so few hold so much?

Should not a campesino too be able to sit under his own "vine and fig tree" and find gainful employment? How can the oppressed who live on the underside of history experience "length of days" for themselves and their children and "dwell in the land" of their inheritance?

For the church of the poor, these are not issues from some ancient century or from some faraway place with strange-sounding names. They are as close and real as where tomorrow's beans and rice and corn tortillas are coming from. In their animated conversations on these laws of Moses, these believers can say to one another, "The word is very near you; it is in your mouth and in your heart, so that you can do it" (30:14). But how can this Word of God become embodied in their conflictual situation?

The Perspective of the Prophets

The sound and fury that reverberated in the words of "my servants, the prophets," as Jahweh called them, still echo today. Their powerful messages speak as eloquently and forcefully to the harsh reality that is Central America today as they did to the oppressive conditions in ancient Israel. With passionate impatience, Israel's prophets summoned the nation to keep covenant with God and with its people: "Seek the Lord and live" (Amos 5:6); "Pour yourself out for the hungry" (Isa. 58:10). Our brothers and sisters in Central America identify easily with this mission of the prophets.

Looking around, the prophets were deeply troubled by what they saw. No sector of Israelite society escaped their probing critique. Their pronouncements of divine judgment read like an almost interminable laundry list of transgressions. The sufferings of the common people were crying aloud to high heaven for vengeance. The God-given basic human rights of the poor and powerless were being trampled underfoot by the rich and powerful. By blatant acts of aggression as well as by subtle manipulation, the wicked were defaming the image of God in their own lives and defacing it in the lives of others. All creation suffered under this intolerable burden. As attorneys before the bar of justice, prophets like Hosea arose to plead their case.

> Hear the word of the Lord, O people of Israel; for the Lord has a controversy with the inhabitants of the land. There is no faithfulness or kindness, and no knowledge of God in the land; there is swearing, lying, killing, stealing, and committing adultery; they break all bounds and murder follows murder. Therefore the land mourns, and all who dwell in it languish, and also the beasts of the field, and the birds of the air; and even the fish of the sea are taken away. (4:1-3)

The prophets openly challenged the power brokers of their day—despotic rulers, corrupted priests, false prophets. With righteous indignation against the oppressors and with compassion for the oppressed, they defended the cause of the dispossessed and disenfranchised, the widows, orphans, sojourners, and refugees in the land. Since God, in the name of justice, takes the side of the poor, his servants, the prophets, could do no less. So they too sided with peasants robbed of their little farms, with day laborers defrauded of their just wages, with all the victims of a cruel caste system which disrupted that solidarity which was to be the mark of a redeemed peoplehood in Israel. Conversely, the prophets never tired of pointing an accusing finger at greedy land barons, unscrupulous merchants, heartless bureaucrats, and all other representatives of ill-gotten gain and those who supplanted right with might. Such a land fares poorly in every way; even the most formally correct acts of worship then lose their meaning (Amos 5:21-23). Given a different set of names and places and faces, these stinging indictments sound strikingly like a broken record playing itself out anew in the Central America we know today.

In an urgent appeal to turn the tide of iniquity, Isaiah called for a fast. But what, he asked with biting sarcasm, is true fasting (58:1-5)? It certainly means more than giving up a little food for a day. Fasting that carries heaven's endorsement involves social, economic, and political repentance, the prerequisites for authentic reformation. In the spirit of jubilee, Isaiah (61:1-3) put the trumpet to his lips to "proclaim liberty throughout the land to all its inhabitants" (Lev. 25:10): "Is not this the fast that I choose [says the Lord]: to loose the bonds of wickedness, to undo the thongs of the yoke, to let the oppressed go free, and to break every yoke? Is it not to share your bread with the hungry, and bring the homeless poor into your house. . . ?" (58:6-7).

A few years ago this moving passage was read at a gathering of

Christians in Central America. Someone, overhearing it, sounded an alarm. For these prophetic echoes from the past come across to those in high places as a frontal attack upon their privileged positions. The ruling powers retaliated. The pastor who led the service was arrested. His only crime was reading from Isaiah. But in the crisis situation of these countries, such words sound dangerously like the subversive language of a revolutionary.

There is weal mixed with woe in the message of Israel's prophets, but only by way of radical and sweeping conversion. The road to true reformation is clearly marked: "He has showed you, O man, what is good; and what does the Lord require of you but to do justice, and to love kindness, and to walk humbly with your God?" (Mic. 6:8). In his typically picturesque fashion, Amos lent added weight to Micah's imperative with these words: "Let justice roll down like waters, and righteousness like an ever-flowing stream" (5:24).

When all was said and done, the message of the prophets fell on deaf ears. So divine judgment descended anew upon Israel. For a second time Israel entered "the house of bondage." This time it was the Babylonian captivity. Eventually, however, God in his grace reopened the doors to new life. Israel experienced another exodus. Liberation a second time! The bottom line in God's way with Israel is this. New life depends on One who is greater than the prophets. Enter the Messiah. In the fullness of the times, Jesus gathered all these prophetic utterances together in his jubilee sermon and, focusing them on himself, declared, "Today this scripture has been fulfilled in your hearing" (Luke 4:21). His life and death and resurrection comprise the final and decisive ground upon which the struggle for new life rests among the peoples of Central America.

Abundant Life versus Cruel Death

In searching the Scriptures, believers in Central America find it easy to enter into the confrontational spirit of Jesus' running encounter with the Jewish leaders of his day (John 8:39-47; 10:7-18). For they too live in a situation of intense conflict. They respond intuitively to the radical antithesis posed by Jesus: the abundant life that he offers versus the stunted life that is their lot, the truth versus the lie, the sacrificial service of the Good Shepherd versus the reign of terror unleashed by the ancient murderer who is also the father of lies.

The church of the poor embraces readily the impact of Jesus' teachings from two thousand years ago and half a world away as though these realities were happening anew in their world of experience today. Instinctively they sense that Jesus' world is much like theirs. They too are like sheep without a shepherd. They too have suffered much at the hand of hirelings who abandon the pastoral care of the sheep. They too bear the enduring scars left by ravenous wolves who snatch their helpless victims and scatter the flock. They too need the disciplining comfort of the Good Shepherd's staff. For they too have been deceived and defrauded by an endless string of lies. The one whom Jesus calls "a murderer from the beginning" (John 8:44) is still among them, and his greedy and power-hungry agents do not cease to exact a heavy toll from the ranks of the poor and powerless. Like the flock under Jesus' care then and there, so his flock here and now has also suffered great loss at the hands of "thieves and robbers" who come only "to steal and kill and destroy" (John 10:8, 10). In the face of rampant death, they embrace, eagerly and often desperately, his standing offer: "I came that they may have life, and have it abundantly" (10:10).

It is precisely this hope which sustains believers in the fellowship of their base communities. For in Jesus' words they hear the call to life eternal, not only as an inheritance awaiting them hereafter but also as an earthly reality in which they too are entitled to participate today and tomorrow. For they claim the presence of Christ among them. And where he is, there is the promise of life in abundance. What remains to be done—and that is indeed a formidable challenge—is to break the grip of death and thus hasten the day when that promised life becomes reality.

Powers of Death

The life-and-death struggle of Central America is more than a "class conflict." That conflict is real, and its reality is already bad enough. But there is more to it than a historical encounter between the oppressors and the oppressed. The struggle has a deeper dimension. For there is in our world a strange host of spiritual forces restlessly at work in, under, with, through, and above the actors engaged in this dramatic struggle for life against death. Paul calls them "principalities and powers." Originally they were designed by their Maker to serve the well-being of human societies. In their fallenness, however, they betray their original right of and reason for existence.

Yet there is hope. For the entire sin-burdened creation is now groaning expectantly in the birth pangs of its eventual restoration (Rom. 8:22-23). Since the coming of Christ, the outcome is no longer in doubt. On Good Friday and Easter the decisive battle was fought and won. The war to ultimately end all warfare is over. This is Paul's good news. In Christ, God "disarmed the principalities and powers and made a public example of them, triumphing over them in him" (Col. 2:15; cf. 1 Cor. 15:24). For the time being, however, this triumph involves a "not yet so" as well as an "already so." The enemies are die-hards. Although fighting in a losing cause, they carry on a frantic rear-guard action. Instead of being agents of justice, peace, and freedom, the "rulers of this age" (1 Cor. 2:8) become instruments of injustice, oppression, and violence. Their ultimate concern is their own security. They act like gods, enforcing their idolatries, which are couched in false ideologies that defame God and demean people. They are not re-mote world-spirits but actual life-threatening, death-dealing magni-tudes, incarnate in ruthless militaries, land-grabbing oligarchies, dic-tatorial governments, corrupt judicial processes, greedy transnational corporations, foreign imperialists, pyramidical church structures, bloody insurgencies, and—sometimes—revolutionary movements. The cumulative impact of these demonic forces goes a long way in ac-counting for the crisis that is Central America.

In facing these formidable foes, the church of the poor takes to heart Paul's exhortation:

> Be strong in the Lord and in the strength of his might. Put on the whole armor of God, that you may be able to stand against the wiles of the devil. For we are not contending [only] against flesh and blood, but against the principalities, against the powers, against the world rulers of this present darkness, against the spiritual hosts of wicked-ness in the heavenly places. Therefore take the whole armor of God, that you may be able to withstand in the evil day, and having done all, to stand. (Eph. 6:10-12)

A New Humanity

The unprecedented surge of new life in Central America in recent years is centered largely in the grass-roots gatherings of Christians. There the churches of the poor—mostly Roman Catholic, some evangelical, others ecumenical—are discovering that the closer they get to Christ, the closer they get to each other. There a profound sense of solidarity as "the people of God" is taking shape in prayer, praise, and biblically illumined reflection on their common lot as people perennially con-signed to life on the underside of history. Now they are being "born anew to a living hope through the resurrection of Jesus Christ from the dead" (1 Pet. 1:3).

These widespread stirrings of new life clearly fit the biblical pic-ture of our corporate history as people of God living together in his world. The base communities are recapturing the original vision of God planting "the first Adam" as the root from which sprang the entire tree of humanity. But that primeval root withered and died, and with it the trunk and its branches. Thus the "old humanity" produced the evil fruits of alienation, oppression, and exploitation. But that is not the end of the story. "There shall come forth a shoot from the stump of Jesse" (Isa. 11:1; 11:10; 53:2). The promise that "the root of Jesse shall come" (Rom. 15:12) was fulfilled in "the last Adam." Christ Jesus is now the root from which a "new humanity" draws its life: "If, because of one man's trespass, death reigned through that one man, much more will those who receive the abundance of grace and the free gift of righteousness reign in life through the one man Jesus Christ" (Rom. 5:17). The Messiah arose from death to life so that his people might "walk in newness of life" (Rom. 6:4).

These are the long-standing promises that give birth to a new and living hope among beleaguered Christians scattered across the face of Central America. In their base communities they see themselves as part of a "new humanity." For "if any one is in Christ, he is a new creation; the old has passed away, behold, the new has come" (2 Cor. 5:17). As the many members who compose a single body, these communions of the saints are seeking to shake off the old way of death and lay hold upon a new way of life as a foretaste of "the new earth" under "new heavens."

A PREVIEW

This chapter opens the door to the rest of the book. Our intent is to introduce the major issues which shape the crisis in Central America from the viewpoint of that vast majority of its inhabitants who experience the crisis from below. To empathize with the aspirations of the majority over against the tyranny of the minority means to face up squarely to the life-and-death struggle that continues to dominate the contemporary history of these five small nations. That struggle touches every facet of their cultures. The coming chapters will focus in greater analytical depth on that multifaceted crisis which is Central America today—taking note along the way of how it bears upon us as North American Christian communities. Looking ahead, then, let us briefly preview the course of things to come.

Chapter 2: Profitable Death or Rich Life

Control of the land lies at the very heart of the crisis in Central America. No complete resolution to this crisis is possible without dealing more equitably with the distribution and use of land and with the societal relations that have emerged from the historic importance of land in Central America. For the rural peoples of Central America, both Indian and mestizo (the racially mixed sector of society), land is more than real estate, more than paper rights to private property, more than an economic commodity to be bought and sold. It represents a spiritual and cultural heritage handed down from generation to generation, much the same as land was treated in Bible times. It is the basis for the rich meaning of productive work, and it is the source of community identity and strength.

This indigenous legacy was undermined by the Spanish colonial regime that sought to alter land use and social patterns for the benefit of the empire. Such pressure on the rural poor of Central America has continued unabated to the present day. Thus the crisis in Central America has very deep roots in the historical development of the region.

The effects of such pressures on the land, labor, and community of rural workers and family farmers in Central America have been devastating, intensifying the life-and-death struggle in the area. The expansion of private property and its use to sustain the profits of international commercial enterprises have come at the expense of the communal concept of landholding and land use. The historic concentration of land for the development of single-crop export agriculture has robbed peasants of farmland they need to feed their families, to sustain their communities, and to nourish their own sense of identity. It has also fostered the abuse of peasant labor. Rather than supporting families and community, work became (and often still is) controlled by rich landowners who have seen it simply as a factor in the profit equation.

This long-standing, insidious crisis in land, labor, and community in Central America was captured by Archbishop Romero when he said,

> The terrible words spoken by the prophets of Israel continue to be verified among us. Among us too there are those who join house to house, and field to field, until they occupy the whole land, and are the only ones there. Amos and Isaiah are not just voices from the distant centuries; their writings are not merely texts that we reverently read in the liturgy. They are everyday realities. (*Voice*, p. 181)

Chapter 3: Development Strategies:
Success Consumed by Failure

The bottom line is poverty—stark, naked, dehumanizing poverty. Families with huts, but no houses; with tables, but no bread. Children with sickness, but no medicine. Without land to work, there is no corn for tortillas. Without jobs, what is there left to do?

To the North, they say, across the great sea, there is plenty of land and food and work and penicillin. Machines and factories make people wealthy. Bring them here, then, and we can have success too: bigger farms, bigger harvests, bigger markets, bigger projects for the future. That is what they promised.

So it happened—development projects. Tractors came, and the insecticide factory, and Coca-Cola, and a cotton mill. But for us, ordinary folk, things stayed monotonously the same. Oh yes, a handful of people got richer: they built large mansions, they bought new cars, they traveled. But for most of us, peasants and laborers, there was no real change: still only huts, empty tables, sickness. If anything, things got worse.

They talk about economic miracles, things we can only dream about, because they rarely come true. If you work hard enough, and save your pennies, and do not waste your money on drink and fast living, you can get ahead. At least that is what some people say. But there is no way around it: what you get, you pay for, even if it means borrowing. So debts pile up: personal debts, and so you mortgage your future; national debts, and so you sell your independence for a mess of paper pottage. And down the line, who will pay but our children's children?

Is there any hope? Does anyone care whether we eat or drink, and do all for the glory of God?

Over the past thirty-five years in Central America, everything has changed, yet ironically everything has stayed the same. Only the rich got richer. But the poor are poorer than before. Economic growth was badly distributed. It did not provide food or houses or healing for the vast majority of the people. What went wrong? What is missing?

Development aid that only increases dependency is not true development. True development comes not through more machines, more exports, more guns, larger bank accounts. It comes through access to land, job openings, the exercise of public justice, the healing of diseases, the elimination of poverty, the freedom to create and to choose and to live. These are the ingredients of an integrally holistic society. What steps can be taken toward meeting these real needs?

Chapter 4: "The Cubans Are Coming! . . . The Cubans Are Coming!"

In the modern history of Central America, crises come and crises go. Washington seems to view each successive crisis as a new emergency, as though it were blind to the historical continuities running through them all. Yet the responses of the U.S. government over the years have been strikingly similar: covert operations, subversion, and armed intervention. Such interventions are regularly justified in the name of maintaining hemispheric stability, establishing democracy, and safeguarding our national security. Repeatedly the enemy is identified as some "unfriendly external force" intruding upon the Americas. In the 1920s it was called "the Bolshevik threat." In the 1980s it is "the communist threat" moving out from the Soviet Union by way of Cuba into Nicaragua and on to El Salvador.

These interventions were long justified in the name of the Monroe Doctrine, updated through endless "corollaries," including the present-day Reagan doctrine. What has plagued all such interventions is their unilateral character. Our foreign policy has flown under the banner "America for the Americans!" But this slogan has only begged the real question: Is the security of the Americas to be genuinely shared among the nations of the Western Hemisphere, or is it to be defined and dictated by Washington? As Chapter 4 will show, this is one of the most important questions facing United States–Latin American relations today.

Back in the 1930s President Franklin Roosevelt declared an end to the days of "gunboat diplomacy" and committed the United States to being a good neighbor in Latin America. After World War II, the United States joined with the Latin American nations in setting up a regional security system through the Organization of American States (OAS), the charter of which emphatically rejects intervention by one American nation in the affairs of any other. National sovereignty, international agreements on noninterference, and the right of peoples to self-determination are therefore among the vital issues at stake in Central America today.

Chapter 5: Expanding War and the Search for Peace

At the very eye of the stormy crisis in Central America is the tragic reality of war, a war in which it is difficult to see how there can be any winners. On every hand there are only losers—especially among the poor and powerless. And all the while, these armed hostilities continue to exact their heavy toll in human lives and resources. A desperate struggle for life in the face of demonic forces of death goes on and on. Families are torn apart. Villages are ransacked. Cooperatives are destroyed. Foreign embassies are converted into fortresses. Military appropriations consume from 40 to 50 percent of national budgets, depriving even more people of the basic needs of life. Thousands are uprooted from their homes and lands. Displaced people move from place to place, and refugee camps spring up in country after country. Prolonged states of emergency deprive people of their fundamental freedoms. Human rights violations abound. All this and more are the immediate and obvious effects of the warring conditions that accentuate the crisis in Central America.

None of these countries is immune to this scourge of death and destruction. But Honduras is certainly among the most hapless victims of war. No matter which way it turns, there is no avenue of escape. It must contend with five armies: its own military, which controls the civilian government; the Sandinistas along its northern border; the Contras occupying its own soil; the bittersweet presence of U.S. military forces; and its own huge army of the unemployed. Meanwhile, in El Salvador the civil war between government forces and the insurgents drags on, with no end in sight. During a single year recently, 1,700 people were killed in combat. Over the past decade, 50,000 to 60,000 citizens were assassinated, including one archbishop, ten priests, and four religious women from North America. In addition, 4,000 to 5,000 people have disappeared, the refugee camps are overcrowded, and about 20 percent of the population has left the country.

Similar life-and-death struggles are going on in and around Nicaragua. The Sandinista government has more soldiers bearing arms than any other Central American nation. The Nicaraguan people are suffering greatly under the pressures of a two-front insurgency—Contra attacks from the south and the north as well as from within the country. Reports abound of Contra atrocities, together with reports of human rights violations by government agencies. The wartime economy is draining off the resources of the people. The newly adopted constitution remains largely suspended. Many sectors of the civilian population are regularly devastated by fearsome acts of aggression. Meanwhile, back in the United States the Contra hearings continue to disclose a sordid story of graft and deception, and the question of Contra aid divides the nation as no other issue since the Vietnam war.

Even Costa Rica, long regarded as an "exceptional case" among the nations of Central America, is steadily losing that honored status.

It is no longer a land without an army. It too is witnessing an ominous escalation in military presence, coupled with increasing dependence on foreign economic aid and a mounting national debt. Thus the entire region is being swept along on a tidal wave of growing militancy. Any hope for a peaceable resolution to the regional crisis must begin with demilitarization.

In this crisis situation there is an alternative to war. A peace process has been launched that grows out of the valiant efforts of Latin Americans to fulfill the hemispheric principles of nonintervention and peaceful resolution of conflicts. Chapter 5 offers a detailed look not only at seemingly endless wars but also at the promising peace initiatives in Central America.

Chapter 6: They Cry "Democracy! Democracy!" But There Is No Democracy

Democracy is like the weather: nearly everyone talks about it, but few do much about it.

For decades the U.S. government has been touting its lofty slogan about "making the world safe for democracy." Meanwhile, the long-suppressed yearning for it is at last welling up strongly among the poor and powerless masses of Central America. Now is the time to stop and ask, What does democracy stand for?

When different parties utter the same word, the meanings they lend it may be miles apart. So it is with the call for democracy. For Central American peasants it conjures up visions of exercising a right—as yet alien to them—to participate in the decision-making processes that shape their own destinies. U.S. foreign policy in these five small nations seems to define democracy very narrowly as a summons to go to the polls from time to time and to cast ballots heavily weighted toward the elites—a process to be monitored only in friendly countries. Is that all there is to democracy?

A Salvadoran bishop analyzed this problem for us. The elections of 1984, he explained, may have attained "the formal part of democracy" in his troubled country. For the first time in their history, Salvadorans really did not know in advance who would win. This was a step forward. But what does this mean, he wondered, for the common people who continue to go hungry or who may still be tortured or killed by faceless men? The simple equation of democracy with elections struck him as very one-dimensional. "It's as if the United States had a musical score in front of it marked 'democracy,'" he said. "Whenever you start playing the music the only note you ever strike is 'elections,' 'elections,' 'elections.'" This, he added, is what U.S. policy sounds like to Central Americans.

What the poor in Central America are asking for is the opportunity to add more notes to the score. Allow us to sing to the varied rhythms of our own music, they say. Taking up the challenge, grassroots Christian communities are beginning to compose new and stirring anthems of hope. Instead of harmony born of trust between rulers and their people, however, their songs of solidarity and liberation are answered by renewed cacophonies of brutality and death.

Chapter 7: When Jubilee and Kingdom Embrace

In this, our concluding chapter, we will seek—in light of our reformational heritage as rooted in the biblical message of jubilee and the coming kingdom—to build bridges of better understanding between the ongoing life-and-death struggle in Central America and the life of Christian communities in North America.

THE NEXT MOVE IS OURS

During our six- to eight-week study tour of Central America, we talked with hundreds of people from every walk of life. At the close of our conversations we would often ask, "What shall we tell our people at home?" Repeatedly the answer came back, "Just tell the truth!" This response was given especially by the poor and powerless, who experience the reality of their world from the bottom looking up.

"Just tell the truth!" That is a tall order. For in dealing with the crisis in Central America, the truth is not easy to come by. How are we to go about sorting out the truth from half-truths and lies, discerning right from wrong? The media bombard us day after day with sharply contrasting, utterly confusing versions of this story, with conflicting visions and widely divergent reports. What are we to make of this contradictory information, misinformation, disinformation? Who and what are we to believe?

This is a basic challenge that you, our readers, will have to face with us as we move through this book together. As believers in Christ, we cannot rightly weigh the question of truth apart from the sovereign claim of him who said, "I am the Truth!"

At its most fundamental level, the struggle the peoples of Central

America are going through is an agonizing quest for a new way of life in the midst of a seemingly endless reign of death. Which will it be: the God of life or the idols of death? Can you begin to sense with us that we too are profoundly involved in this life-and-death struggle? Whose lives are at stake? Theirs alone? Or ours too? Doesn't recognizing our convergent histories mean that in a profound sense we are co-actors in the unfolding of this crisis? Are we in the North prepared to re-examine our way of life in the hope of helping to make a more abundant life possible for our brothers and sisters in the South? Let us not forget that our ultimate accountability in these matters of life and death belongs to him who said, "I am the Life!"

Meeting in a mountain town in Guatemala in February 1987, members of the CCCS team held a lengthy conversation with two Indian leaders—one a pastor, the other a relief worker. Both are active in the six indigenous sectors of the Presbyterian Church. They opened their hearts to us. Is it possible for them as Christians, they asked, to honor their Indian identity and tribal customs within the structures and regulations of their national synod, a church planted by Western missionaries and reflecting a Western Christian tradition? They spoke of "religious colonialism." Furthermore, how are they to cope with the problems of political opposition, social discrimination, the brutalities of paramilitary death squads, and the guerrilla warfare in the region?

The troubles of their evangelical communities are compounded by their government's policy of "active neutrality." However commendable this policy, spiraling inflation is one of its aggravating side effects. Its costs are passed on to the poor. The price of aspirin, for example, has risen (in terms of American currency) from two for five cents to fifteen cents apiece. Guatemalans also feel the pressures of U.S. foreign policy: "We couldn't swing over to the Russian side, even if we wished to." They are becoming enmeshed in an alien cold-war squeeze play between the East and the West. In this oppressive situation, which way should they turn?

Our hosts have decided that the most promising route is to work for the reformation of life from the bottom up. This means committing themselves to holistic evangelization, an integral word-and-deed ministry. But those in power label such service to the poor as "communistic." These men are therefore viewed as "subversives." This is their crisis.

The pastor and relief worker ended our conversation on a surprising note, turning the tables on us. "Whose crisis is it? And where is it located?" they asked. "Only in Central America, or also in North

America?" That pointed question gave us reason for ongoing critical reflection as we went our way.

We share our reflections on Central America with you, our fellow North Americans, in the hope of building better bridges of understanding between these two regions in our common hemisphere. If this hope is to have any chance of becoming reality, we must learn jointly to become truth-seekers, pro-lifers in the full sense of the word, and peacemakers and peacekeepers. So, once more, the call to seek a peaceable kingdom rests upon us in the name of him who said, "I am the Way!"—the way to truth and life and peace. The next move is ours.

We are reminded of the ringing affirmation by Archbishop Romero: "What is most fundamental about the faith is given expression in history: either we believe in a God of life or we serve the idols of death" (*Voice*, p. 185).

2. PROFITABLE DEATH OR RICH LIFE

The Indian woman who sells me the tapestry
is toothless, but her art is colorful:
such juxtapositions are woven into Guatemala
where lines and lives blend in a travesty.

Early Morning, Guatemala by Frank Sawyer

LAND, LABOR, COMMUNITY

The life-and-death struggles of Central Americans take many forms. Some of them are unfamiliar to North Americans. Very few of us have probably heard of, let alone experienced, the murder of a local pastor for political reasons. Other struggles, however—especially those over land, labor, and community—have historical roots that strike a common chord. Traditional ties that bind Central Americans to the land are the wellspring of their culture, just as the social functions of land and working the land gave character for a long time to North American society. Generations of schoolchildren learned and believed the "agrarian myth," the notion that farmers embodied the North American ideals of thrift, hard work, productivity, and community spirit. In both North and Central America, the cultivation of grain has been associated with a spiritual attachment to land and agrarian protest. In both regions, farming has determined the possibilities and the limits of community relationships.

In the late nineteenth century, U.S. farmers felt a serious threat was posed to their properties, their work, and their way of life. They were sure that the federal government had failed them and that Washington politicians had weakened their democratic participation. Neither the Republicans nor the Democrats offered the farmers any hope, so they established their own political party. Its 1892 presidential platform expressed the worries of farmers in the United States. It also made the following charges now being echoed by Central American family farmers:

> We meet in the midst of a nation brought to the verge of moral, political, and material ruin. Corruption dominates the ballot box, the legislatures, the Congress, and touches even [judges on] the bench. The people are demoralized. . . . The newspapers are subsidized or muzzled; public opinion silenced; business prostrate, our homes covered with mortgages, labor impoverished, and the land concentrat[ed] in the hands of capitalists. The urban workingmen are denied the right of organization for self-protection; imported pauperized labor beats down their wages; a hireling standing army, unrecognized by our laws, is established to shoot them down. . . . The fruits of the toil of millions are boldly stolen to build up colossal fortunes, unprecedented in the history of the world, while their possessors despise the republic and endanger liberty. . . . [The United States] builds two great classes—paupers and millionaires.[1]

The eviction of Central American farmers from their land by death-dealing "principalities and powers" in the name of export agriculture is also a long-standing theme of their history. In exploring the current crisis in Central America, we begin, then, by looking first at the profound struggles over the control of labor, the utilization of land, and the dynamics of community life among the common people of the region.

Alfonso and Ricardo

An evangelical missionary tells the true story of two Guatemalan Indian farmers, Alfonso and Ricardo, both of whom became Protestant Christians. Their experience illustrates what is for poor Central American farmers a real life-and-death issue. The troubles faced by Alfonso and Ricardo were complicated by their ethnic identity. Like North America, Central America has not escaped deep-seated racial antipathy toward Native Americans. At the same time, the case of Alfonso and Ricardo points out a fundamental issue for all the poor and powerless of Central America whose access to land of their own is a key to self-expression, self-esteem, self-sufficiency, and hence to life itself.

In the mid-1960s, Alfonso and Ricardo and several hundred of their fellows were forced to move from one part of Guatemala to another. The owners of the land that they had worked to grow food for their families decided to replace corn with cattle and cotton, and to replace people with tractors. This action was designed to bring the landowners greater and easier profit. But it brought only hardship and heartache to the displaced farmers and their families.

These farmers and their families then moved to distant land that the government said was available to them. For fifteen years they cleared it bit by bit and just barely scraped by. It is reported that 85 percent of them were malnourished. So many children died young that parents often waited until a child's sixth birthday to select a name. As they said, "It's a lot easier to bury a nameless child."

Despite tough times, these poor farmers persisted. Then a Protestant missionary visited these families, and many were converted. What emerged was a new Christian congregation built on the already existing community. Christianity actually strengthened the community spirit of these people, enabling them together to fight more strongly for the life that the Bible proclaims as their right.

With a very small economic investment from mission agencies, these farmers were finally able to produce a small surplus of food. They also began to raise animals for sale. But that tiny success caught the attention of outsiders, who claimed to own the land that the farmers lived on. These men began to threaten the community's leaders and pastors in order to force the families to leave their homes. Now that the land was producing, the rich wanted it at any cost. For them it was just a faceless, nameless opportunity for more profit; for the farmers it was the wellspring of their communal and personal existence.

The farmers decided to appeal to their church leadership for help in keeping their land, their livelihood, and their very lives. The church supported the pleas of these poor brothers and sisters in Christ. It set up a committee to look into the matter. Soon it was discovered that these recent claims of outside ownership were completely false. The land that the farmers lived on belonged to the federal government of Guatemala, and this group of Christians had every legal right to be there.

Nevertheless, the farmers continued to be harassed. The committee members were made to suffer too, all because of their work to protect the farmers' rights to use the land properly. Alfonso and Ricardo disappeared. Almost certainly, they were made to disappear—abducted by security agents or soldiers. Without any indictment or even trumped-up charges, they were, in all probability, tortured and then murdered. Their only "crime" had been to take a leadership role in defense of land and life for the poor. Further threats and intimidation from the secret police and the army forced the church's committee members into hiding and eventually into exile. To stay would have meant torture and death. Although small on a cosmic level, this particular Christian effort to foster life based on land use challenged the wealthy landowners and their allied forces. Their response was to use the brute power of the government to squash that life.[2]

In this instance, the Christian community took a stand for life on behalf of a group of poor farmers and their families. In the face of severe opposition, the peasants' traditional ties to the land (farming) and their historic sense of community (group solidarity) were upheld as good structures for healthy living. These actions were in keeping with solid biblical principles, personified ultimately in Christ and exemplified in his mission. And as Christ lives on today in the hearts, minds, and conduct of his followers everywhere, so he lives on in the struggle of valiant bands of farmers in agricultural movements all over Central America. The right to life and the drive to live more abundantly are forces too potent to be eliminated.

Pro-Land Movements

Members of the CCCS team experienced the vibrant expression of such a pursuit of life when they visited the headquarters of the Pro-Land Peasant Movement *(Movimiento Campesino Pro-Tierra),* a Christian organization—based in Tiquisate, Guatemala—dedicated to purchasing land for poor farmers. Tiquisate is located on the Pacific plain in the heart of plantation country. As one would expect in an area that grows cotton and sugar cane, it was a hot, sweaty day when the team pulled up in front of a small clapboard Catholic church that provided rustic office space for the organization. It is the parish priest of this church, Father Andrés Girón, who started and now leads this push for land and life.

We met with Girón's right-hand man, whom we shall call Pedro. Eagerly Pedro explained in detail the goals and strategies of this farmers' movement. Like the work of Alfonso and Ricardo, this Pro-Land action is fighting for the livelihood and the lives of small family farmers. Many in the Tiquisate area were displaced when plantation owners shifted to the cultivation of sorghum and soybeans. Both of these crops need relatively little labor, requiring little more than a worker to drive a tractor. So the owners dismissed the workers and forced them to leave the small fields on which they grew food to eat. Girón felt compelled by his Christian faith and principles to respond to the needs of the displaced farmers. His answer, now known the world over, was to put together (in February 1986) a farmers' organization that would buy land for those who had none or who did not have enough to support their families.

As Pedro continued relating the history of the group, sweat beaded all the listeners' foreheads and soaked into their shirts. But the story of Christian faith and commitment was too compelling for any of his North American visitors to pay much attention to such inconsequential physical discomfort. Pedro explained that the Pro-Land Movement is centered on the purchase of land, the fount of life for farmers. But it also includes more. Land is to be purchased by *communities,* not individuals. In fact, Pedro noted, the strength of the movement lies in its sense of community, its spirit of togetherness. Like the political party that represented U.S. farmers in 1892, these Guatemalan farmers have joined to form a united and organized front for their common good. In their emphasis on communal action, they are responding to the greed that individual ownership of private property has fostered in and around Tiquisate and other plantation areas in Guatemala.

U.S. citizens place great emphasis on owning private property. Some claim that it, above all else, is what has made the United States a rich and powerful nation. But in Guatemala, as elsewhere in Central America, the poor farmers and their families—the majority of the population—have known only the dark side of private property. For hundreds of years they have seen it bring them only misery, poverty, and death. So they chose to work together, not singly as individuals.

The members of the CCCS team listened on. The biblical message of hope for the poor, the common people, the agrarian folk demanded their attention. God does not always work in air-conditioned buildings. So, with Pedro, we remembered that God-fearing people like those he worked with—farmers, fishermen, shepherds, and carpenters—figured prominently in the biblical drama too. Moved by such stories, those involved in today's Pro-Land Movement are making sure that it is well-planned. Not only does it finance the purchase of land; it also envisions building schools for the children, teaching crafts, developing markets for the sale of surplus crops, and organizing business enterprises to handle the financial affairs of the community.

All of these goals are striking a responsive chord among the Guatemalan people. The first Pro-Land meeting attracted 188 people; the movement has now grown to the point that it boasts offices in eighteen of the twenty-two provinces of the country. In April 1986 the Movement sponsored a peaceful five-day march by 16,000 people from Tiquisate to the capital city of Guatemala, an event that recalled the cross-country march on Washington, D.C., by the American Agricultural Movement in early 1979.

This call for land for the landless and life for the dying is grounded in a Christian commitment to economic and social justice, based on the biblical principles of feeding the hungry and giving drink to the thirsty. But the hunger and thirst experienced by the poor in Guatemala and throughout Central America is not limited to empty stomachs and dry throats. The poor living in the rural areas of the region long for something more. They hunger and thirst for self-expression, for creative and productive work, for respect for their agricultural traditions and their spiritual ties to the land, for reinvigoration of community togetherness. All these aspirations are wrapped up in their labor of tilling the land. They desire life in a fuller sense, not mere physical survival. Through organizations such as the Pro-Land Peasant Movement, they are striving to reach that goal. Although Father Girón and other peasant leaders have been threatened, some even murdered, they continue to work for the life abundant that the gospel message supports and that it calls us in North America to respect.

Past, Present, Future

These two episodes reflect several themes that have deep roots in the past and that are at the heart of the current crisis in Central America. We now focus on these key issues in examining the Central American past to better understand its present.

From the days of the Mayan Indians, who have thrived in Central America from ten centuries before the arrival of Christopher Columbus until the present day, tilling the soil has been a crucial source of life in the region. In earlier times, land was communally owned. Labor was a communal enterprise. Working the land not only provided food to eat; the fruits of the common people's labor also represented their expressions of self-worth and self-esteem. Working the land was essential to the very meaning of community—planning together, living together, caring for each other. All this reflects basic biblical principles. As Christians, we too accept the unifying social norm of working together as parts of a single body, none superior and none inferior, whether it be on the farm, in the factory, or in the school.

Historic Christianity brings with it an inherent sense of the relationship between the past, present, and future. "Christ has died, is risen, and will come again" is a historically rooted outlook on reality. Our understanding of Central America should reflect such a perspective. This will help us view events in this country from a Central American perspective, as opposed to an all-too-prevalent North American "top-down" view. One Latin American evangelical now living in North

America has described this view by noting that the United States knows its myths, but Central America knows its history. And, as an Indian Protestant from Guatemala told the team, "Our future lies in our past." If we ignore the past, our perceptions of the present and the future of Central America will be skewed. For the present is built on the reality of the past.

Thus it will be helpful to look at key aspects of Central America's past that have shaped all of its subsequent history—namely, the interrelated themes of land, labor, and community. We will trace them from 1524—the year that the Spanish conquest of Central America began in earnest—to about 1930, the era of the worldwide economic depression, which marked a watershed in Central American experience and the beginning of a new historical era. To do that, we will focus on Guatemala, which in this context is typical of all Central America. Home to the most highly developed, most enduring Indian cultures in Central America—the Mayas—Guatemala represents the fullest expression of the historic struggles between the elite and the poor over the right and proper understanding of land, labor, and community.

The Spanish colonialism of the sixteenth century has left an indelible imprint on Central America, just as early English colonialism has left its mark in the United States and French colonialism in Canada. The institutions, ideas, and goals that took hold in the first century of Spanish rule in Central America molded the entire period of Spanish domination and shaped life there well into the twentieth century. Central America has yet to overcome its colonial legacy, with its disturbance of social structures—of traditional patterns of life pertaining to land, labor, and community—and its resulting economic dependence on export agriculture. Even today there is hardly a break with the past of the Spanish domination in the way in which poor peasants and the working classes are treated by the wealthy and powerful elite. A look at what scholars call a "conquest society" is therefore essential if we are to understand the early contours of Central American life and the legacy that they have left for Central Americans today.

SPANISH CONQUEST AND COLONIZATION

The first European contact with the isthmus that we now call Central America occurred in 1502, when Christopher Columbus, during his fourth voyage to the New World, sighted an island off the coast of Honduras. Eleven years later, in 1513, Vasco Núñez de Balboa became the first Spaniard to view what he christened the Pacific Ocean. Not until

1524, however, did Spanish forces begin the actual military conquest of the Indian inhabitants of the region. This first band of Spanish conquerors was commanded by the capable but cruel Pedro de Alvarado, who led his men to victory despite fierce Indian resistance. By 1540 the Spanish were in control of virtually all of Central America.

The native peoples that Alvarado defeated in Guatemala, Honduras, and El Salvador were Mayan Indians. They may not be as well-known in North America as the Aztecs of Mexico or the Incas of Peru, but their achievements are magnificent nonetheless. They were the most powerful and most advanced Indians in Central America. Centuries before the Spanish arrived, they invented the mathematical concept and use of the zero. Without the advantage of telescopes or clocks they developed a calendar as accurate and precise as the one we use today. As many visitors to Cancun and Cozumel have observed, the Mayas designed and built large and beautiful pyramids, government buildings, temples, and athletic fields that rival any other ancient architecture. They also worked out an agricultural system that has yet to be matched in Central America in terms of sustenance. It demanded hard work by the Mayan farmers, but its efficiency and productivity insured that no one, not even the least of them, went hungry.

Other small, less highly developed Indian cultures were present in southern Nicaragua and Costa Rica. But because they were located in areas of relatively little importance to Spanish colonial authorities, had a more diffuse political structure than did Mayan groups, and were primarily oriented toward hunting and gathering, they did not have the lasting cultural impact on Central American life that the Mayas had. For this reason we focus on the Mayas in Guatemala, where they still comprise about 50 percent of the total population.

Among the Mayas, agriculture was important for reasons beyond simple food production. They cultivated cacao (the plant from which cocoa and chocolate are derived), which they not only consumed but also used as money. Even more important to the life of the Mayas was the corn they grew as their principal crop, their staff of life. They also valued it as a supreme religious symbol, since they considered the land itself sacred and believed that the ultimate owners of the land were the gods. They thought of themselves as stewards of a divine gift, not as owners of a piece of property. Quite naturally, then, agriculture was also the focus of many of their religious rites. The periods of planting, cultivating, and harvesting all had spiritual significance. All these acts of agricultural production—even the work itself—were seen as avenues of worship. The symbolism that Scripture employs when it speaks of seeds as a metaphor for life coming from death was equally important to the native inhabitants of Central America. Individual and community values—indeed, all of life—were centered on the process and results of agricultural labor.

This Native American concept of land use still characterizes the attitudes of small Central American farmers toward land, labor, and life, reflecting the enduring impact of Native American values on the culture of Central America. But then again, all people who work the land—whether they be the sons of Abraham, Native Americans, or Iowa farmers—have a similar respect for and appreciation of the land.

While it is true that indigenous culture continues to shape Central America, it is also true that the colonizing Spaniards tried to re-channel, if not eliminate, the Indian view of land, labor, and community. To the Spanish as well as the English, French, and Dutch of the same period, land and labor were potential sources of profit and power, and native community was a threat to such gain. Thus Spanish colonialism sought to restrict Indian life in order to enhance the accumulation of wealth. The Indians, of course, fought that deadly invasion with whatever weapons their recently overturned world supplied them with.

This tension between Indian and Spanish values implies that the military conquest of Central America was only the first step in the colonization process. As we will see in this chapter and throughout the book, the world of Central America has never been a monolithic, stagnant entity. It has evolved, and is still changing. This historical process is something we must not lose sight of.

Immediately on the heels of the military victories of Alvarado, Spanish colonists and policymakers faced the even greater challenge of organizing Central America into a rural colony. This involved working out the details of governing and exploiting the territory. To Spain's dubious credit as an imperial power, it proved very successful at this. While the English empire in North America lasted only 170 years, the Spanish empire in America lasted between three and four hundred years.

In Central America, as throughout Latin America, this process of colonization focused on the native inhabitants of the region. Central America had little gold and silver. Even Honduras, where most of the region's mining took place, was quite poor compared with Mexico, Peru, and Colombia, which had vast mines. Wealth had to come from something else: agricultural commodities, especially cacao and indigo (the plant source of blue dye). Like bullion from other regions, these products were shipped primarily to Spain. This was in keeping with the vision of all European colonialism in the 1500s and 1600s: colonies were to provide raw materials and sources of wealth while the mother country provided manufactured goods and enjoyed most of the wealth. This was the beginning of the long tradition of Central America's economic dependence on one or two export crops. In the colonial period these were cacao and indigo; in the modern era the principal export crop has been at various times coffee, bananas, or cotton. As Chapter 3 will demonstrate, the export products of Central America have varied over time, but Central America's place in the world economy as a mere supplier of raw materials has scarcely changed in more than four and a half centuries. And that has had a devastating impact on the common folk in the region.

None of this was possible, however, until the Spaniards got control of the means of agricultural production—that is, the land needed to grow these crops and the labor needed to harvest and transport them. The early Spanish conquerors were not about to do manual labor. Like the first settlers at Jamestown, Virginia, they thought they had a much higher calling and station in life. Nor did enough Spanish immigrants come to Central America to provide all the necessary work. But from the Spanish viewpoint, there was really no great need for a Spanish work force because of the sizeable Indian population. The natives would provide the labor that would make them rich. In a backhanded way, then, the Spaniards acknowledged that in Central America the Native American population—the mass of small, poor farmers—was the actual source of wealth derived from the colonization project.

Consequently, Spanish authorities made the goal of gathering and utilizing Native American labor a matter of high priority. Unlike their English counterparts, the Spaniards turned the natives—not lower-class immigrants or indentured servants or African slaves—into their main permanent work-force in colonial Central America. At the same time, they attacked the Indians on two other fronts. They took their land and transformed it into plantations and ranches. And they tried to break down the bonds of Indian community through a variety of methods, including resettlement (which facilitated the seizure of Indian land) and evangelization. What emerged out of the clash between these three focal points of Indian life—labor, land, and community—and Spanish colonialism was a complex of relationships that converged into an ongoing historical process. Labor control was at the heart of the Spanish enterprise, but it was followed closely by the control of land. Land and labor policies affected each other, and together they undercut the bonds of community. By the nineteenth and twentieth centuries, these colonial policies had broadened to include all the poor, both Indians and the descendants of Indian-Spanish marriages called mestizos. These forcibly imposed structures remained intact well into the 1900s. Wealthy white landowners used the rural poor and brought them death. In response, the poor looked desperately for ways to keep their traditional way of life alive.

COLONIAL LABOR POLICIES

During the colonial period (1520-1820), different systems of forced labor developed. Spanish colonists devised what were for them—not for the workers they exploited—increasingly more efficient and more profitable methods of putting Indians to work. None of these labor systems ever existed to the complete exclusion of the others, though generally one predominated at any given time. It is important for us to look at these different systems because they illustrate some of the changes that took place over time in colonial Central America. They also give us a clue about the present strength of the landed elite in Central America. The various means of acquiring labor services in this early era are also tied up with the changes in the use of land and in the structures of rural community life. From the very beginning, however, one thing remained constant: the Indians and the rural poor were always the ones who did most of the work on farms, plantations, ranches, and other places in the country. The different labor systems made little difference to them. Their status remained the same regardless of the dominant labor practices. Abuse is abuse, and exploitation is exploitation, no matter what its name.

Encomienda

The first labor system that Spain put to use in Central America in a large way was called *encomienda*. It made available Indian labor and tribute to benefit Spanish colonists and the imperial treasure, while at the same time theoretically insuring care and guidance for Indian workers and their families. It provided the elite with resources for profit and the poor with "civilization" and Christianization. This particular labor system thus reconciled both the economic and the spiritual mandates of Spanish colonialism.

This is how the *encomienda* worked. The king "commended" a specific group of Indians (a family, a hamlet, or a cluster of Indian villages) to a loyal Spanish officer or a royal official. The recipient of such a grant then received income from the tribute and the work of "his" Indians. By this arrangement he made his living. In return, the Spanish king expected two things of the colonist: he was to provide military service for the state in case of foreign invasion or Indian rebellion, and he was to nurture the Indians under his charge. That second duty—to care for the Indians—had two main components. The Spaniard was to see to it that the Indians were converted to Christianity, which would save their souls, and that they learn to act, dress, and talk like Europeans (to adapt to Spanish culture), which would make them "civilized."

The *encomienda* dominated colonial labor policy in Central America for only fifty years—from about 1525 to 1575—although it continued to exist in some places into the 1700s. Nevertheless, it set the tone for all future labor systems, making exploitation one of their basic characteristics. *Encomienda* epitomized the spirit of Spanish colonialism in the New World, and it shows us clearly what the Spaniards were about in Central America. Like all colonizing peoples, they sought wealth and prestige through conquest and control. At the same time, they had a certain degree of sincere concern for the vanquished Native Americans.

In colonial Central America the *encomienda* was tied directly to export crops, particularly cacao. Widely used by Indians prior to the arrival of the Spaniards, cacao soon became the major source of exportable wealth for the European newcomers. They demanded it in tribute and then shipped it to Mexico and Europe, where it was sold and distributed. Profits from the trade in cacao filled Spanish pockets, but the newly introduced European system of cultivation of the crop brutalized the Indian laborers. It required workers to leave their highland villages and families and travel to the hot and humid coastal areas where cacao was grown. The long journey by foot, the strenuous work, the distance from the communion of family and friends, the different climate, the lack of traditional foods and lack of sufficient food—all these factors debilitated the workers. One Spanish official described the cacao-growing areas in graphic life-and-death terms. They were, he said, a "general sepulcher for all those Indians who came to [them], for great numbers of them die[d]."[3]

Such mistreatment of the rural workers under the *encomienda* system was denounced by a few brave and articulate Catholic clergymen, such as Bartolomé de las Casas, the famous Dominican friar, and Antonio de Valdivieso, the first bishop of Nicaragua. They fought hard for the humane treatment of the Indians, both in Central America and at the royal court in Madrid, Spain. Their efforts bore fruit in official imperial policy when, in 1542, the king of Spain issued a series of decrees called the New Laws, which, among other things, sought to insure that the Indians would be better treated. The king did have more than one goal in establishing the laws, however. He wanted to end the abuse of Indian laborers, true—but he also wanted to assert his royal command over the Spanish American landholders, whose quick financial gain had already made them feel somewhat independent of kingly authority.

Unfortunately for the workers, for those at the bottom of society, the spirit of Las Casas's preaching and of the king's commands (at least some of them) did not translate into practice. Thus we see that the failure of land and labor reforms that has frustrated the rural poor of Central America in the twentieth century afflicted their ancestors in the 1500s and 1600s. The New Laws demonstrate that already by the mid-sixteenth century the foundation had been laid in Central America for the social, political, and economic dominance of the region by a small group of wealthy families, a dominance that still exists today.

Compulsory Labor Drafts

Always looking for new ways to maximize income and minimize labor costs, Central American rulers and landholders turned to forced labor drafts in the second half of the sixteenth century. Ideally, the system of compulsory labor drafts was to reflect work voluntarily done by Indians with "natural and Christian liberty." But from the workers' standpoint it was just another technique of abuse and death. The method of commandeering Indians for physical labor had changed, but the oppression of workers had not. The colonial government required a percentage of all able-bodied Indian men to present themselves, on a rotating basis, in a particular town for labor services. They were then supposed to be hired at a fair wage for moderate tasks such as public works or jobs done for private individuals on farms and ranches and in mines.

Like the *encomienda* before it, forced draft labor also abused all those whom it touched. The following sixteenth-century account accurately describes the experiences of most Central American laborers who sweated under this arrangement:

> The Indians from towns within a distance of ten leagues around [the] city had to come to the capital to be hired by Spanish employers. A common laborer received a wage of 12 ["cents"] a day. An Indian might spend two days in travel to the capital, and then might have to wait for three or four days for some Spaniard to hire him; during this time he must sell the clothes off his back to keep alive. After being hired he got his 12 ["cents"] a day, of which 10 or all had to go for food, and so he had served for nothing and had lost his clothing in the bargain.[4]

Debt Peonage

As with the *encomienda,* so with the compulsory draft system of labor: it failed to meet adequately the rulers and landholders' demand for steady, readily available, and inexpensive manpower. So around 1600 they turned to yet a third form of labor—debt peonage. Much as coal miners and railroad workers in the United States were once beholden to company stores, workers from rural areas in colonial Central America were now made dependent on the landowners through the manipulation of debts. In Guatemala, for example, peasants were advanced as much as six months' salary, which reduced a substantial sector of the Indian population to virtual serfdom.[5] This system worked so much better for the landed elite than the earlier systems that it became the dominant form for the recruitment, use, and control of labor in Central America for the next 350 years. It even survived the collapse of the Spanish empire in the 1820s.

THE RISE OF LARGE ESTATES

It was the use of labor that drove the secular arm of Spanish economic policy in Central America. But, as any farmer knows, labor without land to work is worthless. So, adding to the woes of the poor, the acquisition and exploitation of land became a second major focus of Spanish activity in the region. As soon as Spaniards moved into Indian territories, they began to appropriate Indian lands. The fact that Central America had few mines made control of the land even more important, because it meant that agricultural production would have to furnish the majority of exports from the region.

The Indian population found it difficult to stop Spanish seizure of their lands. They had been militarily defeated and so lacked the might to fight against the loss of their lands. Moreover, from the time of Columbus's landfall in 1502 into the early 1600s, the natives were literally dying by the thousands because they had no immunity to European diseases—such as measles and smallpox—that the Spaniards brought with them. Consequently, they also lacked the numbers and the social cohesion with which to launch a powerful defense of their lands. The Indians also fell prey to the Spanish legal system, which, like ours today, emphasized private ownership verifiable by a legal document. That practice was completely foreign to the Native Americans, as was almost everything Spanish. The Indians worked their lands as a group for the benefit of the group, not as individuals concerned with personal gain. Land was essential to their universe. It gave them life, and it lent meaning to their culture. Analogous to the Judeo-Christian tradition of the creation of Adam from dust was the Indian belief that humankind came forth from the ground. According to the Mayas of Guatemala, El Salvador, and Honduras, their people sprang from corn seeds planted in the soil of their native land. Further explanation is given in the *Popol Vuh,* the sacred book of the Quiché Mayas, written shortly after the Spanish conquest:

> And then grinding the yellow corn and the white corn, Xmucané made nine drinks, and from this food came the strength and the flesh, and with it they created the muscles and the strength of man. This the fore-fathers did, Tepeu and Gucumatz, as they were called.
> After that they began to talk about the creation and the making of our first mother and father; of yellow corn and of white corn they made their flesh; of corn-meal dough they made the arms and legs of man. Only dough of corn meal went into the flesh of our first fathers, the four men, who were created.[6]

To the Spaniards, however, land was principally a source of power, wealth, and prestige. The European conquerors had several forceful weapons at their disposal to insure that Indian land became Spanish land and that land used to grow corn became land used to grow products for international trade. In a very real sense the overriding colonial purpose behind land utilization stressed profitable death over rich life.

Because European colonialism in the sixteenth and seventeenth centuries stressed money-making, colonizers assessed agricultural efficiency in terms of large-scale and small-scale operations. Just as debt peonage was more efficient and more profitable than draft labor, so large-scale operations were more efficient and more profitable than small landholdings. That should surprise no one in North America, where mega-farms are becoming more and more common precisely because they too are more efficient and more profitable for the companies that manage them than are the smaller, family-operated farms. The result in Central America was the typical landholding unit—the large estate.

Often called a *hacienda,* it was much like a plantation in form and function. The Indians were not exactly slaves, though they must have felt that way as they worked in the sepulchers of the cacao and indigo harvests. The Spanish estate was designed to manipulate the Indians, to take away their wealth and to insure that their economic lives were controlled by the Spanish overlords. This was true throughout

Central America, whether in the highlands of Guatemala or on the plains of Nicaragua. To quote a well-known and highly respected North American scholar, the estate "needed and wanted more land, not to raise more crops, but to take the land from the Indians in order to force them to leave their holdings and to become dependent on the hacienda for land and work. . . . Like the slave plantation, [it] was a system designed to produce goods by marshalling human beings regardless of their qualities and involvements as persons."[7]

RE-MAKING A CULTURE

Land, labor, and community—all three were crucial aspects of colonial society in Central America. Taken together, they were inextricably linked to the cruel dynamics of the relationships between the rich and the poor, between the powerful in their fancy houses and the powerless in their shacks, on their small plots, and in the plantation fields. We have noted how Spanish labor systems produced profit for the Europeans but deadly change for peasants. We have also seen how land as the source of life for rural populations was converted into a source of profit for the white landowner. We now turn our attention to the impact of Spanish colonial institutions on the poor Indian farmers' sense of community. How did forced labor and the loss of land affect communal, cooperative living? What other forces attacked native community? How did Native Americans respond to these pressures?

"Civilizing" Native Peoples

Spanish colonialism, like the colonialism of other European powers of the day, sought to rationalize the permanent subjugation of native peoples, making them over into "civilized" beings worthy of living under the rule of Westerners. In the case of Central America, it turned the natives into "Indians." We have already used that descriptive noun several times. But we should pause now to reflect on its full implications. Today, "Indian" is a relatively acceptable term used to identify certain peoples both racially and ethnically. Native Americans themselves in North and Central America use it and use it proudly. But we should be aware that it was first applied to the native peoples of the Americas because Columbus thought that he was somewhere that he really wasn't. Then, from the 1500s onward, the word came to mean an enemy of civilization. You don't have to watch many "B" westerns to sense that connotation of the word. Thus the Spaniards' referring to the natives of Central America as "Indians" implied that they intended to break down the natives' sense of community development as well as abuse their labor and lands.

This made very good sense to the Spaniards because they truly believed that they were superior to the Indians, just as nineteenth-century politicians, businessmen, and soldiers in the United States believed they were superior to Cherokees, Hawaiians, Filipinos, and Cubans. The Spaniards, like our forefathers, felt the paternalistic "white man's burden." Indians were to be the students; Spaniards were to be the teachers. Or, as one famous sixteenth-century Spanish missionary put it, Indians were "sardines" while the Spaniards were "whales."[8]

The Spanish forced-labor systems illustrate well this colonial concept of emphasizing supposed European superiority in order to justify the attempts—in euphemistic terms—to raise the cultural level of the "little brown brother." For example, the *encomienda* and draft labor were rationalized as ways to teach Native Americans the value of hard work, while actually they "guaranteed [the Indians'] subjugation and exploitation and hence their position of inferiority" in Central American society.[9] Forced labor also struck directly at the leadership roles in native communities. The Spaniards' use of village chieftains to oversee tribute and labor payments undermined traditional lines of authority within Indian society. To insure their compliance with Spanish wishes, officials granted the chiefs privileges denied to Indians in general, such as personal exemption from labor services and the right to own land and ride horses. Thus the chieftain came to represent Spanish interests to the Indians rather than representing Indian concerns to the Spaniards. The migration required by forced-labor systems also meant that Indian lands—and, consequently, food production— were neglected by Indian families. That in turn made it easier for Spaniards to acquire the Indians' lands and to attack their sense of identity. The Spaniards could argue that the lands were now underutilized, which was a common European rationale for seizing land. Such seizure was made easier because the men of the families were often far away, working on the plantations, and therefore unable to defend their own properties.

In this way forced-labor practices undercut Indian community and culture. The spirit of life that the Indians felt in union with each other, the land, and the supernatural was undermined by such exploitative tactics.

Evangelizing the Indians

Another intentional frontal assault on rural communities fell to the church, especially its mendicant orders. The church's goals sound laudable: the eternal salvation of Indian souls and the improvement of Indian lifestyles along Western lines. But the church also felt obliged to transform the Indians' identity, tradition, and sense of worth—in sum, to destroy Indian community.

Early evangelization of the Central American Indians was somewhat successful as measured by Spanish imperial goals. Because the friars sought to change not only the Indians' belief systems and ritual expressions but the whole of their lives, including their very names, evangelization affected much more than just native religious rites.[10] The indigenous account of Spanish missionary activity given in the *Popol Vuh* highlights this impact. Its preamble makes the following declaration:

> This is the beginning of the old traditions of this place called Quiché. Here we shall write and we shall begin the old stories, the beginning and the origin of all that was done in the town of Quiché, by the tribes of the Quiché nation. . . .
>
> This we shall write now under the Law of God and Christianity; we shall bring it to light because now the *Popol Vuh*, as it is called, cannot be seen any more, in which was clearly seen the coming from the other side of the sea and the narration of our obscurity, and our life was clearly seen. The original book, written long ago, existed but its sight is [now] hidden to the searcher and to the thinker.[11]

The quick elimination of the Quiché Mayas' oral religious heritage implies a broad disruption of Indian lives and culture by Hispanic Christianity. Of course, Spanish missionaries intended to replace the lost indigenous traditions and customs with something positive. Proselytizing Native Americans was meant first to turn the natives into Christians, but it was also designed to "civilize" them, to teach them Western ways. The friars and their successors saw no conflict between Europeanization and Christianization. In fact, like most Europeans of the day, they presumed the two processes to be essentially the same. (Bartolomé de las Casas, the famous activist Dominican friar, recognized the difference between being Christian and being Spanish, but his was a minority viewpoint.[12]) Through Christianity the missionaries were to indoctrinate the Indians in the arts, skills, and concerns of Western civilization.

Like their Anglo-American counterparts, Spanish colonizers believed that hard work was part of the natives' civilizing process. The

Europeans perceived the Indians as indolent and free of capitalist worry, neither of which was an acceptable trait in a truly civilized society. Little did the newcomers appreciate that the Native Americans had developed effective systems of labor and agricultural production well-suited to their cultures and environments. Accordingly, the church sought to rescue the natives from what it considered to be their ignorant laziness. One missionary explained that the Christian religion should, and would, counteract the backwardness of the Indians:

> As long as legislation fails to discover the secret of inspiring desires and necessities among this indolent caste, it is good that ideas of religion oblige them to labor. . . . If confraternities [religious brotherhoods] and tributes did not exist, the Indians would not need anything; and consequently they would produce nothing, either for society or for the state. A banana grove maintains them with its fruits, and with its leaves it covers their dwelling. Twenty cotton seeds scattered in a field furnish their clothing; and living with disregard for any stimulus of comfort, decency, honor, luxury, etc., they would be happy to vegetate sadly, and in isolation, only for themselves.[13]

The Spaniards believed that when the natives were converted to Christianity, they would want to work in order to acquire things and to support the state. Thus Indian labor both served the economic interests of the empire and prepared the natives for life in Christian society.

Evangelization disrupted Native American traditions of land, labor, and community in other ways as well. Akin to the functioning of forced-labor systems was the way in which missionaries made their first goal the conversion and acculturation of village leaders. Thus Spanish missionary methods weakened traditional indigenous leadership as they attacked traditional indigenous religion. Because both secular and religious Spanish administrators used the chiefs or the leading figures in the Indian communities as their mediators with the people, the outward form of the native polity remained. But the chiefs now received and obeyed orders from their European superiors rather than ruling by internal consensus.

The missionary strategy of these early friars was also focused on the relocation of Indians into new, centralized mission villages. Several factors explain this plan. Mission villages reflect the sixteenth-century Spanish preference for urban life. Moreover, both religious and political leaders recognized that the concentration of a defeated and dispersed population made its rule and domination easier. And Spanish policymakers believed that the relocation of Native Americans facilitated the undermining of Indian community and so facilitated the learning of Christian doctrine and European customs. Such thinking has had a long history in the Americas. It reappeared almost point for point in the United States of the 1800s under the guise of the so-called Peace Policy for Native Americans. In 1873 Columbus Delano, the secretary of the interior, offered this explanation of it:

> [This policy] sought, first, to place the Indians upon reservations as rapidly as possible, where they could be provided for in such manner as the dictates of humanity and Christian civilization require. Being thus placed upon reservations, they will be removed from such contiguity to our frontier settlements as otherwise will lead, necessarily, to frequent outrages, wrongs, and disturbances of the public peace. On these reservations they can be taught, as fast as possible, the arts of agriculture, and such pursuits as are incident to civilization, through the aid of the Christian organizations of the country now engaged in this work, cooperating with the Federal Government. Their intellectual, moral, and religious culture can be prosecuted, and thus it is hoped that humanity and kindness may take the place of barbarity and cruelty. . . . [It] is the further aim of the policy to establish schools, and through the instrumentality of the Christian organizations, acting in harmony with the Government, as fast as possible, to build churches and organize Sabbath schools, whereby these savages may be taught a better way of life than they have heretofore pursued, and be made to understand and appreciate the comforts and benefits of a Christian civilization, and then be prepared ultimately to assume the duties and privileges of citizenship.[14]

The concentration of Indian populations into mission villages reinforced the prevailing colonial policies of the Spanish oligarchy. It freed even more land for Spanish use and occupation, as did forced labor, and it forced further changes in Indian social structures. In the Mayan areas, for example, the clan was the key social and land-tenure unit. Therefore changes in traditional land-use patterns necessarily affected the family structures of Native American societies. Because Spanish colonialism stressed individual ownership and accumulation of land, it undercut the clans' very reason for existence. At best, the disruption of Indian lives, lifestyles, and land-use practices through the process of relocation led to the consolidation of clans, forcing the remnants of clans to merge just to help keep the idea and reality of extended family alive.[15]

That very consolidation, however, reflects something about the process of Indian-white relationships that we must not forget. Indians could, and did, adjust to Spanish colonialism. They found ways to defend themselves against the cultural death that the Spaniards seemed determined to bring upon them. Sometimes this led to armed rebellion against the Spaniards. The Mayas, for example, did not easily succumb to the Spanish invasion; they fought back. Even after 1540 they continued to rebel. In the hundred years prior to political independence from Spain, which came in the 1820s, they launched at least ten major revolts against Spanish rule.[16]

Central American Indians also used less violent means to resist the Spanish and to protect their cultural integrity. They sought, for instance, to press the new religion into the mold of their traditional beliefs. They merged Catholic saints and symbols with their own deities and idols. They correlated the crucifixion of Jesus with their own practices of blood sacrifice. Culturally that seemed easy to do because in both cases the shedding of blood pleased a divine being and insured continued life. Thus the Mayas easily assimilated the death of Jesus into their own belief system. Church officials rebuked such practices of religious syncretism as recurring paganism, but, in reality, it was for the Indians meaningful acculturation on their own terms.[17]

INDEPENDENCE: MORE OF THE SAME

The century following emancipation in Central America (1820-1930) brought about a number of notable changes. Political independence from Spain was achieved. New modern technology was introduced into the region. Investors from Europe and the United States came to Central America. Coffee replaced indigo as the principal export crop and the key to the region's economy. The rural population also became less Indian in racial and ethnic makeup, because in Guatemala, El Salvador, Honduras, and Nicaragua, mestizos (the offspring of Indian and Spanish intermarriages) became increasingly numerous in the countryside. Costa Rica, which for generations had only a small indigenous population, remained substantially white in racial composition. In general, however, racial mixing was a regular part of life in Central America, unlike in the United States. So by the 1800s the rural poor and farm families were both Indian and mestizo.

But these changes did not affect the basic relationships between the rich and the poor, the powerful and the powerless, the landowners and the family farmers. The long-standing tension between profitable death and the hope for a better life remained a constant feature of rural life. The following chapters of the book will demonstrate that this is still characteristic of life in Central America today. Political independence does not mean an easy resolution of major societal problems.

This is clear from the historical process in Central America. Land, labor, and community relations reflect only unbending continuity with the past. Some outward forms of societal relationships may have changed, but in essence the dynamics of established structures have not.

More than any other country in nineteenth-century Central America, Guatemala demonstrated the deadly impact of the elite's continued appropriation of the land and dislocation of the labor and community of poor farmers. El Salvador and Nicaragua were not much more humane in their treatment of the rural population. Things were slightly better in Honduras and Costa Rica. In understanding the current protest from the countryside in Central America, then, the Guatemalan experience continues to serve as the truest index to the life-and-death struggles of the small farmers against the "principalities and powers" that dominate the region.

Shortly after independence, the new "democratic" governments began to simply imitate the old colonial policies in their policies concerning rural land, labor, and community. In the 1830s, for example, the government of Guatemala seized Indian communal lands, claiming that joint ownership and use of farm lands was not "modern." What followed began a pattern that would be repeated again and again: much of this land was put first into coffee production and later into banana and cotton production to expand the export trade of the country.

Similarly, basic labor patterns inherited from the colonial period remained unchanged during the first century of independent rule. The government required Indians to leave their homes and communities to furnish labor for coffee growers. In 1876, for example, the president of Guatemala, Justo Rufino Barrios (1873-1885), ordered local magistrates to help planters round up laborers; if this were not done, the government claimed, all the efforts of the Guatemalan elite to modernize the country would fail "due to the deceit of the Indian." Government security forces then swept through rural areas, forcing as many as one-fourth of all males in a single village onto the fields of wealthy planters. As had happened three hundred years earlier, rulers of Guatemala justified this blatant exploitation by saying that such forced labor taught the rural poor "the habits of work" considered characteristic of Western civilization.[18] Strange that anyone would presume that small farmers have to be force-fed lessons in hard work. But this was an ancient, familiar refrain to people living in the countryside throughout Central America.

In 1877 President Barrios further aided the owners of large estates by rejecting the Indians' claim to communal lands and working to turn the lands into plots of privately owned property. The politicians and the rich landowners believed, as many North Americans do, that private property, like "sober industry," is a sure and universal sign of civilized society. That move, however, was destructive and deadly from the perspective of the poor. Barrios's land policy clearly showed that the government was primarily interested in serving the interests of plantation owners rather than the needs of the majority of the population. It was also a sure sign that the government was committed to large-scale export agriculture as its major source of income and the basis of national development. Together with the forced-labor laws, the outlawing of communal property attacked the very fabric of life among the rural poor and betrayed an underlying racial prejudice among the ruling elite. Once again, as had so often happened in the past, Indians and mestizo farmers were evicted from their lands, which were the source of their food and the roots of their traditions and community. This turned them into displaced and migratory people, dependent on whatever wage the large estates offered. It further facilitated the seizure of their lands by those who already owned a disproportionate share of the land. Thus the land, labor, and community programs of the government greatly expanded the coffee elite's economic base at the expense of those who had little or no land. One Indian farmer who had lost his land and saw his very life threatened responded this way:

> You [the President of Guatemala] have ordered us to leave our lands so that coffee can be grown. You have done us an injustice. . . . You ask us to leave the land where our grandfathers and fathers were born. . . . Is it because we do not know how to grow coffee? You know very well we know how. . . . Are we not the ones who sow the coffee on the [plantations], wash it, harvest it? . . . But we do not want to grow coffee on our lands. We want them only for our corn, our animals, our wood. And we want these lands where our grandfathers and fathers worked. Why should we leave them?[19]

Mortgaging the Future

The permanence of this basic relationship between the rich and the poor was insured by the system of debt peonage that was also carried over from the colonial period. This economic dependence continued to provide the powerful with a ready tool to keep laborers in subjection. With the open consent of the Barrios government, labor contractors and plantation owners traveled throughout the interior of the country extending small loans in return for harvest labor. Because of the high interest rates and the planters' questionable accounting practices, and because the government actually declared debt peonage to be a legally recognized manipulation of labor, these debts quickly became lifelong obligations that passed from generation to generation. The pernicious effects of this abuse of laborers were summed up in a well-known study of Chichicastenango, one of the most famous Indian towns in Guatemala. An in-depth series of interviews with the residents of this town reached the following conclusion: "So effectual [have been] the familiar devices of colonial exploitation, alcoholism, easy credit, debt indenture, and liability for debts to the third generation, that once caught in the system, escape is difficult."[20] All this happened at the expense of the Indians' land, labor, and community, greatly hindering the preservation of their way of life.

In 1934 the government of General Jorge Ubico (1931-1944), the godson of former president Barrios, abolished the laws of debt peonage but did not actually end this practice. It merely replaced old laws with new ones that had the same effect. The words changed, but the results did not. The government continued to compel the poor to work on coffee farms and, increasingly after 1906, banana plantations. In 1906, when the United Fruit Company, a powerful U.S. multinational corporation, established its first banana plantation in Guatemala, the foreign-controlled export agriculture sector solidified its dominance of the country's society and economy. Taking advantage of government concessions, artificially cheap labor, and easy access to land, United Fruit proceeded to create a virtual monopoly of the banana industry in Guatemala, ranging from the control of Indian labor in the fields to the shipping of the product to U.S. consumers. Moreover, by the time of the overthrow of Ubico in 1944, the company managed the ports of Guatemala, ran its railroads and merchant marine, operated its communication system, and was the principal creditor of the government.[21]

Thus the Ubico government actually increased official oppression of the rural poor. It transferred the enforcement of labor laws from the Development Ministry to the National Police. The reason is simple: the political and economic elite of Guatemala recognized the abusive nature of their system, and realized that, ultimately, armed force would be needed to gain compliance. The abolition of forced-labor laws in 1945 demonstrated how much plantations relied on government coercion. Immediately afterwards, the number of Indian laborers working in coffee and banana fields declined by 50 percent.[22]

Exporting Labor

Labor exploitation produced other severe strains on the customs and community traditions of the rural poor as well. Coerced plantation labor meant the sweeping redistribution of Indian populations. By the mid-twentieth century, virtually no Indian community was left untouched by its demands. Chichicastenango was particularly hard hit. Today it is a well-known tourist haunt where traditional Indian ceremonies are performed on the steps of the Catholic church fronting on the town square and where visitors can find both beautiful examples of local crafts and gaudy trinkets. The Mayan inhabitants of Chichicastenango themselves now seem to be as much objects of tourist curiosity as the souvenirs they sell. In 1947 a highly respected anthropologist, specializing in studies of Chichicastenango, highlighted this community's suffering when he wrote that the "chief reason for the decline [of the town's population] is not the death rate but that families have moved to the [coffee plantations]. The beginnings of this migration date back at least thirty years."[23] Chichicastenango actually came to specialize in the export of labor, much as other Indian communities specialized in other commodities. As the CCCS team walked around the square, we could still sense the tremendous pressure that these people have long endured because of assaults on their land, labor, and community.

Besides forcing the relocation of rural workers, the government's labor and land policies concentrated laborers into settlements that facilitated their control and exploitation by growers and local authorities. Like colonial resettlement into mission villages, this tended to break down the traditional ties of extended family in favor of the establishment of single-family households. Some extended family groups did survive, but that was more a function of poverty than the strength of family cohesiveness.[24]

Costly Mammon

Work on the banana plantations especially favored acculturation to the dominant Hispanic culture. Leaving his highland home, the Indian worker entered a hot, humid environment where traditional dress, language, and customs were unwelcome. On the other hand, in terms of higher wages and job advancement, it paid to Westernize, to "civilize." Such economic advancement, however, carried a heavy price. For example, Tiquisate, the prototypical plantation town on the Pacific coastal plain of Guatemala where the Pro-Land Peasant Movement is now based, has been labeled "an outstanding example of productive efficiency and social disorganization. . . . Drunkenness, prostitution, lax family relations, [and] strong social antagonisms are all present."[25]

Driving down the highway that connects Tiquisate with the Pacific coast, the CCCS team saw the ramshackle housing for plantation laborers that now stands in mute but powerful testimony to this living death endured by the migratory workers. This glimpse into plantation life at Tiquisate also illustrates how such living conditions undercut traditional values. Seasonal wage labor no longer fulfills communal obligations. Instead, it is more a means to an end, to the accumulation of private and individual wealth, which well-meaning folk consider to be a mark of being civilized. This positive view of the destruction of Indian life is also evident in our history. In 1896 Merrill E. Gates, then president of Amherst College and of the famed Lake Mohawk Conference of the Friends of the Indian, made the following declaration:

> We have, to begin with, the absolute need of awakening in the savage Indian broader desires and ampler wants. To bring him out of savagery into citizenship we must make the Indian more intelligently selfish before we can make him unselfishly intelligent. We need to *awaken in him wants*. In his dull savagery he must be touched by the wings of the divine angel of discontent. . . . Discontent with the teepee and the starving rations of the Indian camp in winter is needed to get the Indian out of the blankets and into trousers—and trousers with a pocket in them, and with a *pocket that aches to be filled with dollars! . . .*[26]

The pressure to be capitalistic in outlook also contributed to the decline of the Indians' native manufactures. In their place, the Indian workers came to depend on imported goods, ranging from Western-style clothing to liquor. Buying things, an activity oriented to the individual, took the place of customary bartering, a community exercise. Because the head of the family and sometimes even the entire family was uprooted, the cultivation of food crops was given little attention. The workers simply did not have the time or the energy or the means to farm while they labored under the harsh yoke of the planters and their allies in the police force.[27]

SEEDTIME AND HARVEST

As we saw at the beginning of this chapter, the struggle of the rural poor is fundamental to a right understanding of the current crisis in

Central America. And clearly it is a struggle with a long history. The roots of the crisis run very deep. The sickness unto death of Central America in the 1980s cannot be cured with a "bandage" approach that ignores the past and so looks askew at present reality. The long-standing assaults on the life of the poor seen in the recurring seizures of their land, the exploitation of their labor, and the disruption of the bonds of their community life cry aloud for redress. That is the very reason the Pro-Land Peasant Movement was called into existence and now works so hard to find land for the landless of Guatemala. And it is the reason that rural folk all over Central America clamor for agrarian reform. They want to work the land, to make it productive, and to demonstrate their self-worth through planting and harvesting crops, because all of that is their life.

This is a way of life that Jesus understood very well. "A sower went to sow," he said in the parable of the soils. On another occasion he said, "The kingdom of God is as if a man should scatter seed upon the ground, and should sleep and rise night and day, and the seed should sprout and grow, he knows not how. The earth produces of itself, first the blade, then the ear, then the full grain in the ear. But when the grain is ripe, at once he puts in the sickle, because the harvest has come" (Mark 4:26-29). The life of the small farmer in Central America is clearly rooted in the traditions of the past as reflected in the Master's teachings.

Albert Memmi, a Tunisian Jew who, in the middle of this century, lived in an Arab country ruled by the French, provides us with another key to understanding the plight of the poor and powerless in Central America. As a result of his experience, he developed a keen insight into the dynamics of social and economic exploitation, whether that be blatant imperialism or more subtle forms of modern control. In his book entitled *The Colonized and the Colonizer,* he wrote,

> The colonized's liberation must be carried out through a recovery of self and of autonomous dignity. Attempts at imitating the colonizer required self-denial; the colonizer's rejection is the indispensable prelude to self-discovery. That accusing and annihilating image must be shaken off; oppression must be attacked boldly since it is impossible to go around it. After having been rejected for so long by the colonizer, the day has come when it is the colonized who must refuse the colonizer.[28]

Enrique Dussel, a well-known Argentine church historian, summarized the matter when he said, "To cease being 'colonial' is to be liberated."[29]

These observations give us a good clue to the aspirations of people like Alfonso, Ricardo, Pedro, and Father Gíron. For centuries the small and poor farmers of Central America have suffered death in many forms at the hands of powers that treated them as colonial subjects. But the poverty of these people does not make them mere instruments of commercial profit. They have worth as children of God. As Christians they know that; as Christians we should know that too. They are now acting on that belief, claiming their just and proper right to life.

The people of the land realize that their work produces life when it is used rightly and justly and in a stewardly fashion. It is the abuse of their labor, the theft of their land, and the disintegration of their community that brings death in all its tragic forms. It is the violence of that destructive system that denies them, the majority, access to power, wealth, and culture. So it is that the colonized rural poor resist the colonizer—the rich plantation owners, the governmental bureaucracies, and the foreign corporations—in their quest for liberation, self-discovery, and life. For many, like Alfonso and Ricardo and thousands of others, such efforts have ended in murder. But as their work in life demonstrated Christian principles and a kingdom vision, so have their deaths. In their own way they reflect something of Christ's saying that "unless a grain of wheat falls into the earth and dies, it remains alone; but if it dies, it bears much fruit" (John 12:24). Not many saw that fruit during the era of Spanish rule in Central America. Not many saw it in the nineteenth century. As the next chapter shows, even today it is not immediately forthcoming. The grand schemes of economic development and modernization still have not answered the need and call for life among the poor. But God's promises of social and economic justice are sure, and the common people of Central America believe that their labors will eventually bear fruit—if not for them, then for their children or grandchildren.

3. DEVELOPMENT STRATEGIES: SUCCESS CONSUMED BY FAILURE

Why do the crises intensify,
the nations rage,
the powerful increase,
the candles die?

Why is it the babies cry,
the mothers bow,
the boys go off to war,
the men are few?

How can it be—the Prince of peace comes,
the shadows lengthen,
guns at rest,
night falls?

Sidney Rooy

Encarnación del Sur

Under the heat of the early afternoon sun, the Jeep wound its way carefully around the hill. Once we were down in the valley, the driver shifted to low gear. Since it was the dry season, the stream barely touched the vehicle's undersides as we splashed through it. The Jeep labored up the steep hill on the other side, and went round and down again, repeating the process for an hour or more. Finally, near Trinidad, a small village came into view. The people watched curiously as the Jeep pulled in. Some smiled and nodded in greeting.

The rows of whitewashed adobe houses spoke of simplicity and equality. A few thousand villagers called this their home. No one with class pretensions would live under these elemental conditions. Small ruts in the dirt streets testified more to the hardness caused by drought than to frequent rain.

The center for the cooperative was a roomy wooden structure with simple benches for group meetings. The CCCS team met there with about thirty-five people, including a few teenagers and children. Their story was one of vision, suffering, and perseverance. The pastor read the Bible story of the strong-minded widow who sought justice from the judge who respected neither God nor men (Luke 18). Sergio, the president of the cooperative, told their story. The parable fit.

In 1972, Sergio said, twenty-eight village families organized to farm together on communal lands. They planted beans and corn. Like many farmers in Honduras, they sought to reclaim lands that had been expropriated by rich landowners in preceding decades. Often the military government promised measures to help the hungry rural population. More often, however, repressive measures were taken. The organized efforts to occupy lands and to cultivate them were strenuously opposed—sometimes brutally opposed—by soldiers, secret police, or gunmen hired by the landowners. Hundreds were killed. "Thus we also were continually obstructed and frustrated in the '70s," continued Sergio. "Finally we organized again in 1980 and asked for official recognition from the National Agrarian Institute. It approved our request in 1982. A year later we received legal recognition."

"But we had no seed, few tools, and no animals," said Pedro, the secretary. "The government receives money from the U.S. and the International Monetary Fund, but we never see it. The politicians come with promises before elections, but then we never see them again. So we were stuck. Then in 1983 the Evangelical Committee for Development came—except for its help, we would still be the same miserable creatures as before. They gave us seed grain to plant and technical help. The next year we got some cows which have since grown to a herd of thirty-eight head. Before, no one had milk to drink; now all our children do."

Five men go by turns each day to the cooperative, located five kilometers outside the village, to milk the cows and cultivate the land, while others seek jobs to earn money for themselves and for the cooperative. Some harvest coffee, which pays five dollars per day, but the income is seasonal.

Recent gains notwithstanding, these people still face a critical variety of problems. Thirty years ago large landowners took over many of their lands by getting legal titles or fencing in large tracts. The peasants' small plots for growing rice and beans disappeared rapidly. Prior to that there had been enough land for each family to produce its food, and buying was basically an exchange of goods. Now, with attempts by the elite to modernize the economy, cash is necessary—especially since productive lands have been taken over for export crops such as coffee, sugar cane, cotton, beef, and bananas, and people now have little room to raise food for themselves.

Although education is free, many lack money for school expenses such as clothes, pencils, and paper. In some families children must work or are incapacitated due to severe malnutrition. A health center provides basic help. "However, yesterday," said a mother, "a child was diagnosed as having arthritis. But there is no medicine. And right now, food is also scarce due to last year's drought." The land in this area is poor, and rain is usually insufficient. Years ago the hills were stripped of pine cover and burned to create pastureland. In some places, logging operations left them bare.

"Yet we are better off than most others," said another participant. "Those rural folk who have not organized are worse off now than thirty years ago. They have no grain or cows and too little food and money most of the year. They live like beggars. Their children suffer terribly. Yet the political parties and the military do nothing for them. Aid money goes for the bureaucracy and armaments. It never reaches the common people. Even when there are civil governments, it makes no difference; the military decides what to do. The civilians are only a front."

"When aid is given from government to government, it hardly ever gets to the people. It's much better to give through private and church agencies," still another testified. Most nodded their assent. It is the government that still owns the land. It sells it to individuals and groups, giving them twenty years to pay. But without financial help, starting up is almost impossible. "What we need is not more deaths and suffering," said another cooperative member. "Yet the government is more and more militarized. This is wrong. Sometimes those who send us aid through the government impose conditions upon the grants," he continued. "They should let us resolve our own problems. The Honduran people have their own dignity and rights." The community is increasingly aware of the detrimental effects of concentrating on export crops that take over land needed for food production for their families, of the lack of control over foreign annexation of farms and factories in the area, and of the rising price of food and implements with no corresponding increase in wages. And these problems are getting worse.

The thirteen leaders of the co-op are elected from among the members, all of whom participate in the life of their village. Together they are responsible for the planning for and care of the 170 dependents in the group. Eventually, when their economic situation permits, they hope to build homes on their own land. Hope shapes their vision of the future. "We are building our future and doing it for our children. We do not want to leave them the same as before."

From that isolated village in central Honduras we made our way to another village (also near Trinidad) in the fertile fruitlands. There we heard a very different story. The preceding one was told by Honduran peasants; the following one, by a longtime foreign resident of the country.

El Roble

Unending rows of pineapple and banana plants mark off the gentle slopes of hills and valleys in northeastern Honduras. The fertile soil and Gulf moisture, augmented by irrigation, produce lush fruits for export. The general manager of a U.S. company welcomes us into his air-conditioned office and explains the blessing these plantations bring to the underdeveloped Honduran people.

Some malnutrition does exist, he concedes, but starvation is a rare occurrence. The crisis here is not hunger. Although this nation is the second poorest in Latin America, the problem is not lack of food, he explains, but what is culturally accepted as edible. Nutritious foods such as coconut are available but not used. Too many people rely on traditional staples—rice and beans. International agencies such as the Agency for International Development (AID) and other government projects stimulate economic growth. Yet, among the population of four million, although one-half are dependent upon a cash economy, only one-fourth are gainfully employed or related to someone who is—and these figures may actually understate the problem. The unemployment rate for city dwellers is about 40 percent, and there is serious under-employment as well. In rural areas the situation is worse.

Why, we ask, are Hondurans poorer than the rest of the Central Americans? Our host thinks these people are not sufficiently work-oriented, that they have no Protestant work ethic, that they do only enough work to get by. Other Central American countries are different, he says. El Salvador and Costa Rica have European-oriented cultures. In Guatemala a European ethos is superimposed on an Indian culture. Honduras, however, has a machete agriculture and a not-very-aggressive business class, and it places a heavy emphasis on commerce over industry. A true national industry is rare. But "thank God," he continued, North Americans hold large investments here. They own over 90 percent of the agro-industrial sector of the nation.

A "strong, sophisticated labor union movement" has created disproportionately high labor costs for fruit production in Honduras. So its bananas, he said, are the most expensive in the world. Yet, thanks also to the unions, its workers are the "aristocracy" of the peasants—they get decent pay, child care and health care, and education. If only "madam housewife" in the United States would be content to pay more for the fruit she buys!

The solution to poverty, the manager proposed, is the creation of new jobs. That would require a more favorable investment climate, meaning lighter taxation on production and sales. The United States ought to give tax-break incentives to stimulate more investment. Key provisions of such legislation were knocked out by Congress. Nevertheless, industrial growth and commodity production remain the key to progress. A regional common market, though desirable, would not help Honduras—first, because Honduras has few products to offer, and second, because its currency is highly overvalued.

What does Honduras have going for it? The general manager answers his own question. Its strategic commodity is its place on the map! Although the Sandinista situation is a tragedy, it is not without its benefits. Hundreds of millions of U.S. dollars have gone into the military buildup. This creates short-term benefits, but in the long run it is harming the Honduran economy. What is needed is a committed effort on two fronts: military and economic. What is at stake is the welfare of our children and grandchildren, he continues. If communism is allowed to become more entrenched, the military threat to the United States will be enormous. The buildup of airfields and submarine bases across the border in Nicaragua is frightening because of what Russia could do to us. And if "the big game" doesn't go well, we will need a standing army on the Rio Grande.

With those somber words, we were ushered back out into the blistering sun. The sultry air seemed heavier than before.

WHOSE LAND?

These two visions of what is happening in Honduras stand in sharp contrast to each other. Each has its own ideas about what the causes are, where the solution lies, and who the agents are that can bring progress to this poverty-stricken country. In this chapter we will deal with some of the basic economic and social questions to prepare the ground for understanding the political and military crisis of the region in succeeding chapters.

The struggle of the Honduran peasant cooperative to claim a small, remote piece of pastureland raises an urgent question: To whom does the land belong? Until 1950, half of Honduran land was communally owned. But since 1950 this situation has been changing steadily, with the government always having the last word. One wonders why. Hadn't the land always belonged to the people? First to the Indian forebears, then to the dominant mixed race (mestizo) that now constitutes 87 percent of the population in Honduras? Could they not still claim it as their own?

For campesinos (peasant farmers) who have learned to listen to the Bible, it seems so. The great Lord made the earth for all. He gave it to humankind to cultivate and to receive its fruits. Didn't Joshua distribute land to the families of Israel? Weren't they charged to cultivate it for food for themselves and for their beasts? Didn't the prophets condemn those who seized large tracts of land for themselves and left other people hungry? And was not freedom from economic servitude to be granted every seven years, and restoration of family lands to be made in the years of jubilee? Life flows from the land. All have God-given rights to it. Surely grass for cows to produce milk for the children is the campesinos' too, as well as the little rocky garden plots where stunted corn and rice and beans fight drought till harvesttime.

By Use or by Title?

Deeply rooted in the collective memory and practice of the peasant people is the right of every family to a small parcel of land—if not here, then somewhere else. For decades, and often for generations, enough food was grown on such plots to keep the children from going hungry and to keep malnutrition within limits. Land is there for the sustenance and furtherance of life. The right to plant and harvest derives from the right to live, to provide for one's children, to guarantee life for future generations. According to this view, not only these lands but all idle, unused lands rightfully belong to those who need food, who like all others have a right to live. This is not just a secular matter but a religious matter. God has given humankind land to use for the production of food, and when hungry families claim it and work it for this purpose, it is a denial of life and a sin to take it away.

When possible, particularly in recent decades, some peasants have sought titles to the lands they are using in order to avoid losing their traditional source of life. Traditional agrarian laws in Central America sometimes give legal recognition and titles to the occupied lands, provided the occupants can demonstrate that they have used them for a period of time. But the peasants believe that cultivation—

even apart from legal titles—constitutes substantial proof of their right to use and to live on the land.

But this view, so firmly rooted in Judeo-Christian tradition, has found little favor among powerful groups in the changing Honduras of recent decades. Another view, an imported one, defines land ownership by legal title. In colonial times sections of land were assigned to the Spanish conquerors, the gentry, the church, and later to Creoles (Spaniards born in the New World). These landowners became the oligarchy, the wealthy elite who have played such an important role in Central American history. They have controlled the government, become the hierarchy of the church, occupied the key positions in the military, handled economic affairs with foreign-interest groups, and used the Indians, blacks, and mestizos for carrying out their agricultural enterprises. Through this combination of control over land and control over labor, plantations for gainful export commodities became common.

Since the turn of the century, Central American governments have sold or ceded many land rights to multinational U.S.-based companies for export crop production. Fruit companies came first; others followed. The view that legal title rather than family or tribal use determines ownership was thus extended to foreign business. Any understanding of the Central American crisis must take account of the two conflicting perspectives on land ownership that exist there. Even the emerging agribusiness sector of society and the processing of by-products from export commodities need to be seen against the background of this conflict.[1]

The peasantry really has no choice in this matter. Lands they need to produce their food have been taken from them by the local and foreign elite, who use an imported system of laws to legalize their actions. Now the peasants must use the same legal system to survive. But they find working in this bureaucratic maze expensive and terribly difficult. (The crucial question of harmonizing the rule of law with peasant participation in government is considered in Chapter 6.)

One reason for the relatively low level of tension in Honduran and Costa Rican societies, in contrast to those of the other three nations, has been their somewhat less stringent policy toward the land claims of peasants based on the principle of use. However, in all five nations, when opportunities have opened up for increasing export commodities, governments have been quick to title lands to those who could produce the stipulated crops. National armies or police forces have implemented and enforced these decisions. Landowners have frequently fenced off thousands of acres of contiguous lands, usually communal, for their own use without having legal titles. They have formed their own plantation guard or hired teams of armed men to keep squatters or peasants from invading the land. Clashes have been few in the case of landowners who have cultivated their lands for many years. But peasant invasions of idle lands have become more frequent as evictions and poverty have increased.

Where Is Your Title, José?

In the 1950s, the 1960s, and the early 1970s, peasants in Honduras and Nicaragua (prior to the rule of "Tachito," the last of the Somozas) made repeated attempts to reclaim land they needed for family food production. The following is typical of such scenarios:

> Don Miguel, a local cattle rancher, gets a loan from the government development bank. He purchases barbed wire and hires a team of men to fence in an area contiguous to his existing cattle ranch. The area includes a peasant settlement, with its cluster of palm-front dwellings surrounded by cornfields. The peasants are notified that the land is Don Miguel's and that they must leave.
>
> The peasants have lived on the land for some time and have not previously been bothered by Don Miguel. They are the ones who cleared the area of forest, and from their perspective, the land is rightfully theirs. So they do not move from the settlement.
>
> After repeated threats fail to budge the peasants, Don Miguel decides to wait until a few weeks before the time for harvesting corn. Then he instructs his men to turn cattle loose into the peasants' cornfields, trampling the crops and munching on the corn.
>
> The peasants drive the cattle from the fields. With barbed wire from a section of Don Miguel's fence they enclose the fields to prevent the cattle from reentering and further destroying the crops.
>
> In retaliation, Don Miguel's men cut the peasants' fence and drive cattle onto their cornfields once more.
>
> By this time the peasants have formed an action committee and have notified peasants in neighboring communities as well as priests, school-teachers, and other sympathetic people in the closest town.
>
> If the peasants have not moved after the second or third trampling, Don Miguel sends for the police in the nearest town. The young men are arrested, roughed up, and imprisoned.
>
> If the peasants do not move when the cattle are turned onto the fields at this point, Don Miguel has his men block the road or path into the peasant settlement to prevent people and supplies from passing. If the peasants still refuse to move, Don Miguel sends for the armed militia. The militia arrives with reinforcements from the

nearest army or national guard unit. The peasants are removed by force, and dwellings and cornfields are set afire. An armed guard is stationed day and night at the burned settlement to prevent the return of the evicted people.

Those evicted move in with relatives in a nearby village. They enlist the support of sympathetic townspeople. They pressure the town government for the release of the imprisoned. They have a priest, a lawyer, or some other sympathetic townsperson who can read go to the registry of deeds to do a little search. They have someone who can write literate Spanish help them draw up a list of grievances to submit to government officials.

In the meantime Don Miguel has united with other cattle ranchers in the vicinity. Peasants and persons sympathetic with the peasants are harassed by the police. If direct harassment is not possible, a team of off-duty policemen is hired to intimidate the peasants and their supporters in an attempt to crush the movement before it goes to the next level.

The peasants, in turn, build a case to take to the land court or land-reform agency in the departmental or national capital. The list of grievances is submitted, and the peasants begin to seek out support for their case from national peasant organizations, churches, universities, labor unions, and other national institutions that may show sympathy for their case.

The cattlemen, in turn, gather their forces at a national level. They unite with other agricultural and business groups, apply pressure through their allies in the military, and they do whatever they can to defeat the peasants and their sympathizers.

At any step the chain reaction may be broken, or it may escalate until extreme levels of violence are reached. The paths taken in particular struggles vary in important ways from one cattle-boom zone to the next depending on local and national conditions.[2]

Such encounters lead to repeated outbreaks of violence. Three massacres of peasants by ranchers occurred in the province of Olancho, Honduras, in recent years: one in El Jute in 1965, one in La Talanquera in 1972, and one in Los Horcones in 1975. These purges took place in spite of and in defiance of the national agrarian law of 1962 (subsequently modified), which recognized the right of the peasants to settle on undeveloped national lands. Since there were large tracts of public lands in Olancho—nearly one-half of the area was still untitled in 1974—settling there was particularly attractive to the peasants.

Similar violence surged in the rural Nicaraguan province of Matagalpa during the late 1960s and throughout the next decade. There, too, peasants occupied large sections of land without title, leading to the massacre of Pancasan. In retaliation, rural guerrilla activity increased. Brutal counterinsurgency measures were employed by Somoza's National Guard, and new government "land grants" were given, 88 percent of which went to forty individuals (1,670 acres each). The previous land tillers who had not been eliminated either fled or were relocated for "security" reasons to colonization projects in the tropical zone of Zelaya.[3]

With the nuances appropriate to different areas, the same story was being repeated in Guatemala in the 1960s and 1970s. During this time the cattle boom, particularly in northeast Guatemala, produced unbelievable repression of the native population. Whole villages were relocated or eliminated. In 1975 thirty-seven members of a rural cooperative in Quiché were abducted and flown away in helicopters. They were never seen again. The defense ministry later claimed responsibility for this antisubversive operation. This was followed by an increasing repression of Indian families who had settled in that area. During 1976 and 1977, 168 more community and cooperative leaders were killed in three neighboring towns. Up to this point, few Indians had joined the guerrilla movement. They had opted instead for official investigations and legal defense.

But on 29 May 1978, the situation changed dramatically. Kekchi Indian farmers from three neighboring towns came to Panzós to press title claims for the lands they were farming. Rich landowners came to oppose them. The landowners called in the military, claiming that the land was theirs. Fighting broke out, in which the army massacred over a hundred people and wounded many more. Since the Indians had only sticks and machetes with which to defend themselves, army casualties were light. Some soldiers were wounded, but none were killed. After the Panzós massacre, the guerrilla ranks multiplied with the influx of angry Indian farmers.[4]

Los Horcones, Pancasan, and Panzós all tell the same story: they are tragedies of the recent past that continue to be re-enacted in the present throughout the area.[5] Counterinsurgency forces armed by the United States forced the eviction of the peasants, insured the "rights" of the oligarchy to the land, and thereby assured the heightening of a crisis in the countryside. Only in Honduras and Costa Rica, as noted previously, did governments intervene in such a way as to lessen, though not eliminate, the effects of the conflicts and thus avoid open hostilities.

Repeatedly the question of "whose land?" has been answered to the advantage of the elite. Peasants and small landowners have progressively been forced off their little plots and communal lands. Rights to land by use have not been recognized, and titles have not been granted. Efforts to reclaim family and traditional properties have frequently been met with violence and repression. What went wrong? Had these peasant Christians misread their Bibles? Did God not intend the land for all—the fields for corn, the pastures for milk-giving cows, the rivers for fish?

SHOULD WE MIGRATE?

More and more during recent years, peasants were being forced to ask themselves a series of basic questions: What can we do? Where can we go? How can we feed and care for our children? Some said, "We must migrate to find new opportunities." Others replied, "Better stay where we are; perhaps things will improve." The question for those who chose to move was—where? There were really only three options: to move to a region near one of the banana companies, to move to the city, or to emigrate *al norte* (to the North). But how real are these alternatives?

Going Bananas

Turning to the first option, let's take the case of the United Fruit Company (UFCO).[6] Its roots go back to the late nineteenth century. Small companies merged to form this U.S. multinational conglomerate, which soon dominated the banana industry of the isthmus. It built a network of railroads in all the countries from the plantations to the ports. The UFCO then founded a steamship company whose trade dominated the ports. It also established and controlled telegraph and radio communications and food-processing plants.

To meet the increasing world demand for bananas, the UFCO needed large acreages. In their eagerness to imitate the economic development of England and the United States, development-minded governments willingly offered large grants of land, gave railway concessions, approved shipping and port facilities, and provided exemption from taxes and customs duties. However, the land grants were on the hot, humid coastal plain where few national workers cared to go. So the fruit companies imported Caribbean blacks, giving rise to sharp social conflicts that still exist today.[7] Diseases were also a major problem for the labor force.

The inherent weaknesses of the Central American economies became obvious during the Great Depression. Because of the enormous power wielded by the fruit companies, their decrease in profits had disastrous effects on the national economies. In Honduras, for example, bananas constituted 88 percent of the total export value during the period from 1925 to 1939, and they were the only source of new capital for the country. Between 1931 and 1938, however, profits from bananas decreased by more than 50 percent. The government responded by giving the fruit companies even more generous concessions in order to gain more investments and to increase production.[8] In Guatemala the fruit companies were responsible for 30 percent of the total value of exports in 1924. The economic crash of 1929 meant a sharp drop in the demand for and price of bananas and a subsequent dramatic decrease in the income of plantation owners and workers. The entire economy went on the skids. The government took drastic measures, including making a 50 percent cut in the salaries of all workers, prohibiting pay increases, and constructing highways by the forced labor of hundreds of thousands of Indians. This was followed by the granting of still more lands to foreign companies in the Pacific area, which created still greater dependency.

By 1950 the U.S. companies had an almost complete monopoly on Central American fruit production: they controlled about 80 percent of it. This gave them enormous power over political decisions in the various countries. Pacts between the oligarchy and the companies contributed to the political instability of the region. The framer of early U.S.-Nicaraguan relations, former U.S. Secretary of State Henry Stimson, had said at an earlier tense moment in these relations in 1931, "Up to the present, Central America knows that no government which does not have our recognition can remain in power and . . . those which we do not recognize will fall." The truth of this statement was confirmed in 1954, when the U.S. government overthrew Guatemalan president Jacobo Arbenz, partly because he expropriated United Fruit lands as part of his land-reform program. During the 1940s and 1950s the governments of Honduras and Guatemala alike depended upon Washington's approval and that of the fruit companies to remain in power.[9]

Rather than influencing local governments for good, the fruit companies perpetuated and strengthened the inequitable social structures of Central American society. Located in isolated areas, the companies were dependent in large part on imported labor. Workers within these areas generally received better wages, health care, and basic education, but this had little beneficial effect on the rest of the nation's poor. Few of the rural masses were able to enter the areas.[10] Moreover, the nation received little recompense in taxes. The companies' exemption from paying national taxes on their profits lasted until 1945, and from 1945 to 1970 they were taxed merely a token amount. Between

1966 and 1970 these taxes averaged out to only .004 of the product's export value, certainly an insufficient amount to stimulate government public-service activities on behalf of the rest of the population.[11]

Going to Town

The second option for the campesino is to migrate to the city. In recent decades large numbers of rural folk did just this, seeking a better life. As a consequence, urban populations in Central America grew from 1.3 million in 1950 to nearly 9 million in 1980. Thus 43 percent of the total population now lives in urban areas, compared with only 16 percent thirty years ago. Of the five countries, Nicaragua has the highest percentage of people living in cities (54 percent), while the lowest belongs to Guatemala (38 percent).[12] There are both push and pull motives at work here. Due to mechanization on the plantations and the difficulty of producing enough food on their own small plots to meet basic subsistence needs, the peasants are pushed off the land. Others are drawn to the cities in the hope of pulling themselves out of abject poverty.

The cities were not prepared for this invasion, however. They doubled, even tripled their size in the last generation. A similar experience occurred in the United States at the turn of the century. The great difference is that the Central American migration was neither preceded nor accompanied by significant industrial growth. Therefore, few jobs and little housing were available—and that remains the case. Most migrants build precarious homes with makeshift materials (cardboard, plastic, boards, tin, adobe, cane) in open areas around the cities. Called *tugurios,*[13] these shantytowns lack even the basic urban services of electricity, roads, water, sewage facilities, and police and fire protection. *Tugurios* are usually built illegally on public or private lands, often on steep hillsides, in flood areas, or near city dumps. Their residents are often subject to harassment and forced eviction by police or military forces.

In Costa Rica, the land on which these new villages are built is sometimes named after the landowner and bought from him by the government to maintain civil peace. Low payments and long-term loans are made available to the migrant families. By contrast, in Honduras members of our team visited a *tugurio* named La Lucha, which is built on the fringe of an inland industrial city. In 1982 more than 150 families moved there as squatters on open pastureland. In May 1983 the landowners came with soldiers and tractors to destroy the huts and drive the inhabitants out. Many of the settlers were beaten, some imprisoned. Finally the owners agreed to sell the land, and a cooperative was formed. Each family is paying a small amount per month until the debt is paid. The people have practically nothing to call their own: their houses are shacks; their roads, dirt paths; their sewage system, open ditches; their water-supply system, old cans; their clothes, mended rags; their food supply, uncertain. One by one they tell their story:

- I was selling coffee in the street. The devil attacked me. I fell and broke my arm. He that perseveres to the end will be saved. Sometimes I work in houses. Then I get sick and Jesus heals me. I have epilepsia and three children. My mother lost her sight.
- We came a year ago. We have only a *chozita* (hut), not a house (= wooden frame). We are rich in Christ. What is most important is to finish the church, make the walls—when it rains or it's cold we suffer. The only thing that is of value in life is to serve the Lord. We work when we can, he gives health. Praise the Lord always and in every place.
- Brothers, this life is of little value, and it gives us nothing. But since we know Christ Jesus, we must build him a church so we can place our burdens, our lives in His hands. I am poor, but we are rich in the Lord. God is preparing us for that place to which He will rapture us to be with Him forever.
- Two years ago we came from Copán. Eleven live in our little hut. But God has a dwelling place prepared for us. Our land is poor; few live well. But our Lord knows. He is ready to listen.

For an hour our team members listened to these and many similar testimonies. It was always the same: suffering now, with the only hope a bright future. From the depths of poverty they could only conjure up visions of a world beyond. For now, faith serves as a refuge to help cope with the brutality of the storm.

Going Elsewhere

Some migrate to the compounds of the fruit companies only to be sorely disappointed. Many migrate to *tugurios* to suffer even worse misery and hunger. Still others seek to escape altogether to greener pastures, to the relative security of a neighboring country, or, if dreams and visions are big enough, to that beautiful land of cowboys and skyscrapers where food abounds and, so it is said, little children do not die.

But migration is not easy. Internal moves within one's own country mean giving up a web of social and family relationships that serve as a cushion when hunger and tragedy strike. Moreover, people who move may well end up substituting one desperate situation for another. Yet hunger itself and suffering children have impelled about two million people to make such decisions during the past three decades.[14] Perhaps an even more urgent factor forcing personal and family flight is the persecution by the military and the death squads. In El Salvador most of the half-million displaced people are rural peasants who fled in search of greater security in urban areas. Estimates place the number of displaced people in Guatemala at close to a million, most of them Indian campesinos. Unknown numbers of Hondurans and Nicaraguans have been displaced by a protracted war that affects both lands.

Homelessness is not only an internal problem within each country. There is also large-scale emigration to other lands due to political and economic chaos and the destruction of societal structures. Some migrants become undocumented and often unwelcome guests in a neighboring country. Many find a temporary (or semipermanent) home in refugee camps under the United Nations High Commissioner on Refugees (UNHCR). Conservative estimates place the number of such refugees on the isthmus at 300,000.[15] Still others head for the United States, where the promise of economic and political security beckons.[16] During the debate on the new immigration law in 1986, U.S. government officials estimated the number of resident illegal Salvadorans in the United States at half a million, while officials in El Salvador were putting the number at 700,000.[17]

HOW THEN SHALL WE LIVE?

The alternatives have been exhausted. The fruit companies modernize and discharge workers. Urban areas are overcrowded and jobs nonexistent. Emigration means separation from roots and families, illegal entry, living as unwanted and hunted aliens in strange lands, and possible deportation due to ever-stricter immigration laws in the North.

For a majority of the people, emigration is neither desirable nor feasible. They must seek to survive by other means. The question of how to live cries aloud for an answer. For generations on end, as far back as the people's collective memory reaches, there has been only one response—work the land. Do it on your own, if possible, however small the parcel of ground. For the rest, one works for *el capataz* (the plantation boss) in the coffee harvest. That means up to three months of work each year, between May and October, depending upon the weather, coffee prices, and other factors beyond the peasant's control. At best it is a precarious existence.

Of Cotton and Hamburgers

The years following World War II intensified the abrupt changes in economic patterns. For centuries cotton could not be produced profitably in Central America because of insects, plant diseases, and soil conditions. However, with the introduction of insecticides, herbicides, and chemical fertilizers, these problems were overcome. The availability of agricultural equipment and cheap labor and the fertilization of volcanic soil combined to make the Pacific coastal plain of Central America an ideal location for producing cotton. A support system of roads, credit for machines and insecticides, and subsidies from national governments and international banks helped to get the industry started. World demand was great. So before long, cotton became an important export commodity. From World War II to 1980, the value of cotton exports increased 31 times, while production increased a whopping 70 times.[18]

A rapid return on investments helped to boost cotton production. Coffee trees require four or five years to mature, while cotton can be harvested within a year. However, the risks are greater. The whitefly struck in the mid-sixties. In the early eighties the market tumbled, due in part to the oil crisis, the tight money policies of the U.S. administration, high interest rates, and a general recessionary trend. As a result, many small and medium-sized cotton growers went bankrupt. Only the large and powerful withstood the storm and and were able to arrange the needed financing to continue production.

This led to a further concentration of profits in the hands of a few. They included not only the traditional oligarchy but now also a new and growing elite group—one made up of businessmen and professionals who live in the city, rent land, and become weekend supervisors of their enterprises. These urban-based producers from the capital cities were incorporated into the new agribusiness elite that share in the benefits of modern technology.

However, the change from coffee and other traditional crops (corn, rice, sugar, sesame) to cotton seriously affected the peasant class. As long as farming was done by hand and with oxen, some plantation workers could stay on their subsistence plots. During the 1950s, however, the owners mechanized production, which diminished the need for workers. Forced evictions followed.

Meanwhile, a similar boom developed in cattle-raising. The

years following World War II witnessed the rise of the so-called hamburger connection. The fast-food business in the United States stimulated an insatiable demand for low-cost beef. Cheaply produced grass-fed meat found ready access to U.S. markets. Several factors made this possible: newly developed refrigeration techniques for shipping, the building of new roads in Central America to open up new areas, and the necessary credit subsidies to build the essential support system, with Washington development agencies in league with local governments providing the necessary capital.

The results were clear and rapid. Whereas prior to the 1950s farmers sold their products to the few local markets they could find, in the 1950s and 1960s meat production and sales became an organized international business. Many conservative ranch owners in Central America had formerly used cattle as a capital investment to bring dividends once a year. Now the goal became efficiently "producing" cattle for rapid sales and quick profits.

The beef business expanded as rapidly as cotton production. In 1957 Costa Rica alone provided a limited quantity of beef to the United States. But soon Nicaragua and Honduras became important sources as well. The total dollar value of beef exports to all nations rose twenty-six times in the twenty-year period from 1960 to 1980. The number of packing plants in the five countries that were apporoved by the U.S. Department of Agriculture grew from zero in 1956 to twenty-eight in 1978. Regional beef exports to the United States rose from 805,000 pounds in 1957 to nearly 28 million in 1960 and to 264 million in 1979.

From the perspective of many experts in Third World development, post–World War II Central America was a tremendous success story. The nation had been excessively dependent on coffee, sugar, and bananas; the addition of cotton and beef resulted in a significant diversification of products. The introduction of roads, subsidiary industries, and modern technology achieved a significant measure of modernization. More important still from the viewpoint of the international aid agencies and banking interests, foreign exchange increased greatly. This was considered essential in generating continued economic growth.

All Out for Economic Growth

The development of Central American countries has been calculated in global economic terms. From 1950 to 1978 this region had nearly the highest economic growth rates in the world, exceeding those of the United States and even postwar Japan and Taiwan. But significant questions arise: What was the net effect of this rapid economic growth?

How were its benefits distributed? Why wasn't it sustained? How did it affect the fabric of Central American society? How does this growth relate to the crisis?

The cotton and beef booms brought increased wealth to the Central American countries. But what did the new export products mean for the common people? As production was mechanized, less and less peasant labor was needed. So no choice remained to the peasants but to move. Dispossessing peasants from their traditional lands and annexing them for export crops had dramatic effects on land ownership and devastating consequences for peasant well-being.

Only during harvest season was there an urgent cry for workers. All available labor power then traveled on foot or was transported to the open fields. The seasonal labor demand in Central America expanded from 15,000 workers at the beginning of the cotton boom in the early fifties to more than 400,000 in the mid-seventies. The rest of the year peasants now living in the cities were able to pick up only occasional day labor or hourly jobs. Most of the rural population moved to the poorest land areas, where mountainous terrain, deforested and eroded land, and rocky soil provide little or no room for subsistence farming.

The resulting creation of a growing class of landless workers transformed rural society. No longer did the peasant family have a small patch of corn to assure tortillas for the hungry children the year round. The place of women in the social structure became increasingly precarious. They no longer cared for pigs, chickens, and the family cow. Produce for family food was not available. There were no more fruits, vegetables, eggs, and milk for the village market. While the men scoured the countryside for seasonal jobs, the women often migrated to town. Only there could they hope to earn a wage by scrubbing floors, washing dishes, or working as sales clerks, seamstresses, street vendors, and factory hands. The economic and social links of community life were thus broken. Traditional family unity was destroyed by the forced separation of its members. Often children had to fend for themselves. The number of matriarchal households rose sharply.

The unraveling of the social fabric extended from the family to the social classes. The unwritten code of mutual loyalty between landowners and peasants disappeared. Previously the peasant offered long-time service in exchange for the landowner's promise of protection from life's vicissitudes: hunger, illness, imprisonment for thievery or drunkenness. The prevailing religious perspective of the peasant taught him to believe that meekness on earth brings reward in the hereafter.

For the landlord, charity to those entrusted to his care opened the door to heaven.

For many the social plight became the soil for the germination of a new type of religion that contrasted sharply with such futuristic hopes. Whereas the old-time religion taught obedience and submission to the status quo and hope for the hereafter, the new religion aroused dreams of the beginnings of the kingdom of God here and now. The greater the breakdown of the traditional fabric of society, the more urgent the search for its reconstruction along new lines. The new religion defined faith as hope for earthly change and transformation and a better life for future generations. These views on life and society are further developed in Chapters 6 and 7.

A paternalistic and benevolent attitude toward the handful of year-round employees still remaining on the family plantation was quite possible. But such attitudes disappeared when the only contract was a wage paid for hard work at harvesttime "to dirty, anonymous faces." And why should the laborer respect an unknown boss, himself hired by an absentee landowner, who had no care or worry for the laborer's plight beyond the paying of a minimum salary for as few days as possible once a year?[19]

There is one more step that figured in the breakdown of the social fabric. The coffee boom of the 1800s, the banana empire that lasted from 1890 to 1940, the on-again, off-again sugar plantations, and the postwar cotton explosion all required very rich soil and special climatic conditions to be profitable. But the cattle business, which boomed in the 1960s and 1970s, prospered wherever grass could be grown. As a consequence, vast areas of land, previously unusable for export crop production, were pressed into service. Large idle tracts of land, properties of the multinationals and the elite alike, were turned into pasture. In addition, huge sections of communal and public lands were fenced off for grazing, and the peasants living there were evicted by force. The earlier story of Don Miguel illustrates this procedure.

In the past the forests had offered rich resources for peasant life, providing game, lumber, firewood, fresh water, and opportunities for fishing. Now forests were being cut down and burned to make way for grass and cattle. With the sharp depletion of forest preserves, possibilities for subsistence living were greatly decreased. From 1955 to 1975 the number of cattle increased two-and-a-half times, while the total acreage dedicated to pasturelands increased from eight-and-a-half million to over twenty million acres. By 1975 cattle exports required the use of more land than all other export crops combined. In 1950 three-fourths of Costa Rica was covered by forests; a quarter of a century later that figure stood at less than one-third. The ecological as well as the social consequences of this development are disastrous.

Likewise, the change from coffee to sugar to cotton to beef as the principal export has seriously affected the job market. Coffee is more labor-intensive than the other export commodities: it requires seventy man-days per acre annually. Sugar requires forty, cotton thirty, and cattle only five. That is, land dedicated to cotton provides employment for six times more workers than does land devoted to cattle-raising; sugar gives employment to eight times more workers, and coffee to fourteen times more. One sociologist describes these social consequences as "a qualitative redistribution of rural misery."[20] The quality of life itself, sustenance, and hope for future improvement were all seriously affected. Rural misery accelerated. The number of landless peasants in El Salvador tripled between 1960 and 1975, so that only 6 percent of rural families could eke out enough to live on. More than half of the country's workers were unemployed two-thirds of the year. In Guatemala, although export agriculture grew by 45 percent between 1965 and 1979, peasant landholdings dropped by 26 percent. Domestic food production fell significantly. During the 1950s in Nicaragua, then under Somoza, similar circumstances forced 180,000 small farmers into seasonal harvest work.

Although Honduras and Costa Rica also experienced an increased exploitation of land and displacement of small landholders—Honduras through the fencing in of communal land and Costa Rica through the continued growth of the banana industry—these countries maintained a relatively stable political economy. The moderate land reforms in both countries and the lower population density resulted in the expulsion of fewer rural families from traditional subsistence plots. Since, therefore, their life patterns were not as drastically disrupted and they were able to retain relatively more control over their livelihoods, peasants from these two lands did not respond with the explosive force that erupted in Nicaragua, Guatemala, and El Salvador.

More Children, Less Food

Another factor that conspired to increase unemployment and decrease the food supply was population growth. The growth rate for the Central American countries (excluding Costa Rica) averages about 3.4 percent annually. William and Elizabeth Paddock, who have examined this problem, make the obvious point: "One draws back in consternation, wondering how a nation, any nation, can keep from sinking into complete anarchy when, just to stand still, it must double all its facilities—power supply, housing, portable water, schools, medical facilities—in the next nineteen years."[21]

During the last three decades, El Salvador's situation of misery has steadily worsened. Food supplies have failed to keep up with population growth. Land depletion and erosion, increased export crop production, less access to family subsistence plots, flight to the city, lack of jobs, high malnutrition rates, decreasing life services (health, housing, education), growing psychological stress—all these factors have conspired to make the life story for hundreds of thousands of Salvadorans a heroic yet often futile struggle against the forces of death.

Yet it was the growing concentration of land in the hands of a few and the inaccessibility of it to the many that had a perhaps even greater negative effect than did the population explosion. Rural people comprise half of the total population of El Salvador. In 1892 there was an 18.8 acre-per-person land base; by 1971 it had shrunk to .9 acres.[22] The result was migration. The capital city of San Salvador nearly tripled in size in twenty years. Hundreds of thousands more left El Salvador altogether. What happened there was repeated to varying degrees in Nicaragua, Honduras, Guatemala, and Costa Rica. Moreover, the cross-movement of estranged, politicized, and hungry thousands throughout the region served only to further strain local resources and spread social unrest and strife.

Although life expectancy has increased and infant mortality rates have decreased during the last thirty years, the changes in other life factors are negative. Illiteracy remains high for the rural population (about 55 percent), the production of food per person is less than it was twenty years ago, and the percentage of national budgets spent on health and education has also declined. Extreme poverty rates for 1980 in Central America (excluding Costa Rica) averaged 45.4 percent of the population (56.6 percent in rural areas); the rates of those living below subsistence levels averaged 67.2 percent (80.1 percent in rural areas).[23]

Life often seems hopeless to the urban and rural poor. As victims of underdevelopment—sometimes torn by internal disputes about what to do, and repressed by conservative landowners, businessmen, and reactionary governments—it often seems best to some to *aguantar* (just bear up under it). Others have answered this violence with counterviolence. Back in the 1930s, after the Great Depression, dramatic peasant revolts sparked strong loyalty to local cooperative movements. These uprisings were much like the hundreds that had occurred during the colonial and national history of these various countries, and they were repressed with similar violence. Yet such revolutionary impulses are still alive.

Organizing for Action

As industries were established and the public sector grew, labor unions and peasant organizations became more viable. However, they were usually dependent upon government authorization for their right to exist. They were therefore often linked to political groups and used for political and bureaucratic ends. Several factors contributed to the early rise of unions: outside pressures from the League of Nations and its International Labor Organization, growing nationalism, and university reforms, with students participating in union administrative roles. However, repressive dictatorships in Central America in the 1930s and early 1940s tended to keep the unions tame. For this reason these organizations were few. Some worked underground; some were inspired by Marxist principles; all were suspect.

Early on, Costa Rica stood alone in accommodating these popular concerns. From 1909 onward it taxed foreign interests. After the progressive revolution of 1948, it placed restraints on the United Fruit Company, enacted social legislation, and permitted union activities. This is remarkable, since the leader of the revolution, José "Pepe" Figueres, belonged to the elite land-owning class and was opposed by communist-dominated unions. Figueres outlawed the Communist Party until after the writing of the new constitution and its adoption in 1949, at which time the party was once again permitted to function (and it continues to do so). The unions, however, did not participate in that revolution.

Throughout Central America limited rights to organize and the adoption of limited labor legislation advanced during the 1940s. Guatemala's new constitution of 1945 gave unions the right to organize. As in Costa Rica, this right included communist labor unions and political parties. Social reforms inaugurated in Guatemala by President Arbenz included higher wages, social insurance, increased taxes on capital goods, basic rights for labor unions, and a reduction in the military budget. In 1954 these reforms were severely curtailed with the overthrow of the Arbenz government.

That very year a Honduran strike against the UFCO achieved significant worker benefits. Several factors made this strike successful. Compared with other Central American nations, Honduras had many unions, spread over widely diverse parts of its economy. The initial impulse to strike came in the 1920s, with national organizations stimulating the united action of local groups. After strikes that were partially successful during the Great Depression, labor organizations were declared illegal for sixteen years under Tiburcio Carías's dictatorial rule (1933-1949). After 1950 a limited measure of political moderation created an opportunity for the historic 1954 strike, which sent shock waves throughout the region. Yet success did not come without sacrifice. Union leaders were threatened, persecuted, and imprisoned by the government. Eventually they were replaced by a more docile leadership. Then the UFCO fired large numbers of workers, often accusing them of communistic tendencies. It was in the midst of this strike that the CIA-supported invasion of Guatemala was launched from Honduras.

Historically, therefore, labor movements throughout Central America made only slow progress, suffering many setbacks and generally lacking strong popular support. Despite the economic changes of recent decades, these countries failed to develop a solid industrial base to undergird the cause of laboring people. Relatively few citizens were involved in union activities. Nor did organized labor make a substantial, lasting impact upon society at large. The precarious nature of labor's slow advance was confirmed by the crushing blow dealt the labor movement in El Salvador in 1945. That urban labor sometimes accepted a form of communistic leadership is not surprising. The average worker wanted help to escape exploitation and grinding poverty, and other quarters showed little willingness to sacrifice and actively defend his cause.[24]

The attempts of the peasants to organize were fraught with difficulties even greater than those of their urban brothers. The history of the region recalls violence and revolt, frequently sealed by blood. Recently land reforms have been announced again in Honduras and El Salvador, but these promises remain largely unfulfilled. To date, only neighboring Mexico and Nicaragua have achieved significant land reforms.

A question forces itself upon us: How can campesinos organize to affect their country's policy? They are separated from urban unions, both geographically and ethnically, and they cannot finance their own organizations. Their enemies exploit these weaknesses and disadvantages. Attempts to link urban insurgents with peasant organizations in the struggle for better living possibilities have been crushed with unusual brutality. Even when peasants are not involved in direct guerrilla action, they are suspect. It is not uncommon to find villages in the Guatemalan highlands that look like ghost towns, the families having fled or been massacred.[25]

Campesino movements began to coalesce in Honduras during the 1960s. They participated in the signing of the land reform act of 1962. It had only limited objectives, but it did recognize the right to organize and carry on the activities of social organizations. Yet the almost immediate result was repression, red-baiting, and persecution. Several hundred campesinos were killed during the decade. Nonetheless, the room to maneuver, though circumscribed, served to diffuse the kind of polarizations manifest in its three neighboring lands. In this way Honduras, together with Costa Rica, has—at least until now—avoided the terrible civil wars that rage in its sister countries.

Unlike Nicaragua, El Salvador has experienced neither the overtaking of large tracts of land by fruit companies nor U.S. military occupation. But for decades rural unions were illegal. Where they did exist, they were under very close surveillance. The Workers Confederation of Central America (COCA) began its work there in the 1920s, as it did in Honduras. In El Salvador too the struggle for economic betterment soon became political in character. Since the government is the means by which the landowners, the export businesses, and the military maintain their dominance, this could hardly be otherwise. After years of dictatorship and varying degrees of rigorous repression, the new constitution of 1950 provided more moderate working conditions for a minority of the laboring class. But no legal protection was forthcoming for the mass of rural workers. Although this was promised, and although on occasion limited freedoms were granted, labor organizations and campesino movements were regularly repressed, suspected of communistic tendencies, and persecuted. This has been the case even in recent decades.

The policy of allowing limited space and power to labor movements and of repressing those who exceeded such prescribed limits was aimed at resisting basic change in societal structures. This is clear in the case of Guatemala. With the invasion of Castillo Armas in 1954, severe measures were taken: the repeal of the congressionally approved constitution of 1945, the dissolution of the congress, the reversal of land reforms, the reformulation of the labor code to eliminate many guarantees of workers' rights, the outlawing of all labor movements, and the establishment of the National Defense Committee to direct the witch hunt of "communists" and to institutionalize terror as an instrument of societal control. As its reward, the Armas government received eighty million dollars in U.S. aid, plus additional loans from the World Bank. The new Guatemala was coerced into following a strict laissez-faire policy, which resulted in lowering the purchasing power of salaries and fully respecting the rights of private enterprise and industrialization by foreign capital.[26] These actions show the methods imposed and the measures taken to guarantee the maintenance of the status quo, methods and measures not strange to Central American history.

Can we organize? This is the question both urban and rural workers ask. The answer is yes and no. Organizations that merely ask for reforms of the existing situation, that do not threaten the existing structure of society, that frequently leave the poor poorer and the wealthy elite in charge of their national and personal destinies—such organizations have with great effort gained a place in society. But cooperatives that ask for serious land reform, unions that demand radical change in the share that workers receive from production, military and political leaders who propose national independence with real taxation of foreign and local capital—for such organizations there is no room. Such threats to the establishment—threats that would significantly alter the endemic poverty of the land, with its debilitating malnutrition and its retardation of the capacity of millions of God's children—must be eliminated.

CAN WE HOPE FOR BETTER TIMES?

Life is hard on the majority of people in Central America. And what does it offer in return? Are there reasons to hope for better times in the upcoming years? Conflicting answers are given to these questions.

Some believe that reforms sweeping enough to alter significantly the life-and-death struggle of twenty million Central Americans are possible within the existing structures of society. What is needed, they propose, is modernization. Some who hold this view advocate substantial structural changes, a position that we call "progressive modernization." Others argue that the existing structures and policies need to be improved only so as to generate more "trickle-down" benefits to the poor. This view we call "conservative modernization."

Another school of thought claims that only through fundamental structural change can the long-standing crisis be alleviated. Traditional approaches have all failed. For, as these critics point out, the growing dominance of elite national groups and international power interests has resulted in a growing dependence of the powerless upon the powerful in each country and a growing dependence of the entire region upon stronger foreign nations. This analysis we call the "dominance-dependency" theory. Those who hold this view fall into two groups: those who are convinced that violent means are necessary and inevitable in achieving greater justice, and those who cling to the hope that significant structural reforms can be effected by peaceful, democratic processes.

All these responses are addressed to the same deep-seated crisis. Moreover, these parties to the dispute are all agreed that the development strategies—those going back to colonial times and those introduced during the pre–World War II era—have fallen far short of meeting the needs of the majority of Central Americans.

Before World War II the economic development strategy that was believed best for people's needs was the primary-product-export strategy.[27] Central America was to produce agricultural commodities and minerals in exchange for manufactured goods from Europe and North America. Foreign investors would provide ships, ports, railroads, and even the needed sources of energy. Some Central Americans became wealthy in the process, especially with intensification in the production of coffee, cotton, grains, beef, and fruit. But the overall economic structure remained fragile. The Great Depression of the 1930s and the effects of World War II made people sense the need for a change.

Attempts at Reform:
Progressive Modernization

At the close of World War II theorists began working on a new model called *progressive modernization*. Its goals were to diversify the economy and to control excessive dependence on foreign markets, and thus to overcome widespread poverty and economic instability. The inspiration came from a number of contemporary sources: Catholic Social Action, Roosevelt's New Deal, the Mexican Revolution. This model called for new structures to redistribute income and increase domestic consumption. It would thus create demand for goods and the capacity to buy from below, bringing the poorer classes into the cash economy. Since the elite were not likely to cooperate in such redistribution of income, its advocates looked to the laborers in industry and the peasants as the base of support for this program.

In order to achieve these goals, especially for the benefit of the poor, a three-step plan was outlined. Basic to it all was land reform, the breaking up of large estates and their redistribution to peasants and small farmers, who would then be instructed in the improvement of production techniques and the diversification of crops. Second, a broad program of industrialization and the manufacturing of national goods was needed to replace the importation of foreign goods. This would then lead to the third step: a reduction in economic dependence upon foreign nations and foreign capital.

During the three decades since midcentury, however, severe obstacles have obstructed the implementation of this model. The most formidable of these is the militant and effective opposition to land reform by the large landowners. How could these obstacles be overcome?

The only way to proceed is for regional governments to expropriate these estates and, if possible, to purchase them either at current market price or at the declared tax value. The latter is usually far below market value but coincides with what owners have been willing to pay in taxes over the years. It is also a far more realistic figure for poor countries. In addition, land reform requires credit for tools, fertilizers, necessary technology and instruction in its use, and access to markets. Where would these governments get enough independence from the influential elite, enough power, and enough money to effectuate such change? At center stage must remain the central objective: the redistribution of assets and opportunities to both the urban and the rural poor.

Thus far the obstacles standing in the way of this program have frustrated the realization of this goal. Such attempts at more radical social reform have always been brutally repressed. Domestic and foreign pressures have therefore forced this progressive modernization model into an increasingly conservative mold. Yet they have also served to kindle hope for a better future.

More lasting results came from the reforms in Costa Rica adopted after 1948 through the "little revolution" carried off by José "Pepe" Figueres. Resources were significantly redistributed and effective political participation was introduced through the nationalization of banks, the promotion of cooperatives, the universalization of education, the adoption of social security, the suppression of the army, the organization of a civil-service program, the taxation of capital gains, and the establishment of an election tribunal.

Paralleling the general failure of land reform in most Central American countries was, anomalously, their rapid economic growth from the 1950s through the 1970s. Foreign aid and investment stimulated a measure of small-scale industrialization. The establishment of the Central American Common Market fostered more dynamic trade in the region. However, most of the industrialization was related to businesses that grew from the agro-export sector or to household and luxury commodities within the reach of only the upper classes and the small but growing middle class. Few benefits came to the poor. In fact, their conditions worsened.

The United States played a vital role in all these developments. Much of the export and import trade as well as capital investments came from and went to the North. In 1950 three-fourths of the total

Central American commerce was U.S.-related. Seventy percent of present Honduran businesses were established between 1950 and 1968, with nearly half of the investments coming from U.S. sources. Of the seventy foreign companies in that country, fifty-eight were owned by the United States. By 1982 thirty-one multinational companies with seventy-one subsidiaries were operating in Honduras. U.S. investments in that country grew from 4.6 percent of the gross national product in 1943 to 32 percent in 1971.[28]

This dramatic switch from the production of subsistence crops to export-import trade significantly altered the internal structure of the entire region. A coalition of the military, the oligarchy, technocrats, and industrial groups were the strongest supporters of the progressive modernization project. However, its success at one level of society was largely consumed by failure at another level. It had ironic and destabilizing consequences. From 1952 to 1965 in Central America, the production of rice and beans—both basic food items—declined in volume by 8 percent and 18 percent respectively. In the same period, coffee production increased by 256 percent, banana production by 163 percent, and cotton production by 2,440 percent. The elitist export sector expanded its capital rapidly, while steadily the poor had less and less to eat. In the face of these developments, a shift gradually took place toward more conservative policies.

Pulling Back: Conservative Modernization

The multinationals began manufacturing goods in Central America that had previously been imported. After 1960, U.S. investments decreased in agriculture and increased sharply in the industrial sector. Proposals were also made for the economic integration of the five countries. In the 1950s the United States resisted this move. It later gave its approval only after certain restrictions on foreign investments and protective tariffs were scratched. Thus in 1961 the Central American Common Market (MCCA) was born with the blessing of the multinationals. Foreign companies continued to invest in Central American industries because of the ready availability of low-paid workers and cheap support services such as rent, electricity, and upkeep.[29] Although the MCCA effectively stimulated trade and investments in the region, its objectives were only partially realized, due largely to the U.S. demand for the elimination of protective tariffs that would have stimulated internal industrial growth. Their elimination increased Central America's vulnerability to international commerce and foreign control of investments. The result was a tremendous growth in dependence and an increasing distortion in the balance of payments.

Yet this era is known as the "decade of development." Initiated by President Kennedy in 1961, the Alliance for Progress took its place alongside the MCCA with the goal of stimulating economic growth in the Americas. Motivation came principally from two sources. First, Kennedy was optimistic and concerned about the possibilities of improving the situation of the underdeveloped countries. Second, there was the fear that the Cuban revolution would spread throughout Latin America.

The negative side effects of these more conservative policies soon became apparent. The shipping of surplus U.S. grain to Central America undercut local food production. Agencies established by Washington to administer the social-economic programs rapidly grew into bureaucratic giants. Capital injected as loans soon became part of the mushrooming international debt. U.S. representatives of the Agency for International Development (AID) began to wield significant power in the domestic policies of local governments.

The interlacing power that the various finance agencies exercise on the countries where they operate added to the problems of Central America. Suppose the International Monetary Fund pressures a country to devalue its currency, and that government refuses. The World Bank would then likely refuse further loans, no further U.S. AID credit would be forthcoming, and U.S. private banks would deny applications for financial assistance. By such means, outside agencies effectively control the domestic policies of small countries. The power that the United States wields via the AID in the Central American countries was and is very significant. For the sake of protecting its investments and for geopolitical reasons, the United States has markedly increased military aid to Central America at the expense of economic aid.[30] In Honduras in 1949, economic aid totaled $213 million, compared with $28 million it received in military aid; in 1985, according to figures requested by President Reagan, economic aid had declined to $45 million, while military aid had risen to $138 million.

The five-day war between Honduras and El Salvador in 1969 (the so-called Soccer War) effectively broke the back of the Common Market. Honduras lost a prime market for raw materials (El Salvador), and El Salvador lost its largest market for industrial goods (Honduras). Moreover, the recurring rise and fall in the world prices of export commodities dramatized the continuing dependence of the region on external factors. In the countryside the modernization project meant less concern for the lot of the rapidly growing sector of landless peasants.

Migrants swelled slum areas around the cities, areas without basic public services, and they had little hope for work.

Military intervention in the Dominican Republic in 1965 by 25,000 U.S. Marines and paratroopers signaled the beginning of the end of the earlier democratic goals of the Kennedy presidency and the Alliance for Progress. The Nixon administration then terminated the program.

Significant changes have indeed taken place in the Central American societies. Over the past three decades the population has tripled, the per-capita income has doubled, and foreign trade has grown sixteen times. Economies have become diversified; there is urbanization and expanded use of land resources. Yet these changes have not ameliorated the core problems of society, since they have not altered the drastic inequality in the distribution of wealth and power in the region. New social, economic, and political relations have been superimposed on the old ones in a kind of "additive development." But the fruits of modernization have been limited to the traditional oligarchy and the new bureaucratic class of technocrats, businessmen, and industrialists. These individuals in turn have become dependent largely upon the infusion of foreign capital for the continuance of the modernization project and have tended to transfer their own capital to foreign banks for lack of confidence in the region's economy. They are more loyal to external trade and aid than to internal reform. They don't need the poor—they only fear them.

The More Things Change, the More They Stay the Same

For these reasons many have turned pessimistic. How can we hope for better times, they ask, when "the more things change, the more they stay the same"? The picture comes into sharp focus when we take a closer look at the external public debt generated by the modernization projects. Increased spending was financed by increased borrowing rather than by raising the levels of taxation and by internal economic growth. The oil crisis hit Third World economies hard with its steep increase in prices, but at the same time made OPEC dollars available for increased loans. Banks were eager to increase lending in order to invest the flush of petrodollars from the OPEC countries. But as the loans continued to grow, so did the interest and service charges on the debts. More and more export earnings were needed to finance the payments of previous loans. As long as financial aid was poured into the economies, the gross national products continued to increase.

But several negative factors conspired to turn the tables on this "economic miracle."

First, the terms of trade steadily prejudiced the exchange of crop exports for manufactured goods. For example, in 1960, 160 bags of coffee would purchase a tractor, but by 1970, 400 bags were needed to make the same purchase.[31]

Second, loans were made at a floating interest rate, which was adjusted every six months to ensure a profit for the banks. Interest rates rose to as high as 20 percent in the early 1980s, imposing a heavy burden on Central American countries. In 1983, for example, Costa Rica had to use 44 percent of all its export earnings just to service the interest charges on its debts.[32]

Third, the austerity programs required by the IMF as a condition for receiving loans are having very real negative social consequences on the lower classes and give impetus to protests and riots. National governments are required to freeze wages, increase the cost of public services to consumers to eliminate deficit spending, and remove protective tariffs on imports. These programs, together with the general economic recession, have severely lowered the standard of living for common people, brought a marked upswing in unemployment rates, and caused a strong decrease in the real value of salaries.

Fourth, due to its unfavorable balance of trade, Central America was obliged to reduce its imports severely. Imports of consumer goods dropped 49 percent between 1981 and 1983.[33] This plunged much of the internal industry, as subsidiaries of foreign corporations, into a spiral of employee layoffs and bankruptcy. Likewise, the decrease in export goods by local industry due to the recession closed off the fuel needed to generate new or expanded economic growth. These urban conditions, plus the desperate situation of the rural population, are behind much of the social unrest that has erupted in guerrilla movements.

Fifth, high interest rates and internal economic pressures are forcing the devaluation of national currencies in relation to the dollar. This only worsens the external debt situation, since repayment must be made in dollars. Nations that threaten nonpayment are warned of the dire consequences of such action. The chairman of President Reagan's Economic Policy Advisory Board has stated that if Latin America "attempted to default, credit would be cut off for all of their imports, all their ships would be liable and aircraft would be seized when they landed and every bag of coffee and every other thing. . . . I know it would happen, the papers are drawn."[34]

Sixth, regional governments seek ways to reduce public spending. This means that the state's demand for products drops and national industry suffers. Thus the vicious circle continues.

Crisis is the order of the day in Central America. The gross national products of the five countries have taken a turn for the worse over the past five years. Every year since 1978 has witnessed a persistent deficit in the balance of payments. The international debt for Central America multiplied four times between 1977 and 1983. To date, Honduras and Costa Rica have been spared the civil wars and political violence raging in their sister republics. But they have in no way escaped a similar economic tragedy. Costa Rica has the highest per-capita debt of any nation in the Western Hemisphere, while Honduras suffers some of the most abject poverty in all of Latin America. Neither geographical location nor political alliances are able to guarantee escape from the gravity of the crisis.

The proposed programs of progressive modernization with land reform and redistribution of income to the urban and rural poor were rejected by the national power brokers. At the same time, conservative modernization (reinforced by recent U.S. economic policies), with its emphasis on light industrialization supported by injections of foreign capital, has brought increasing concentration of wealth in the hands of a small percentage of the population, while the societal distance between them and the poor two-thirds of the people has become steadily greater. As a result, the number of malnourished, poverty-stricken people is higher today than it was thirty years ago.

In order to maintain control of labor unions, peasant organizations, university groups, and popular political parties, the military becomes the base of support for the status quo. Often it takes the reins of power directly. Defenders of conservative modernization are prepared to impose repressive measures upon their own citizens. Thus a new cost has to be paid: the cost of national security and loss of life in the spreading political violence. These costs are not calculated into economic balance sheets, but they must still be reckoned as terribly crucial factors in the regional crisis. The bottom-line question becomes this: How many resources and how much effort can a government afford to expend in protecting itself from its own citizens?

Radical Change: Dominance and Dependence

Many in Central America today have concluded that "reformism," whether progressive or conservative, really makes little difference. They are but two slightly adjusted ways of maintaining the status quo. What Central America needs, these individuals would insist, is to radically restructure society in order to end exploitation and to promote a better distribution of resources.[35] A tourist's view of new modern airports, high-rise apartments, luxury hotels, and congested city streets does not tell the true story of any of these countries. We must come face to face with the suffering faces of mothers and children, the armies of the unemployed, and the hungry majority that lives outside these enclaves of modernity.

In judging the success of a nation, the redistribution of resources to meet the basic needs of all the people should have priority over indicators of economic growth. But many think that such redistribution can be achieved only by revolutionizing the present societal structures. Government of the people, by the people, and for the people is, for them, a revolutionary idea. For it shifts the decision-making center from the elite to the citizenry as a whole. This, they believe, is the first step on the long, long road to a truly participatory democracy.

Such ideas pose a basic question: What measures must be taken to make it possible for all sectors of society to participate in the governing of their nations? Some adherents of societal revolution calling for radical structural change insist that change ought to come about by democratic and peaceful means. Only when people are conscious of their rightful place and role in society are they prepared for participatory democracy. Others insist that, by definition, the elite's tenacious resistance to change makes peaceful transition impossible. Only by an open display of force—violence, if you will—can the structures of society be changed. Even Costa Rica, the proponents are quick to point out, had its "little revolution" in 1948, though it was not radical enough. But who wants violence? To this question they respond, How is less violence done—by incessant exploitation and repression or by revolutionary change?

A second problem has to do with international relations. Proponents of revolutionary structural change, violent and nonviolent alike, believe that poverty has international roots. They are careful not to claim that these are the only roots. Yet poverty and its continued growth are intensified and nurtured by international forces. The economic development and industrialization of the West were made possible in part by its unbalanced trade relations with Third World nations and its exploitation of their primary resources. In the bargain the value of the resources bought was most often relatively minimal compared with the industrial goods that were sold in return. Third World economics have evolved not in isolation from the industrialized nations but in dependence upon them. This dependency has not decreased with development projects, as promised by the progressive and conservative modernization experts;

rather, it has resulted in "the development of underdevelopment."[36] The incredible burden of international debts accumulated over the past twenty years is shocking testimony to this fact.

In the process, not only do rich nations become richer and the poor nations relatively poorer on the international scale, but polarization intensifies within the dependent nations. As this social crisis deepens, so also does the restlessness of the urban and rural poor, who suffer the most. Historically it is true that the most severe and violent of uprisings and rebellions from the lower classes occur among those most desperate for life's basic needs. According to this dependency view of development, we must expect social revolutions in Central America to remain chronic and to intensify until the structural oppression held in place by the repressive force of arms is overcome and democratic participation by the majority is assured.

In sum, there are two prevailing ways of understanding the social, political, and economic crisis in Central America today. Somewhere along the way each nation must choose between slow change and radical change, between helping the rich and aiding the poor. Each of these analyses has already come to historical expression in Central America and continues today. It seems clear that there is no single messianic solution which holds for every nation. There is rather the diligent search for justice and peace, the taking of risks for right causes, the moving forward by faith in a history still in the making.

What criteria can Christians use to make concrete judgments and choices in the face of suffering, policy conflicts, and the uncertainties of tomorrow? What ought the rural families in Encarnación del Sur take as their guiding light as they struggle against "principalities and powers" in their day-to-day existence? And what of the plantation owners—the producers of the principal exports of bananas, cotton, sugar, and beef—and their workers?

Where Does All This Leave Us?

Christian leaders in Central America urge us to seek nonideological solutions to their very concrete problems. Polarization—the right and the left, capitalism and communism, private enterprise and governmental centralism—paralyzes effective action in implementing policies of reformation. We must rather define concrete objectives and seek ways to achieve them that are appropriate to the region in its historical moment. Priority should be given to (1) satisfying the basic needs of the impoverished majorities, (2) attaining greater independence from the industrialized countries on both national and regional levels, and (3) achieving cooperation among the Central American countries on production and commerce to stimulate internal growth.[37]

In responding to these goals, it is essential to set priorities for action. Among the many laudable goals aimed at achieving more pluralistic, participatory, and democratic societies, which comes first? If we choose a more equitable distribution of the earth's resources among all members of society, what do we emphasize? Some might say, let us have agrarian reform, more investment of public funds in social services, and periodic salary adjustment, even though these policies may discourage private investment and economic growth. Others respond that this puts the wagon before the horse. First there must be investment for economic growth; then the fruits of economic growth will "trickle down" and benefit all members of society.

Our review of the past three decades of experience in Central America has shown that economic growth in itself does not stimulate adequate and meaningful participation in society, nor does it necessarily benefit a large segment of the population or reduce social polarization. On the contrary, such participatory benefits have decreased dramatically. A different approach to the crisis is needed. Our Central American consultants conclude that what is urgently needed above all else is the room and the freedom for each nation and for the Central American nations together to formulate their own social, political, and economic programs and thus to forge their own destinies. This would reduce their vulnerability to outside pressures and interests. Economically this involves a series of concrete measures that these nations should pursue and should be given the freedom to pursue:

1. Achieving as much self-sufficiency in food production, with as much efficiency, as possible.
2. Developing appropriate technologies for the present level of Central American development.
3. Diversifying and broadening exports.
4. Stimulating consumption patterns not dependent upon imported goods.
5. Adopting production models that are less dependent upon capital and energy.
6. Using labor intensively, as this is the most abundant resource of the area, to assure the incorporation of all sectors of society into the productive process.
7. Taking measures to effect a more equitable distribution of national resources through adequate land reform, progressive taxation, and social services.

8. Establishing avenues to promote grass-roots participation by small group and community organizations in the decision-making processes within their local, regional, and national areas.[38]

Despite growing ideological polarization about how to achieve these basic goals, certain concrete objectives could unite the Central American nations in joint efforts to move ahead. If there is a call for austerity, its burden should be borne by all sectors of society. If food and industrial development are essential, funds should be used for this instead of for military purposes. If severe unemployment continues, labor-intensive modes of production must have priority over machines. If markets are too small to stimulate efficient production, cooperative regional solutions need to be found. If more centralized planning becomes advisable, governments should limit the extent of their control of the economy to measures that advance the public good.[39]

With this the political dimension enters the picture. Most basic economic problems remain insoluble apart from the political will and power to effect constructive change. These issues are addressed in the following chapters. Effective change calls for radical transformation. Only then can genuine participatory democracy be achieved for those who live on the underside of history—a democratic way of life as different as day and night from the democratic masquerade that now prevails, in which grown men and women are able to do no more than place an X on a ballot they cannot read and then return to their villages as anonymous and forgotten as before.

The question then remains: What would these practical guidelines mean in the everyday life of common people if they were put into practice?

For members of the cooperative in Encarnación del Sur, the guidelines would mean a variety of significant changes: growing crops for community use would be given priority; their taxes would be relatively low compared with those of the large landowners; money currently budgeted for military purposes would be rechanneled into health and education; planting, cultivating, and harvesting would, for now, be done by hand rather than by large machines; and their cooperative would unite with others in order to market their products for a fair price.

For the banana plantations in northern Honduras, the guidelines would translate differently: the banana crop would be partially replaced by other crops less susceptible to market fluctuations; some of the presently idle lands held by the company would be set aside by the government for local food needs and profitable export production;

taxes would be adjusted to assure equitable upper-class and foreign participation in government programs for the public good; prices on export products would increase for North American consumers; wages and benefit programs would reach better levels; labor union activities would be safeguarded by law; the formation of cooperatives on reclaimed lands would be encouraged in order to generate healthy competition with the large fruit-growers.

For big coffee, cattle, and cotton farmers like Don Miguel, the guidelines would offer new possibilities for farming methods that promote the common good. Again, a diversification of crops would have to be considered, with a certain percentage of all lands dedicated to local food production; beans and rice would be given preference over cattle; upper-class farmers would be taxed in proportion to their wealth; the legality of all land titles would be closely examined; farm mechanization would be limited by concern for unemployment levels and zonal family needs, with priority given to human subsistence over technical efficiency; and campesino organizations would be licensed so that participation of the poor in national economies could be encouraged.

For the *tugurio* of La Lucha in northern Honduras, the guidelines would spell new hope. Social services, such as education and health clinics, would become a priority government concern; increased local production rather than importation of food staples would lower purchasing prices; labor-intensive industry would make more jobs available; the burden of austerity programs would be shifted equitably to those best able to bear it (both the local elite and foreign companies), thus helping to alleviate the disparity between rich and poor; regional cooperation in the establishment of small businesses and industries would stimulate employment; and the organization of local cooperatives and other popular agencies would give the poor a voice in their own future. The God to whom the needy cry also answers through the action of their brothers: Inasmuch as you minister to one of these, you do it unto me.

Echoing the apt phrase by the Swiss theologian Oscar Cullmann, "already . . . and not yet," we close on this note:

> *Already the battle done;*
> *Not yet peace on earth.*
>
> *Already the assurance of victory;*
> *Not yet the end of suffering.*
>
> *Already redemption for the children of God;*
> *Not yet the more abundant life.*

Already the crushing of devil power;
Not yet the prisoner's freedom.

Already the Spirit's outpouring;
Not yet food for the hungry.

Why do the crises intensify,
the nations rage,
the powerful increase,
the candles die?

Why is it the babies cry,
the mothers bow,
the boys go off to war,
the men are few?

How can it be—the Prince of peace comes,
the shadows lengthen,
guns at rest,
night falls?

Sidney Rooy

4. "THE CUBANS ARE COMING! . . . THE CUBANS ARE COMING!"

There is a point where the national pride and independence of one people cease to be a threat to the pride and independence of others.

Jorge Abadia Arias

NEGLECT AND INTERVENTION

The United States has long been the "great power" in Central America and the Caribbean. Behaving as a great power, it has interfered often in the affairs of its smaller neighbors. The earliest direct intervention took place in Nicaragua in 1855. Since that time, over 130 years ago, the United States has felt justified to intervene in the political affairs of Central America on dozens of occasions. Such interventions have not followed any regular calendar. More typically, periods of disinterest and neglect have been interrupted by periods of frenzied preoccupation in the face of some perceived crisis. The present is clearly one such moment. In 1979, after more than a decade of relative neglect, leaders in Washington became frantically alarmed that Central America was about to be "lost" through external aggression. Since then the United States has pursued an increasingly aggressive policy of intervention.

Because interventionism has such a long history in inter-American relations, present U.S. policy toward Central America must be seen in the light of past U.S. interventions. Before we turn to that history, however, two important points need to be made.

First, when inter-American relations are viewed historically from a Central American perspective, it is clear that Washington's view of Central American history is discontinuous. Every crisis is treated as a new one, unconnected to the past. The only element of continuity is that in each "new" crisis Washington discovers some form of "foreign aggression" as the underlying cause to be combatted. By contrast, Central Americans see their history as a single fabric. The past is woven into the present. Each crisis that breaks out has roots in some earlier tumult, in the broad patterns of conflict and injustice that for generations have left their deep imprint on Central American society. Moreover, to Central Americans, Washington's reaction to each new tremor on the political Richter scale is as predictable as the coming of the rainy season.

Second, the historic relationship between the United States and Central America has been badly distorted by a severe imbalance of power. For more than a century the United States has loomed as an overwhelmingly powerful force in relation to any individual nation in Central America, and even in relation to all of them taken together. The Central American countries have been weak and vulnerable. This lack of balance is not only a matter of size or military might, although these are important factors. But strength or weakness in a nation also stems from the soundness or lack of soundness of its political institutions. In this respect the United States had gotten a significant head start on Central America. When that first U.S. intervention occurred in Nicaragua in the 1850s, the United States had already benefited from seven decades of self-government and national development. Nicaragua, with a tiny population of a few hundred thousand, had achieved its independence only two decades earlier. Like the rest of Central America, it had not yet achieved a consensus on how the nation was to be governed. This left it vulnerable to foreign intervention at the hands of more powerful and aggressive nations.

Central American independence coincided with the rise of the Manifest Destiny mentality in the United States. The United States was beginning its period of expansion, acquiring new interests abroad and assigning to itself new responsibilities. The United States was, in fact, on its way to becoming an imperial power, and Central America lay directly within its expanding sphere of influence. The point to be made here is a simple but important one. If we view the past 130 years as a whole, we will see that the United States has had a far greater impact on Central America than Central America's five tiny nations have had on the United States. Actions taken in Washington have had devastating and lasting effects in Central America, effects that have hardly been noticed in the United States itself. In this way the imbalance of power has had a distorting effect on national development in Central America and on the character of inter-American relations. The result is an unwanted estrangement between the peoples of North America and Central America. For this reason, proper stewardship of the immense power available to the United States today is a great challenge to us as citizens and as members of Christian communities in North America.

MARTYRS AND REFUGEES

Perhaps one way we can think clearly and compassionately about the stewardship of our power is to engage Central America, as much as possible, at the level of individual and communal living and concrete personal experiences. After all, the life-and-death struggles of real people compose the historical patterns discussed in this book, and these people are surprisingly like us in their hopes, fears, and deepest convictions. Most of us in the United States are aware of the present crisis in Central America because of initiatives undertaken by our government. The crisis came to our attention as a problem of "foreign policy." But foreign policy too often becomes an abstraction for us. In reality it refers to concrete actions, taken or forsworn by a government, that can have direct repercussions on people's lives. U.S. foreign policy toward Central America is a concrete link between each of us and the millions of mostly poor people who inhabit the five nations of the isthmus. Therefore, Washington's "official" view of the crisis and the policies designed to respond to it should be subjected to the scrutiny of personal experience and appraised in the light of "ground level" consequences.

There are many ways to learn about Central America. One method to which more and more North Americans are turning today is simply visiting the region and meeting directly with ordinary people. Such contacts often lead to the sharing of extraordinary experiences. Firsthand observation and personal testimony reveal events that North Americans, accustomed to living in a stable and orderly society, can scarcely imagine. At the same time, such experiences open up new ways to understand present events.

The Church Comes to Life in La Union

The church came to life on a sparkling morning in January 1987. A group of North Americans, members of the CCCS team, drove to the university town of Heredia near San José, Costa Rica. There they met with members of a Salvadoran pastoral team made up of Christians who in recent years had fled El Salvador's soaring political violence. This pastoral team works with the more than 15,000 Salvadorans who have sought refuge in Costa Rica since 1980. That morning they gathered with us to sing, pray, and recount the experiences that had turned them into refugees. Here is the story of one of their members, a Delegate of the Word (a Catholic lay leader) whom we shall call Pablo.

Pablo is from the province of La Union, a poor area in the extreme eastern part of El Salvador. Like the majority of his countrymen, he grew up in a campesino family that owned some land but not enough to meet the family's basic needs. He and his brothers followed in their father's footsteps, working as laborers on large plantations for as little as fifty cents per day because there was no other option open to them. Between 1965 and 1968, the waning years of the Alliance for Progress, Pablo's father lost half of the small parcel of land he owned to the land-grabbing tactics of the oligarchy. At that time the production of export crops such as coffee, cotton, and beef was expanding rapidly so that more and more land was needed for their cultivation. In tiny, densely populated El Salvador, additional land could be gotten only by dispossessing men like Pablo's father—at least that was the easiest way to do it in a society where military governments were accustomed to serving the landed elite. So, instead of improving the economic condition of families such as Pablo's, the boom years of the Alliance for Progress only brought greater hardship.

At about this time, in 1968, Pablo's own life took a new direction. Priests in the nearby town of San Miguel set up a center for campesino development. Its primary goal was to train local campesinos to lead Bible study groups in their own villages and to serve as facilitators of community development projects. The reading and discussion of Scripture led by these Delegates of the Word was the common point of reference and the point of departure in these community activities.

Pablo became a Delegate, and over the next five years he served his community and his church in this capacity. With his assistance the villagers set up regular meetings that eventually led to a series of self-help projects. They built a school and launched a basic health program. People began to speak out about oppressive conditions. Before long the whole community took on a new sense of organization. In short order this wave of campesino activism attracted the attention of the government. In the Salvadoran countryside, government authority is exercised primarily by the armed forces. For Pablo this turn of events led to a summons to appear at the local military garrison. The commander warned Pablo that if he persisted in organizing such meetings, the security forces would not be able to guarantee his safety. The thinly veiled threat was all too clear.

In the face of this warning, Pablo and his family moved to the capital city of San Salvador. There Pablo continued his work of organizing Christian base communities, eventually working directly under the supervision of Archbishop Oscar Romero. In the archdiocese, Christians such as Pablo enjoyed the open support of the church and its highest spokesmen. Even so, they were not safe in their work. Church leaders themselves were becoming victims of the country's escalating political violence. In 1978 government security forces murdered Ernesto Barrera, the priest of Pablo's parish. In March 1980 Archbishop Romero himself was assassinated. In the following months a reign of terror engulfed the Christian communities. One day a friend who worked in the government came to tell Pablo that he had seen Pablo's name on a list, always an ominous sign in El Salvador. He recommended that Pablo consider leaving the country. Alarmed for his family's safety, Pablo decided to seek refuge in Costa Rica. No sooner had he and his family left the country than five members of the pastoral team who had stayed behind were taken prisoner by the National Guard, one of El Salvador's five uniformed military forces. The guardsmen murdered the five and mutilated their bodies. In the aftermath, the network of grass-roots communities began to disintegrate. Eventually the meeting house where they had studied the Bible and prayed together was simply taken over by the military and is presently serving as a post for the National Guard.

As Pablo, meeting with us, reflected on these painful events in his life, two themes emerged from his story.

On the one hand, he realized that the pain and injustice inflicted on him, his family, and his community were related directly to their pastoral work. They were persecuted because they sought to live out the gospel's command to love their neighbors as themselves and because they expressed that love by teaching each other and by organizing their neighbors so that in working together they became a community. The authorities viewed these activities with great suspicion because for them order in the countryside depended on campesino passivity and resignation. In fact, for fifty years, since the infamous Matanza ("The Massacre") of 1932, the elites and the military forces that protected them had dreaded the prospect of campesino unity.

On the other hand, Pablo was inspired not only by Salvadoran church leaders but also by North American Christians who had chosen to live and work among the poor of El Salvador. Pablo spoke with special affection of Dorothy Kazel, an Ursuline sister from the United States who had been his teacher during the early days of his training as a lay leader in the church. Her connection with Pablo pointed to one of several enduring links between North Americans and the people of El Salvador.

The North American Connection

Dorothy Kazel had come to El Salvador many years earlier from Cleveland, Ohio. She worked with Father Paul Schindler, also a Catholic missionary from Cleveland, and a pastoral team based in the small town of La Libertad. Dorothy was representative of the many U.S. citizens who had heeded President Kennedy's call to go abroad and share the best traditions of the United States. She personified a generation of North Americans who went to poor, conflict-ridden countries convinced that they could do good for others. In this sense Dorothy was a quintessential North American, motivated by religious faith and patriotism and optimistic about the possibility of making a difference in the lives of others. In fact, she was what one friend described as a "flag-waver." During the Bicentennial celebrations of the U.S. Declaration of Independence in 1976, she and Sister Martha Owen "climbed the tallest mountain in El Salvador and hoisted an American flag there."[1]

There was also another sense in which Dorothy reflected an experience common to North Americans who commit themselves to working with the poor in countries like El Salvador. Despite the escalating violence and the pleas of her family, she was unable to leave the villagers with whom she had shared so much and return to the safety and security of the United States. As family members later reported, "She felt she had a commitment to helping those people which she could not forsake. . . . She would say, 'I must go back. They need me too much.'"[2] And so she chose to continue her religious work in El Salvador. Ironically, in those very days the U.S. government was resolving to guarantee the security of El Salvador by making a massive military commitment to it. The country's military forces, including the National Guard, were coming under the direct tutelage of U.S. advisors. They were being trained to combat the growing "subversion" that so frightened both Washington and the ruling class in El Salvador.

On the evening of 3 December 1980, as Dorothy and three other North American religious workers drove from the airport to their home in La Libertad (a town ironically named for the liberty that has yet to come to El Salvador), they were abducted, raped, and murdered by security forces of the Salvadoran government. Subsequent investigation showed that a detail of National Guards planned and carried out this scandalous crime under orders from higher authorities. Why? Because, as the sergeant who supervised their executions later said, "they were subversives."[3]

Dorothy Kazel, Ita Ford, Maura Clark, and Jean Donovan were all labeled subversives because they were working with poor Salvadorans like Pablo and his family, helping them to organize and encouraging them to stand up for their own dignity. For this "crime" they were violated and then murdered in cold blood by government security forces. As North Americans and as Christian brothers and sisters of Dorothy, Pablo, and countless other victims of political brutality, we must try to understand why Central American governments, including such U.S. allies as El Salvador, unleash such unrestrained violence on their people. We must also ask why the government of the United States has for so long supported such governments both materially and morally.

THE FRUIT OF STOLEN ELECTIONS

Pablo, along with thousands of other citizens, fled El Salvador in 1980, the same year in which Dorothy Kazel and her three companions were murdered. They were only four of more than ten thousand people who would die as a result of political violence at the hands of the Salvadoran government during the next ten months. At that juncture it was obvious that the country was unstable. In fact, the government seemed to be in imminent danger of collapse. U.S. public officials, who had been rudely awakened to the present crisis in Central America by the Nicaraguan revolution in 1979, now became deeply alarmed about the situation in El Salvador. Suddenly they found it necessary to explain what went wrong in Central America, and they began a frantic search for policies that could restore stability as quickly as possible. The explanation soon put forward had a familiar ring to it, because this was not the first time it had been advanced in Washington. Central America faced a hostile threat from abroad. The policy solution that immediately took shape placed strong emphasis on military security as the key to all other reforms. This also had a familiar ring because it too had been tried before in Central America. Yet in Washington the crisis emerging in the 1980s was treated as though it were unprecedented: little thought was given to whether the proposed solutions had been tried before and found wanting. Such an approach ignores historical truths that must be confronted if the present crisis is to be resolved successfully.

Electoral Fraud in El Salvador

Just eight years before these events took place, El Salvador had already reached a historic turning point, one that went almost unnoticed in Washington. In 1972, the year of President Nixon's re-election, the United States had other, seemingly more important foreign-policy concerns. We were preoccupied with the war in Southeast Asia and with an elected but Marxist government in Chile. We were not concerned about El Salvador or Nicaragua.

As the war in Vietnam was winding down, Washington was actively engaged in undermining the government of Chile. This policy bore fruit in September 1973, when the Chilean military revolted and overthrew the government of Salvador Allende.[4] Thus, while the United States worked to bring down this popularly elected government in Chile that it disliked because of its social and economic programs, it did nothing to protect the election of a popularly chosen and potentially democratic government in El Salvador.

In that country the presidential election of 1972 was won by the candidate of the Christian Democratic party, Jose Napoleon Duarte, who headed a reform-oriented coalition. Duarte had campaigned on a platform of land reform and democracy. His opponents, a typical coalition of the oligarchy and the military, branded him a communist on the basis of this platform. Although Washington was to hail Duarte as the great democrat of El Salvador in the 1980s, it did nothing to protect him or the democratic opening he represented in 1972. When Duarte's electoral triumph became obvious, the military intervened and declared its own candidate victorious. Eventually they arrested Duarte, beat him, and expelled him from the country.

Following this blatant electoral fraud, El Salvador seemed to settle back into its ancient pattern of military rule. Such rule guaranteed stability by denying most Salvadorans any opportunity to participate in political life. Until the outbreak of the Nicaraguan revolution in 1979, there was almost no coverage of these events in El Salvador by the U.S. media. No public officials spoke of El Salvador's strategic importance to the United States. Neither U.S. officials nor rank-and-file citizens saw that the crisis of the 1980s was already taking shape. They were oblivious to the crucial reality of Salvadoran politics. In that country the political space had been so narrowed by military rule that the government saw any expression of popular demands as a potentially mortal threat to its own survival. Consequently, the government routinely answered all attempts at legitimate popular expression with violence and brutality. These were the seeds of the present crisis.

When the Nicaraguan revolution broke out, we in the United States suddenly realized that trouble was brewing in Central America. But we failed to perceive that the emerging crisis had much to do with those stolen elections and those archaic military dictatorships. Instead, we described it as the threat of "external subversion." We issued a cry of alarm that had been sounded many times before in Washington. Even though subsequent scrutiny often exposed the cry as exaggerated or completely groundless, it has continued to be raised anew whenever authoritarian governments have been challenged by an abused citizenry. Nor has the fact that U.S. intervention has often left a sordid legacy of corrupt and unpopular political institutions served to inject an appropriate note of caution into Washington's assessment of each "new" crisis. A brief review of Central American history will illustrate the point.

"THOSE MEXICAN BOLSHEVIKS ARE COMING!"

Consider the following description of an emerging crisis in Central America:

> I have the most conclusive evidence that arms and munitions in large quantities . . . have been shipped to the revolutionists. . . . The United States cannot fail to view with deep concern any serious threat to stability and constitutional government . . . tending toward anarchy and jeopardizing American interests, especially if such a state of affairs is contributed to or brought about by outside influence or a foreign power.[5]

A reader who is keeping up with current events might guess that the crisis being described is occurring in Central America in the 1980s. The speaker sounds like the president or some other high official, informing the public about an urgent foreign-policy problem. The reader would be correct about the location of the crisis and the source of the information, but would be off by sixty years on the date. This statement was made by President Calvin Coolidge in 1927. President Coolidge responded to the perceived crisis by sending the Marines into Central America—on this occasion into Nicaragua.

The Nicaraguan crisis of the 1920s originated in an earlier military occupation of Nicaragua. U.S. troops had been stationed in Nicaragua since 1909. That year they were sent to support the rebellion of a Nicaraguan leader approved of in Washington—Juan Estrada of the Conservative Party—against his opponent, the Liberal president José Santos Zelaya. Finally, in August 1925, these troops were withdrawn. From then on the protection of U.S. interests in the country was assigned to a U.S.-trained National Guard and a coalition government led by carefully selected men. An election arranged and supervised by the United States in June 1925 installed Conservative Party leader José Solórzano as president and Juan Sacasa of the Liberal Party as vice-president.[6]

However, this plan failed to take into account the long-standing bitterness and suspicion between the two political parties and the personal ambitions of their leaders. Almost immediately after U.S. troops withdrew, the coalition began to break down. First the Conservatives purged the Liberals, and in October Sacasa fled the country. Then Emiliano Chamorro, the real power in the Conservative Party, demanded Solórzano's resignation. In January 1926 Chamorro assumed the presidency and took control of the National Guard, which was supposed to ensure a pro-U.S. political stability in Nicaragua.[7] These events triggered a series of revolts by the Liberals. Thus the political instability the United States had tried so hard to prevent immediately resumed in Nicaragua.

President Coolidge Fights a Guerrilla War

Meanwhile, the Liberal cause was receiving a sympathetic hearing in Mexico, a nation that had recently undergone a revolution of its own. Mexico had tense relations with the United States because of its own experiences with U.S. intervention. During the Mexican Revolution (1910-1917), President Wilson sent 6,000 Marines to occupy Veracruz, and General "Black Jack" Pershing marched through the northern Mexican province of Chihuahua. Against this background Mexico's president, Plutarco Elías Calles, agreed to provide "money and arms" to the Liberal faction in Nicaragua.[8] For nearly a year the struggle in Nicaragua continued inconclusively. Alarmed by Mexican support for the Liberals and fearful of the spread of Mexican "bolshevism," President Coolidge sent U.S. Marines back into Nicaragua in January 1927, seeking to stabilize the country, check Mexican influence in Central America, and prevent the spread of any alien political ideology such as communism.

The fact that there was no evidence at the time of any Soviet influence on Mexican foreign policy did not prevent President Coolidge from using that excuse to justify intervention in Nicaragua. But sending in U.S. troops did not yield a quick solution. Instead, it led to nearly six years of guerrilla warfare against the U.S. occupation led by Augusto César Sandino, a general of the Liberal Party. That war was ended only by the withdrawal of U.S. forces in 1933. What the United States left behind was a legacy that continued to bedevil Nicaragua long into the future. The United States entrusted Nicaragua's fate to the National Guard, as it had done in 1925. This time it handpicked Anastasio Somoza Garcia to be the Guard's commander. From that power base Somoza built a political dynasty that dominated and exploited Nicaragua for forty-five years. In the late 1970s the hatred of Nicaraguans for that repressive dynasty became so widespread that it led to the Sandinista revolution, thus triggering another great crisis in Central America.

The Matanza and Its Tragic Legacy

While the United States was caught up in a guerrilla war in Nicaragua, a second crisis broke out, this one in El Salvador. This crisis was less the result of U.S. intervention and inter-party squabbling than its counterpart in Nicaragua. Its roots lay in popular dissatisfaction with the oligarchy's long-standing control over land, a problem that was severely aggravated by the onset of the Great Depression. The Depression devastated countries like El Salvador that depended on agricultural exports and were vulnerable to fluctuations in world prices. When the bottom fell out of the coffee market, the hardship typically endured by the Salvadoran peasant soon turned into desperation. In this setting peasant and labor groups began to press the government for programs to alleviate their suffering. These developments coincided with a cautious opening up of the nation's political process. According to T. S. Montgomery, a scholar of Salvadoran history, "El Salvador was in the midst of the first presidential administration in its history committed to allowing political organizations of all stripes to participate in the political life of the country."[9] Peasant and labor unions became more active, particularly the Regional Federation of Salvadoran Workers (FRTS). One of its leaders and propagandists was a young radical named Augustin Farabundo Martí. By the beginning of 1931 the FRTS had organized nearly 80,000 peasants, most of them in the western part of the country.

The presidential election of 1931 brought to office a wealthy landowner named Arturo Araujo, who had promised to respond to workers' most pressing demands. Araujo was a moderate reformer who had no intention of making significant changes in the status quo. But his public posture raised peasant hopes while creating suspicion and fear in the landed oligarchy. His limited efforts to distribute a few parcels of land to peasants succeeded only in fueling their demands. Meanwhile, the country's economic situation continued to deteriorate. When the government was unable to pay the army during the autumn months, a military coup ousted Araujo and brought to power his vice-president, General Maximiliano Hernández Martínez.[10]

Legislative and municipal elections, which had already been scheduled for January 1932, were carried out as planned. But these

113

elections were riddled with fraud. In the rural western areas where popular groups were now well organized, their candidates did well, "but the government refused to certify the elections."[11] Now convinced that the government had no intention of actually allowing them to participate in a competitive political process, leaders of labor and peasant groups, including the newly established Salvadoran Communist Party (PCT), planned an insurrection.

The government learned that an uprising was in the offing several days before it was to take place. Martí and several other leaders were arrested, and communications among the insurrectionists broke down. When the revolt finally began, it was unorganized and ineffective. The insurgents captured five small towns, but within a few days the towns had been retaken by the security forces. The rebellion was over almost as quickly as it had begun. In its aftermath, at the urging of the Salvadoran oligarchy, General Martínez unleashed a violent campaign of repression against the Indian population in the western part of the country. At least 10,000 peasants were slaughtered in the orgy of reprisals that has come to be known as La Matanza. According to one survivor of the Matanza, "the government exacted reprisals [at] the rate of about one hundred to one," since the rebels themselves had been responsible for the deaths of about one hundred people.

The United States was eager to indicate its support for the Salvadoran government against this supposed threat of peasant subversion. Ironically, President Hoover had been unwilling initially to recognize the Martínez government because it came to power by force. But now the United States sent battleships to anchor off the Salvadoran coast in a demonstration of military and political support.[12] The U.S. government saw in El Salvador, as it had in Nicaragua, the serious danger of communist subversion, aided and abetted by revolutionary Mexico. John Gunther, a contemporary American observer, made this observation after a visit to San Salvador during the crisis: "The official story is that this was a 'communist' revolt, inspired by Mexican agents; in actuality the poverty-blighted peasants, no more communists than Martinez is an eskimo, agitated for land reform, and were shot for their pains."[13]

The United States did not sponsor or assist in carrying out the Matanza, but neither did it intervene to halt it. When the Matanza had run its course, the government of El Salvador announced a series of political and economic reforms, including a land reform. Having stood by while the Salvadoran government sowed terror in the countryside, the United States now tried to insure the return of order and stability. Bowing to U.S. pressure, Martínez resigned so that "democratic" elections could be held. This done, the loans on which El Salvador had defaulted in early 1932 were quickly renegotiated, and U.S. recognition was granted to the new government.

But neither meaningful land reform nor democracy came to El Salvador in the 1930s. The oligarchy and General Martínez were the primary beneficiaries of the land reform. Within a matter of months Martínez had also returned himself to the presidency by overthrowing the elected president. Now that order was restored, the United States acquiesced in this anti-democratic turn of events.[14] For the next fifty years El Salvador went from one military dictatorship to another. Land, the source of livelihood for most Salvadorans, became more and more concentrated in the hands of the oligarchy.

When the next crisis came, it took the form of a much more coherent and broadly based political opposition, one that truly challenged the political system. That opposition movement, which formed and grew after the election fraud of 1972, took the name of Farabundo Martí, one of the first to be executed in the Matanza of 1932. Martí thus became an enduring symbol of opposition to dictatorship in El Salvador. In the same way, Augusto César Sandino, a contemporary of Martí's and the leader of the guerrilla struggle against U.S. occupation of Nicaragua in the 1930s, became the symbol and rallying point for the Nicaraguan revolution four decades later.

"Operation Success"

The "stabilization" of governments in El Salvador and Nicaragua in the early 1930s led to decades of uninterrupted dictatorship that relied on the military to prevent popular participation in political life. This militarization of politics became a sad and brutalizing fact of life. This is not to say that elections were abandoned; on the contrary, they were held regularly. However, they merely provided a thin facade of respectability for actual military rule. Elites dominated politics throughout Central America until the late 1940s. At that time elections brought a reformist, democratizing government to power in Guatemala. A brief revolution achieved the same goal in Costa Rica. There revolution took the unexpected turn of abolishing the army, thereby removing the obstacle that had long been the greatest impediment to securing democratic reforms in Central America. The revolutionaries also managed to avoid U.S. intervention. As a consequence, Costa Rica has managed until very recently to remain stable and democratic.

Meanwhile, events in Guatemala followed a different course. Between 1944 (when a coup overthrew the dictatorship of General

Jorge Ubico) and 1954 (when a CIA-sponsored invasion force precipitated the resignation of President Jacobo Arbenz), Guatemala enjoyed a rare moment of political reform aimed at benefiting the mass of ordinary people. Two successive popularly elected governments tried to open up the political system of the country and respond to popular needs. To that end the administration of Juan José Arévalo (1945-1951) sponsored legislation repealing Guatemala's draconian labor laws. Under these laws Guatemala's indigenous population had been kept in debt peonage that obligated them to work for large landowners at starvation wages. Arévalo passed laws that established a minimum wage, that recognized the rights of workers to strike and to engage in collective bargaining, and that granted near universal suffrage. These measures were all achieved legally and peacefully, and were important first steps toward broadening the popular base of Guatemalan politics.

In 1951 Arévalo's successor, Jacobo Arbenz, was elected with more than 63 percent of the vote. Arbenz carried these reforms further, broadening access to education and health care and creating a modest system of social security. All these reforms hinged on one further reform—that of the land-tenure system. In Guatemala the distribution of land was among the most unequal in all of Latin America. For example, in 1950 one-tenth of one percent of Guatemalan landowners owned 40 percent of the nation's farmland, while 88 percent of the landowners held just 14 percent of the land.[15] This extreme concentration of land translated into great suffering and hardship for most rural people because they depended on access to land for their livelihood. One irony of the situation was that the single largest landowner in the country was a foreign company, the United Fruit Company (UFCO). It owned more land than the combined holdings of half of Guatemala's landholding population.[16] Yet at times as much as 85 percent of UFCO lands were left uncultivated.

The agrarian reform initiated by President Arbenz was a first modest step aimed at rectifying the extreme distortions in landholding patterns in Guatemala. Herein lies another irony. Arbenz conceived of his land reform as a necessary prerequisite to converting Guatemala into a modern capitalist country. Land reform was seen as a key to stimulating increased savings for capital investment as well as a means of strengthening the incomes of potential consumers. An added, tragic irony is that the Arbenz program was later taken up and endorsed by the United States during the reformist days of the Alliance for Progress.

Inevitably, the reform of the early 1950s affected the UFCO. The Guatemalan government nationalized its idle lands and compensated the company at the level of value declared by the company itself. But,

given the amount of idle land held by the UFCO, the total expropria-
tion ran to over 400,000 acres. While this reform was extremely popular among the tens of thousands of peasants who received land, it
caused fear and anger in Washington. Soon the machinery of the U.S.
government was engaged, both overtly and covertly, in seeking
redress. The UFCO found sympathetic parties in both the Truman and
the Eisenhower administrations. Shaped by an emerging cold-war
ethos, they were easily persuaded that Guatemala's reform programs
signaled the lurking danger of communism. The tragic dilemma this
created for Guatemala is cogently described by Richard Immerman,
who has written a compelling study of the CIA's role in the overthrow
of the Arbenz government: "The leaders of the 1944 revolution
founded their economic and social programs on their analysis of
Guatemala's developmental needs. In doing so, they unwittingly
turned their country into a battleground of the Cold War."[17]

It is important to stress that Guatemala did not become a cold-
war battleground because its government was in fact communist or because it was aligned with the Soviet Union. As several exhaustive studies have shown, it became a battleground because the United States
subjected it to a hostile scrutiny that "discovered" communists
wherever nationalist and populist leaders advocated policies—such as
the nationalization of idle UFCO lands—that were seen as harmful to
U.S. business interests or incompatible with U.S. foreign policy. What
is so disquieting about this period in U.S.-Guatemalan relations is that
the State Department, congressional committees, and the White House
went to extreme lengths to prove an a priori assumption about
Guatemala. In their view, if Guatemalan leaders acted against U.S. interests, they had to be communist, or at least under communist influence. This assumption led the United States to engineer the overthrow
of the Guatemalan government. Such actions can be attributed in part
to the cold-war hysteria of the late 1940s and early 1950s. But the CIA's
overthrow of Arbenz can hardly be treated as an aberration. It reflects
a disturbing continuity with the earlier interventions in Nicaragua and
El Salvador, and with the present intervention in Central America that
has so absorbed our nation's attention in recent years.

The practical effect of labeling Arbenz pro-communist was to
justify the United States' seeking to discredit and finally to overthrow
his government. A massive propaganda campaign was organized in
1951 and 1952 to shape opinion in the United States and Guatemala
so that public perceptions would correspond to those of U.S. officials.
Then, in early 1953, the new Eisenhower administration began to plan
a direct intervention, which was called "Operation Success."[18] Over

the next twelve months this plan evolved into a CIA-created invasion army that was set up in Honduras. The CIA chose its leadership, trained it, provided intelligence, and guaranteed air support. A reporter who visited this "army's" training camp in Honduras saw the troops "receiving wads of dollar bills passed out by men who were unmistakeably American."[19] The pilots of its "air force" were U.S. citizens. Even so, this "liberation force," which was led by the right-wing military officer Colonel Castillo Armas, was incapable of bringing off the coup by feat of arms. However, its presence on Guatemalan soil, together with the intense propaganda and diplomatic war waged by the U.S. government, succeeded in undercutting Arbenz to the point that he resigned at the end of June 1954. With his resignation came an end to ten years of reform in Guatemala and the beginning of thirty years of brutal military rule. The legacy of "Operation Success" was not freedom but captivity and terror for thousands of ordinary Guatemalans.

THE ARMY IS THE ANSWER

At various times in this century the United States has tried to stabilize Central American governments by creating or restructuring their national armies. As seen in the classic case of Nicaragua, that approach proved disastrous for the country's long-term political development. During the late 1930s and through the period of World War II, the United States was preoccupied with Europe and Asia. This was the era of the Good Neighbor Policy in relations with Latin America, under which the United States exercised restraint in Central America. However, after World War II, and with the dawning of the cold war, the United States again took an active interest in the problem of political stability in the Western Hemisphere, as the intervention in Guatemala demonstrated so starkly.

In 1951 Congress passed the Mutual Security Act, which pledged long-term military aid to Latin America. Through the Military Assistance Program (MAP), hundreds of millions of dollars' worth of training and supplies have been channeled into the region. However, from time to time Congress grew disenchanted with the MAP because military aid did not seem to make the military more professional and thereby more inclined to stay out of politics. Instead, it enabled the military to intervene even more decisively. In this respect the military dictatorship that followed in the wake of the Arbenz overthrow in Guatemala generated caution in Congress about military-aid programs to Central America. At the end of the 1950s, in response to congressional criticism,

President Eisenhower appointed the Draper Committee to look into the problem. "The Committee argued that for economic development to occur, order and stability were essential. For the first time in U.S. public policy, a close link between security assistance and economic progress was made. . . . The Committee advocated an expansion of U.S. training of Third World military personnel."[20]

The Draper Committee's recommendations were soon incorporated into U.S. policy toward Latin America. A major vehicle for implementation was the Alliance for Progress, a program of development assistance to Latin America modeled somewhat after the Marshall Plan for Europe, but on a much more modest scale. The alliance was inaugurated under President Kennedy as a direct response to the Cuban revolution of 1959. In order to prevent the outbreak of further revolutions and to diminish the appeal of the Cuban example, the United States offered a package of economic aid and technical assistance designed to stimulate economic development and encourage political reform. The alliance has recently been characterized as "history's boldest venture of regionwide development."[21] This bold venture did help to stimulate economic growth, as noted in Chapter 3. But it failed to redress the deep social inequalities in Central America. One reason is that there was another side to the Alliance for Progress: it was a major instrument for pursuing U.S. security goals in the region. The flow of military aid increased sharply in the 1960s, accompanied by extensive training programs geared to "riot control, intelligence gathering, surveillance techniques, and psychological warfare."[22] The strengthening of the military through these programs worked at cross-purposes with the goals of political reform because it failed to reform the military itself. The army continued to play its traditional role as arbiter of national politics, but now with an enhanced capacity to do so.

The same scenario was repeated by the Nixon administration. When President Nixon encountered congressional resistance to his efforts to send military aid to Latin America, he created the Rockefeller Commission to study the Latin American military. *The Rockefeller Report on Latin America,* which was presented to Congress in the fall of 1969, spoke of "a new type of military man" who was "becoming a major force for constructive social change in the American republics."[23] According to this view, aid to security forces in Latin American nations promised to avert instability (the very instability that occurred in the 1970s). Although Congress was not entirely persuaded, and reduced allocations for training security forces, the Nixon administration nevertheless managed to increase the sale of military equipment sharply.

In 1983 President Reagan appointed yet another presidential

commission—this time with a focus on the crisis in Central America—to make recommendations on U.S. policy. The National Bipartisan Commission on Central America was chaired by former Secretary of State Henry Kissinger. It is therefore commonly referred to as the Kissinger Commission. The commission issued its report to President Reagan in early 1984, a half-century after Sandino's assassination in Nicaragua and the establishment of Somoza's dictatorship based on the National Guard. That fifty-year legacy of militarism made no impression whatever on the commission. Like its predecessors, it focused heavily on present security issues and made strong recommendations concerning aid to the security forces in friendly Central American nations. Its recommendations were made in the light of strong affirmations of recent progress toward democracy alleged to have taken place in El Salvador, Honduras, and Guatemala. Military aid, the commission argued, was necessary to safeguard that progress and to protect U.S. interests. The commission did not acknowledge that in El Salvador and Guatemala that aid would flow to governments that are dominated by the military, thanks in no small measure to the previous decades of strong U.S. support for their armed forces.

What was most alarming was that the armies of El Salvador and Guatemala were, at that very time, at war with large sectors of their own populace. These wars were directed at indigenous groups—at peasants and peasant leaders, trade unionists, teachers, the clergy, opposition party leaders, and lay Christians. People from all walks of life despaired of finding political space in which to express their demands and meet their needs. So, like the people in Nicaragua prior to the revolution there, they joined political coalitions that took the form of broad popular organizations. These organizations were deeply inspired by democratic political values and by Christian principles. The Catholic Church was a major source of inspiration to them. They were struggling to create the political space that all individuals and groups need, that the citizens of free nations cherish, and to expand the representative base of the political system. This was a goal that the report of the Kissinger Commission also endorsed. But, in the eyes of the military regimes to which the commission now wished to commit massive resources, these groups had no legitimate standing in the political arena. Their members, tens of thousands of humble campesinos like Pablo in La Union, were labeled "subversives," agents of communism, to be suppressed or eliminated. The commission's report makes no mention of these popular organizations, arguably the most important political development in modern Central American history. We will come back to the Kissinger Commission's account of the crisis in Central America. First, we can get a still more complete picture of U.S. attitudes and behavior toward Latin America by taking a look at the Monroe Doctrine.

FROM MR. MONROE TO MR. REAGAN

During its visit to Honduras, the CCCS team spent an afternoon at Palmerola Air Force Base, which stands as one of the most vivid signs of the growing U.S. military presence in Central America today. Tens of thousands of U.S. soldiers have been trained at Palmerola in recent years. To many Central Americans it appears that they are being trained for a direct invasion of Nicaragua. During our visit a briefing officer, an army lieutenant colonel, commented on the importance of this military preparedness. Such readiness is important right now, he argued, in order to resist the aggressions of such adversaries as Cuba and Nicaragua. But he also felt the urgency of this show of strength because the next president of the United States might be a supporter of the Monroe Doctrine. A president with those sentiments, he felt, might be reluctant to show the U.S. flag in Central America.

We were struck by the colonel's references to the Monroe Doctrine. It is not surprising that an army public-relations officer should be aware of the Monroe Doctrine. It is, after all, a keystone of U.S. history, especially with respect to our role in the Americas. What surprised us was that the colonel had such a muddled understanding of the doctrine. He had reversed its common interpretation. He presented it to us as a precedent *against* intervention, when it has long been cited as the classic justification *for* intervention. Yet strangely, the colonel was far closer to the truth than he knew. Let us turn now to that story.

The Monroe Doctrine and Its Corollaries

Earlier we spoke of 130 years of U.S. intervention in Latin America. The seeds of intervention actually go back even further. In the early decades of the nineteenth century, the fledgling United States of America was still a weak nation, but its leaders envisioned it becoming a great power. In 1803 Thomas Jefferson acquired the Louisiana Territory. In 1811 James Madison issued the so-called No-Transfer Resolution, in which he declared that European nations could not transfer among themselves any territory in the Western Hemisphere. At that time the countries of Central and South America were still under Spain's control, although they were moving toward independence.

Madison's declaration was probably unenforceable, but it did give notice of the emerging U.S. attitude toward the Americas.

Then, in 1823, President James Monroe sent a message to Congress that had been drafted by John Quincy Adams, his secretary of state. In the light of Latin America's successful fight for independence from Spain, which was just concluding, the Monroe administration felt it was important to warn European powers not to try to take advantage of the turmoil to renew their colonial aspirations in the Western Hemisphere. Monroe promised not to meddle in European affairs and pointedly told the Europeans to follow the same hands-off policy in the Americas. It is important to understand what concerned President Monroe and Secretary Adams in 1823: they feared that Britain intended to settle the Oregon Territory on North America's West Coast. U.S. leaders were already dreaming of extending our nation's frontiers all the way to the Pacific Ocean. Further European colonization would be an obstacle to U.S. ambitions to expand its territory.[24] In short, the original intent of Monroe's "doctrine" was to safeguard this nation's expanding Western frontier. It was not a pledge to guarantee Latin American independence or to assure democracy in other American nations. However, in the light of actions taken by later U.S. presidents, it has come to be understood that way. On the basis of such an understanding, it seemed to follow that if the United States has the right to guarantee another nation's sovereignty, then we are also entitled to intervene in its internal affairs when they threaten to get out of hand. Let's see how that understanding gained acceptance in the United States, while remembering that it never was accepted in Latin America.

In the mid-nineteenth century and again at the beginning of the twentieth, aggressively expansionist U.S. presidents invoked Monroe's declaration of 1823 as a precedent to justify direct interventions in Latin America. Their "corollaries" actually recreated the Monroe Doctrine. In 1844 James K. Polk campaigned on a pledge of winning the entire Oregon Territory for the United States. However, Texas was annexed before he took office, and Britain was too strong to confront militarily in the Northwest. So Polk negotiated a deal with the British in which they agreed to claim only what is today the Canadian province of British Columbia. That left the huge California Territory, which was then under Mexican control, standing between the United States and its access to the Pacific. Now the way was cleared to add a new dimension to the Monroe message of 1823. On the pretext that Mexico was engaged in aggressions against U.S. citizens and property, Polk rushed troops to the Mexican border to restore order. His real intent was to provoke war with Mexico, and his goal was to win territory for the United States. In this aim he succeeded thoroughly. The entire California Territory came under U.S. control in the wake of our defeat of the Mexican army. In a sad and ironic footnote to the episode, Massachusetts congressman John Quincy Adams, author of the Monroe Doctrine, collapsed on the floor of the House of Representatives while opposing President Polk's intervention against a Latin American neighbor.[25] Yet Polk's intervention was only the first of many to come.

The U.S. Civil War brought a lull in further interventions during the second half of the nineteenth century. But by the turn of the century, the United States was ready once again to assert itself vigorously in the Americas and around the world. The Spanish-American War of 1898 launched the period known as the "Era of Imperialism."[26] As a direct result of this war against a badly overmatched foe, the United States acquired Puerto Rico, occupied Cuba, and precipitated Panamanian independence from Colombia. In the following decades the United States went on to intervene in the Dominican Republic and occupied Nicaragua and Haiti for lengthy periods of time. President Roosevelt provided the rationale for these actions. He told Congress that the Monroe Doctrine entitled the president of the United States to "the exercise of an international police power."[27] This view bore little resemblance to the original Monroe message. Had John Quincy Adams been present to hear these words, he would undoubtedly have repudiated them. But Roosevelt was successful in effecting this metamorphosis of the Monroe Doctrine. Later presidents followed his lead, not Adams', as the United States became a superpower and the decisive political actor in the Americas.

By mistake, the colonel at Palmerola was actually correct: the original Monroe Doctrine was not a call for intervention in Latin America. But the Monroe Doctrine of the Polk and Roosevelt corollaries stands squarely behind the colonel's presence in Honduras. This Monroe Doctrine has justified countless interventions in Latin America, many of them in Central America. We have already examined interventions of the 1920s and 1950s. Let us now look at more recent events.

The Compulsion to Intervene

Of the six presidents who have followed Dwight Eisenhower to the White House, four have presided over a major intervention in Latin America. The Cuban revolution, which took place while Eisenhower was still in office, was a crucial event in these developments. A Cuba allied with the Soviet Union has worried all six of these presidents.

Only President Carter made any attempt to normalize relations with Cuba; all the others have regarded Cuba with hostility and contempt. The very existence of a revolutionary Cuba has been treated as an affront to the Monroe Doctrine and a threat to the rest of Latin America. Each of Eisenhower's successors was resolved that there would be no more Cubas. To this end President Kennedy initiated the Alliance for Progress. He also oversaw the unsuccessful attempt to invade Cuba at the Bay of Pigs in April 1961. President Johnson sent 20,000 U.S. troops to the Dominican Republic in 1965 to assure that another Cuba did not develop there. Under Richard Nixon the CIA worked behind the scenes in an attempt to prevent Salvador Allende's election as president of Chile because he headed a leftist coalition. Then, after he was elected, the CIA worked to undermine the effectiveness and credibility of his government. The CIA's actions contributed to Allende's overthrow by a military coup in September 1973.[28] In each of these cases the threat of communism and Soviet influence in the Americas was a central justification of U.S. policy.

In early 1979 President Carter faced a new wave of political instability in a Central American neighbor. The Somoza dynasty in Nicaragua hovered on the brink of collapse due to a growing armed uprising of the populace led by the Sandinista Front for National Liberation (FSLN). As the insurgent forces advanced, rallying more and more popular support each time they clashed with the National Guard, Somoza's hated army, the Carter administration strove frantically to find a way to get Somoza out of power without permitting a military victory by the guerrilla forces. These efforts failed, and President Carter faced a difficult decision. Should he accept the new government and try to work with it, relying on U.S. diplomatic skill and on material incentives to influence the course of events? Or should the United States reject the new government and look for ways to get rid of it?

Had President Carter chosen the second alternative, his actions would have been consistent with those of several predecessors in the Oval Office. He chose instead to pursue the first option. For the final eighteen months of his presidency, Carter tried to shape events in Central America by preserving U.S. influence in Nicaragua through positive incentives. He did not begin covert actions to overthrow the revolutionary government, although his administration did try to encourage the formation and strengthening of opposition groups within Nicaragua by quietly providing funds to them. He was also determined that there would be no more Nicaraguas in Central America. To that end he set about to shore up other governments in the region that also faced popular uprisings. Most conspicuous in this category was Nicaragua's neighbor, El Salvador. So the Carter administration renewed military aid to the government of El Salvador at the very moment when the repression that produced so much bitter fruit—the exile of Pablo and his family, the murder of his mentor, Dorothy Kazel, and the assassination of Archbishop Romero—began to intensify.

"The Most Important Place in the World"

Despite these efforts by the Carter team, the Reagan administration came into office deeply anguished by what it regarded as the complete failure of the Carter policy. To the Reagan administration the very fact that the Sandinista government was a revolutionary government meant that Nicaragua was "lost" to the community of free nations. Along with Cuba, this represented another breach in the protective wall of the Monroe Doctrine. Since a guerrilla insurgency also posed a serious threat in El Salvador, it too was in danger of being lost to nationalist forces. What had brought Central America to such a condition, and what should the United States do about it? This question gripped the Reagan administration from its very first days in office. President Reagan's approach proved to be much like that of earlier presidents who chose intervention and force as the way to peace and stability.

The president's ambassador to the United Nations, Jeane Kirkpatrick, was one of the first to set forth the administration's perspective. She must have startled many Americans when she announced in early 1981 that "Central America is the most important place in the world for the United States today."[29] For several years U.S. attention had been riveted on the Middle East due to a series of crises that began with the fall of the shah of Iran. Now suddenly it was Central America that threatened us. Secretary of State Alexander Haig tried to explain why. Speaking to NATO officials in February 1981, Haig argued that there was danger for the United States in Central America because "a well orchestrated Communist campaign designed to transform the Salvadoran crisis from the internal conflict to an increasingly internationalized confrontation is underway."[30] The secretary's remarks highlighted two points. First, already in the winter of 1980-1981 a political crisis gripped the Salvadoran government. Given that time frame, Nicaragua had hardly had time to create that crisis. Second, in the administration's view there was a real danger that the crisis would be exploited by external forces hostile to U.S. interests.

This interpretation of Central American events had been urged on a projected Reagan administration months before it was elected to office. In "A New Inter-American Policy for the Eighties," a policy document on Latin America written for the 1980 Republican campaign by the so-called Committee of Santa Fe, candidate Reagan was advised that "the Americas are under attack."[31] The attack was directed at Central America and the Caribbean, where the United States was "being shoved aside . . . by a sophisticated, but brutal, extracontinental power manipulating client states."[32] In the committee's view the Central American policy of the Carter administration had invited Soviet expansion into the Western Hemisphere. The Nicaraguan revolution was the alleged proof. Nicaragua had followed the example of Cuba by passing into the Soviet orbit to become a proxy or client state, doing the work of the Soviet Union. El Salvador was the next country on what Secretary Haig later called the Soviet "hit list."

When the president finally spoke out on Central America in April 1983, he chose a spectacular way of doing so. He called the two houses of Congress together in special session. Since joint-session speeches are rare, this action underscored the importance that his administration attached to Central America. In his speech the president portrayed El Salvador as a nation struggling gallantly to achieve democratic reforms. To succeed it needed only a firm commitment of political support from the United States, together with an ample infusion of economic and military aid. The chief obstacle to El Salvador's transition to democracy was the presence of guerrilla forces fighting to overthrow the government. These forces were being instigated, supplied, and perhaps even directed by Nicaragua. On these grounds the president summoned Congress to support his policy of opposing Nicaragua and aiding El Salvador. Such support was necessary, he explained near the end of his speech, because "the national security of all the Americas is at stake in Central America. If we cannot defend ourselves there, we cannot expect to prevail elsewhere. Our credibility would collapse, our alliances would crumble."[33]

To skeptical members of Congress, this dramatic conclusion seemed exaggerated. Why was our credibility placed at risk by these events in Nicaragua and El Salvador, two small and exceedingly poor countries that possessed neither the precious raw materials nor the strategic location that had made Iran, for example, so important to us? What caused the political upheaval in these countries? What if any connection was there between Nicaragua, El Salvador, Cuba, and the Soviet Union? The Kissinger Commission was created to provide persuasive answers to these questions, answers that could vindicate the president's claims and justify his policies. Let us examine the commission's findings and recommendations.

DRAWING A BEAD ON REVOLUTION

The report of the Kissinger Commission is a fascinating mixture of factual description and appeal to moral values. It tries to bring moral principles and hardheaded, pragmatic common sense together in a single vision. It appeals to the most positive features of the historic relationship between North America and Latin America. On a superficial reading it appears sophisticated, well informed, and firmly grounded on the highest ideals of the Americas. But a more careful reading reveals that the report is seriously deficient in its portrayal of the Central American crisis and its origins in an earlier history; that it is carefully selective in its treatment of cause and effect, ignoring many crucial factors; and that there are deep contradictions between the ideals it affirms and the policies it recommends. In the final analysis, the report is overwhelmingly concerned with the security of Central America as defined by the United States. To this end, it recommends a strong U.S. commitment to the militarization of the region. The intervention into the internal affairs of Central American nations that accompanies such militarization is justified, oddly enough, in the name of democratic self-determination.

"Powerful Forces Are on the March"

According to the Kissinger Report, Central America poses both an economic and a political challenge to the United States. The economic challenge derives from "the contraction of the hemisphere's economies, and the impoverishment of its people."[34] This downturn is attributed to international market forces that adversely affected Central America in the 1970s. The report suggests that the United States must invest in Central America in order to restore its economic growth.

The political challenge, it was claimed, "centers on the legitimacy of government. . . . Powerful forces are on the march in nearly every country . . . testing how nations shall be organized and by what processes authority shall be established and legitimized."[35] This observation is perceptive because in a crucial sense Central America's crisis *is* political in nature. As suggested previously, it arose from a breakdown in the legitimacy of existing political systems. But the commission is unnecessarily vague about specifying the source of the political challenge. What, we might ask, is meant by the phrase "powerful forces"? Does it refer to hostile foreign armies? If so, why doesn't the commission tell us who they are? Suppose we take a different tack, substituting the terms "revolution" and "counterrevolution," as the commission itself does almost immediately after mentioning "power-ful forces." These terms give a different sense of the "powerful forces." They point to local rebellions against tyranny and the struggle of local elites to maintain a privileged way of life. Consider how the commission confronts the reality of revolution in Central America:

> The issue is not what particular system a nation might choose when it votes. The issue is rather that nations should choose for themselves, free of outside pressure, force or threat. There is room in the hemisphere for differing forms of governance and different political economies. Authentically indigenous changes, and even indigenous revolutions, are not incompatible with international harmony in the Americas. They are not incompatible even with the mutual security of the members of the inter-American system—if they are truly indigenous.[36]

This is an intriguing paragraph, and an important one. It is typical of much of the argument in the commission's report. One can only applaud every line—except the last one. The last line gives the argument away. It is the escape clause that activates the Monroe Doctrine. It reminds us, if we are watching for it, that Washington will decide whether or not Central American revolutions are truly indigenous. Based on the facts of Central American history, a history marred by repeated U.S. interventions, we realize that the paragraph just cited describes a Central America that Washington has never permitted to exist. We begin to suspect that the real aim of the Kissinger Commission is to justify yet another intervention, and therefore the goal of its argument will be to persuade us that the present revolutionary upheavals in Central America are not "truly indigenous."

The "Inter-American System"

Clearly it is the threat of revolution in Central America that has precipitated a sense of crisis in Washington. The threat is present because existing political systems have lost legitimacy. The commission does not acknowledge what this means—because it means that revolution is an effect and not a cause of the crisis. The revolutionary movements arose in such countries as Nicaragua and El Salvador in response to the crisis created by electoral fraud and abusive, authoritarian government. Accordingly, the revolutionary struggles led by these movements are directed at the old regimes, not at the United States. Neither are they inspired by Cuba or the Soviet Union, but rather by the oppression and brutality within these countries themselves.

Given the importance the United States supposedly attaches to the principle of self-determination, why does this sort of crisis concern the United States at all? It is important to recognize how the commission handles this question. When laying the groundwork for U.S. intervention in the crisis, it speaks not of individual countries challenged by particular revolutionary movements but of the "inter-American system" and of "powerful forces." The term "powerful forces" is used to obscure the historical roots and the broadly based, indigenous nature of revolutionary movements like the FSLN in Nicaragua and similar guerrilla groups in neighboring countries. Such vague terms are used in order to forge a plausible link between these movements and the efforts by Cuba and the Soviet Union to export subversion to Central America.

In the same way, the term "inter-American system" does not refer to the Organization of American States or any other collective body of American states. The term is intentionally vague because the commission wishes to imply a broad sense of agreement about Central America among the nations of the Western Hemisphere, an agreement that does not exist. The report relies heavily on this inference. It wishes to equate U.S. interests with those of the Central American nations. But these countries are individually unique, and have different interests that separate each from the others. Profound differences also separate them from the United States itself. The Kissinger Commission's view is untenable because, in fact, virtually all of our neighbors in the Western Hemisphere see the crisis in Central America differently than Washington does. Their disagreement with the United States about Central America will be discussed in the last section of this chapter.

According to the commission's report, revolution is necessary at times to fulfill one of the major principles of the Inter-American system, which is self-determination. The United States' own revolution was undertaken in the interest of self-determination. Apparently some of our small neighbors want to follow our example. Why, then, is the present revolutionary movement in Central America incompatible with inter-American security and a danger to the United States? Why would it threaten legitimate political systems? The commission's answer to these questions is really what the report is all about. But the commission did not discover the answer in Central America. It had the answer when it went there.

REWRITING HISTORY

The Kissinger Commission's portrayal of Central American history is brief, but it does grasp some key threads. It recognizes that Central

American economies have long depended entirely on agriculture, that landholdings have been highly concentrated, and that government has been authoritarian. The landed elite has dominated national life. After World War II the military became an increasingly influential political actor. Even so, the commission suggests that "the trend seemed to favor the growth of centrist political forces and to be leading toward greater pluralism and more representative political orders." Unfortunately, what the commission saw as "moderately progressive" tendencies were never consolidated. Instead, they "gave way in the 1970's to a succession of extremely repressive regimes."[37]

What happened in Central America in the 1970s to cause this turn toward political repression? The report gives the following answer. Through the formation of the Central American Common Market (the CACM, designed to promote regional trade and economic cooperation), and under the stimulus of the Alliance for Progress, Central America experienced rapid economic growth for more than a decade. With economic growth came rising expectations on the part of ordinary people. However, these expectations were never fulfilled. Instead, "the fruits of the long period of economic expansion were distributed in a flagrantly inequitable manner." The result was that "during the 1970's about half of the urban population and three-quarters of the rural population could not satisfy their basic needs in terms of nutrition, housing, health, and education."[38]

In statements such as these the commission clearly identified *what* happened in Central America. What the commission did not do was explain *why* it happened. In fact, one of the report's most striking features is that it never even tried to do so. It never acknowledged the contradiction between its portrayal of Central American regimes in the 1960s as "moderately progressive" and the violently authoritarian course they took in the 1970s. In fact, these regimes did not really change during the 1960s and 1970s. Only the political conditions in which they functioned changed. During this period popular expectations rose but were dashed by repressive governments. But the populace was increasingly unwilling to bow to this repression. As popular organizations spread, so did popular resistance. This story will be told more fully in Chapter 6. But the commission ignored these changing political conditions, as it ignored the U.S. role in creating them.

The closest the Kissinger Report comes to finding a cause of the crisis within Central America itself is to mention the pressures of rapid population growth and migration to the cities: "Except in Costa Rica, rapid urbanization and population growth overwhelmed the limited resources that governments were prepared to devote to social services."[39]

This analysis begs several important questions. Why were peasants streaming into the cities during those decades? Why did existing governments devote only scant resources to such serious problems? It would have been appropriate to ask whether these governments were investing any resources at all in improving the living conditions of campesinos. Had they ever done so? Were these regimes structured to respond in any way, other than violently, to the problems of the poor? The commission did not provide answers to these questions because it never asked them. It was content to explain the domestic roots of the crisis by blaming it on overpopulation. This enabled the commission to avoid the difficult questions about the legitimacy and popularity of governments that the United States supported throughout this period.

Asking the Right Questions

Had the Kissinger Commission been willing to ask these hard questions, it would have uncovered some vital things about the local roots of Central American conflict. This would have enabled it to provide the president with badly needed perspective on the region. With the exception of Costa Rica, each of these countries has a long record of violent, fraudulent elections. During the period in question, elections were repeatedly rigged, stolen, or canceled to avoid democratization. Such evidence directly contradicts the commission's claim that in El Salvador, Nicaragua, and Guatemala, "where the crisis for U.S. policy is centered . . . a trend toward more open, pluralistic, and democratic societies [in the 1960s] gave way [in the 1970s] to oppression and polarization."[40] The fact is that in all of these countries electoral fraud had been occurring long before the 1960s, and continued without interruption throughout that decade.

Earlier in this chapter we mentioned the case of El Salvador. In Guatemala the presidential election of 1958 brought to power a candidate who received votes from only 12.7 percent of the adult population; this occurred because of the narrowness of the political system and because a large number of people simply refused to honor the elections by casting their votes. The 1963 elections were canceled due to a military coup. In 1966 and 1970, winning candidates received only 10 percent and 10.5 percent of the vote respectively, with the rate of abstention climbing to almost 50 percent. It is true that these figures became even more extreme in the 1970s, but that reflects a *continuity* with the past, not a new development, as the commission implies. A more accurate picture of the status of elections in Guatemala during the 1960s and 1970s was given by that nation's vice-president in 1979:

"The people do not care about elections because of their experiences in the past. We cannot talk about an electoral method of change."[41]

The elites who held power in the 1960s and 1970s had no interest in the kind of reform that truly representative political institutions might bring about. They were not reformist. They were reactionary, and among these reactionary elements one of the most prominent was the military. The armed forces played a vital role in this history of electoral fraud. Increasingly during those years it was military men, or those whom the military supported, who attained office. The army contributed not to reform and progress but to continuity with the past. This situation meant that ultimately the demand for change would explode in revolution.

Meanwhile, the Kissinger Commission told the Reagan administration what it already believed. The real threat to democracy and development in Central America, it claimed, lies outside El Salvador, Honduras, and Guatemala. The real threat is Cuba, acting as a proxy for the Soviet Union. Not only are the Cubans coming—they have already arrived in Nicaragua. Thus, in the middle of its chapter on the history of Central America, the commission abandons that study in order to get on to the issue that is really its exclusive concern: what it sees as the growth of a communist insurgency in Central America, fostered by Cuba and Nicaragua. The commission never mentions the Matanza of 1932, and thus it never considers the possibility that this event might have some connection with the crisis in El Salvador in the 1980s. Nor does it consider that a study of the Matanza and its legacy might afford useful instruction to the present generation of U.S. policymakers. Neither does the commission dwell on the legacy of Sandino, the history of U.S. intervention in Nicaragua and Guatemala, or the unseemly closeness of our ties to the Somoza dynasty that the Sandinista revolution destroyed. Instead, it clears the decks for a discussion of the Central American crisis that ignores such crucial historical factors entirely, together with the lessons they might hold. In this way the Kissinger Commission facilitates a repetition of the old cry from the 1930s: the crisis in Central America is primarily a problem of external aggression.

PATHS TO WAR AND PEACE

In December 1986 Dr. Jorge Abadia Arias, Panama's foreign minister, gave a speech at Harvard University entitled "Simplicity and Peace in Central America." In that speech he tried to cut through the inflamed rhetoric that surrounds the crisis in Central America and to identify basic principles that all nations in the Western Hemisphere can embrace. One such principle, enshrined in all hemispheric agreements, is self-determination. That principle is particularly cherished by Latin Americans, who embrace their tortured memories of the Monroe Doctrine and the legacy of U.S. interventions. There is growing sentiment throughout Latin America that the days of such intervention must come to an end. As Dr. Abadia put it, "There is a point where the national pride and independence of one people cease to be a threat to the pride and independence of others." For Latin American leaders throughout the continent, this has become a compelling viewpoint. It applies with great force to the role of the United States in Central America today—above all to our attitude and actions toward Nicaragua. Our friends and neighbors do not agree with our policy of supporting armed counter-revolution against Nicaragua. They have actively mobilized against it. Perhaps a glance at several episodes in U.S.-Nicaraguan relations during the past few years will help to illustrate why, and will prepare us for a deeper examination of the alternatives in Central America: war or peace.

The Attack on Ocotal

On 1 June 1984, Secretary of State George Shultz visited the Nicaraguan capital of Managua for consultations with Sandinista leaders. He came to explain what concerns his government had about Nicaraguan policies and what was demanded of the Sandinistas if Nicaragua was to live in peace with the United States. Secretary Shultz's one-day trip is important for several reasons. It is the *only* visit to Nicaragua by a U.S. official of cabinet rank. It was made without prior notice, either to the Nicaraguan government or to the U.S. public, because there was strong opposition within the Reagan administration to any effort to have talks with the Sandinista government. While in Managua, Secretary Shultz made two key demands of the Sandinistas. First, they must significantly reduce the size of their army because it threatened their neighbors. Second, they must take immediate steps to restore democracy to Nicaragua, because only then could the United States and the rest of Central America feel secure.

On the same day that Secretary Shultz was lecturing the Sandinistas on U.S. security concerns, a force of about 600 counterrevolutionary soldiers, the Contras, attacked the northern Nicaraguan city of Ocotal. (This was the same city where U.S. Marines had been based in 1927 during the guerrilla war led by Sandino.) The Contras swarmed into Ocotal wearing U.S.-made uniforms and carrying U.S.-supplied weapons. They had been trained and prepared by the CIA for this attack, only one of hundreds that have occurred throughout Nicaragua since 1982. The attack destroyed a saw mill that employed 250 workers and supported an additional 250 families indirectly. It destroyed the offices and generating station of the local electrical plant. It severely damaged a coffee-processing plant and a granary that held nearly a year's supply of basic grains. Including Contra casualties, about 65 people were killed and another 35 wounded. Throughout the attack Contra troops fired indiscriminately on the civilian population, and during their retreat they fired on the local hospital.[42] The purpose of a large Nicaraguan army is to defend the civilian population against such external aggression. Moreover, to demand the expansion of democratic liberties in a nation while simultaneously waging war against it is illogical and unrealistic. In such a situation the army will grow, and liberties that one can expect in times of peace are likely to be restricted. As José Figueres, the great elder statesman of Costa Rican democracy, told the members of the CCCS team, "How could it be different? They are in a war situation. When Somoza invaded Costa Rica we also had censorship!"

When Secretary Shultz visited Managua in June 1984, the covert war against Nicaragua had already been underway for more than three years. Nicaraguan harbors had been mined, seaports and airports had been bombed, and hundreds of lives had been lost in Contra assaults. Most of the victims were noncombatants. Across the border in Honduras, the United States was carrying on almost continuous military exercises while building up an elaborate network of military installations and facilities that could be used to launch a full-scale invasion of Nicaragua. Secretary Shultz and other officials in Washington describe these U.S. actions as "defensive." In Latin America, however, these actions look decidedly offensive.

To counteract these hostilities, leading statesmen from throughout the region have been working since January 1983 to achieve a diplomatic solution to the conflict between Nicaragua and the United States. By late 1985 eight Latin American nations, together representing 85 percent of the region's people, had joined in this diplomatic effort, known as the Contadora peace initiative. The key to its success is Washington's willingness to cooperate.

Going "All Out" for Contra Aid

On 10 February 1986, the foreign ministers of the Contadora nations, together with the foreign ministers of the Lima Support Group, visited

Washington. They came representing such Latin American nations as Mexico and Venezuela, which have long been stable and dependable allies of the United States. They represented the large South American nations of Brazil, Argentina, and Peru, which had only recently been hailed by Washington for ending long periods of military rule and returning to democratic forms of government. They came to speak for Latin America and on behalf of Central America. Their message was simple but urgent. Please, they implored Secretary Shultz, persuade your government to halt aid to the Contras and resume direct talks with Nicaragua. Covert wars are in no one's interest. Differences between nations can and should be settled peacefully.

Secretary Shultz listened to his Latin American visitors, but he offered them no encouragement in response to their entreaties. The foreign-policy momentum in the administration he served was moving very much the other way. As this meeting was taking place, another meeting was being held at the White House. There President Reagan was telling a reporter from the *Washington Post* that he intended "to go all out" to persuade Congress to provide more military aid for the Contras. During the spring of 1986 he did just that, all the while expressing support for the Contadora peace process. In June the House of Representatives voted by a narrow margin for Contra aid, and the Senate followed in July. Interestingly, when the Senate passed the measure, it attached a statement urging that the United States continue to support the Contadora diplomatic initiative.

Latin Americans have been trying to tell us that these words and actions are irreconcilable. We cannot continue to speak of our commitment to peace while waging war. We cannot pledge our belief in self-determination at the same time that we intervene in the affairs of our neighbors and repeatedly ignore their counsel. In the next chapter we will look more closely at the Central American war that we are so deeply involved in. We will confront its costs to Central Americans and its costs to the United States. It is a war for which we must take our measure of responsibility. It is also a war that can be ended. A peaceful alternative is waiting. Our Latin neighbors have seized it already and call for our cooperation.

5. EXPANDING WAR AND THE SEARCH FOR PEACE

You will hear of wars and rumors of wars. . . . Nation will rise against nation, and kingdom against kingdom. There will be famines and earthquakes in various places. All these are the beginning of the birth pains. Then you will be handed over to be persecuted and put to death.

Matthew 24:6-9

A View from Honduras

The cameras of "Sixty Minutes" whirred silently as the journalist interviewed a circle of angry Hondurans gathered in the middle of a dusty road. Across the street, more people lounged about in front of the ramshackle, barn-like wooden building that had become their temporary home. The name of the group's run-down shelter was *El Dolar* ("The Dollar"). Ironically, their grief and anger had a lot to do with dollars—specifically the millions of dollars in military assistance that had been passing between Washington and the Honduran-based Contras, an armed force fighting against the government of Nicaragua.

It was Sunday morning, 8 February 1987. "Sixty Minutes" had come to the town of Danlí in southern Honduras because these angry farmers had a message for the people of the United States. Until recently they had been prosperous, self-employed coffee growers on small farms in the province of El Paraiso, the country's second-best zone for raising coffee. But that was before the Contras came and took over about forty villages in their area, occupying some 180 square kilometers of territory. The Contras were supposed to move into Nicaragua to fight the Sandinista government. Instead, they settled permanently enough in the region around El Paraiso to drive these Hondurans off their lands. With cruel irony this Honduran territory was coming to be known as "Free Nicaragua."[1] Thus this group of hardworking, self-sufficient Hondurans joined the estimated 15,000 internal Honduran refugees who are today displaced within their own country by the Contra war.[2]

A few weeks before, under the sponsorship of AHPROCAFE (Honduran Association of Coffee Growers), these victims of the Contra war had sent a delegation to the U.S. Embassy in the Honduran capital of Tegucigalpa. There they presented a petition to U.S. diplomats. Inasmuch as U.S. funds financed the Contras, and the Contras had driven the Hondurans from their lands, would the United States provide financial assistance to help them relocate or in some other way overcome their desperate situation? Embassy officials replied that the United States was not responsible for what the Contras did and therefore could render no assistance to the farmers of Danlí.

So here they were, standing before the cameras of "Sixty Minutes," hoping to get their message through to the North American people. (The program was aired on 28 March 1987.) Their story dramatized the tragic consequences of the widening war in Central America. People who had no desire to wage war were nevertheless caught up in one. Being in the path of the Contras meant threats, assaults, stolen cattle and crops, rape, torture, and even murder.[3] One woman told how her husband had been murdered by the Contras and her son killed in battle by the Sandinistas. An Assembly of God pastor reported that sixteen church buildings had been destroyed in the area. The leader of AHPROCAFE added a bitter note of irony to the situation when he informed the farmers that one of their activists had been detained by the Honduran police for protesting their predicament. Their anguished and indignant response was understandable. "This is completely backward," said one. "They ought to put the Contras in jail, and give us money to rebuild our lives; instead they give money to the Contras, who aren't even Hondurans, and throw us in jail!"

Not far from Danlí, heading due west, lies a refugee camp near Jacaleapa. There almost 4,500 Nicaraguan Ladinos (Spanish-speaking Latin Americans) while away the day wishing the war would end. Some of the young men in the camp fled Nicaragua to avoid the draft. Other refugees are family members of Contra combatants. A number of people complained about the Sandinistas; others complained about the Contras, saying they had nothing against the Sandinistas.

We wandered through the camp talking to people at random, collecting an array of vivid, piercing images of people displaced by war. There was radiant-faced Carmen, a teenager, who lived with her mother and handicapped brother. She had been in the camp for years and had heard that her father died fighting with the Contras, but she wasn't sure. She still hoped to see him one day. In one of the tents for the recently arrived, a wizened old grandmother said she had three sons with the Contras. She was praying for their triumph; "God is with us," she said. Like the others, she was eager for the war to end. A man in his mid-thirties stood beside a wooden wheelbarrow that he had made himself. He wished that the camp administration would come through with a water pump they had promised two years ago. "Look how dry this ground is," he said. "Without that pump we can't make it produce anything." On second thought he added, "What we need most, though, is peace." Then he could return to the cultivation of his own, more fertile land in Nicaragua.

The testimony from both Danlí and Jacaleapa made clear that the immediate victims of the Contra war are both Nicaraguans and Hondurans. They are humble people on both sides of the border who were never consulted about the war, only subjected to it. Their overriding concern is for the peace that will enable them to mend their broken lives.

Meanwhile, all across Honduras were signs of preparation for more war. Returning from Jacaleapa to Tegucigalpa, we met U.S. army engineers who were building a large airport at San Lorenzo, on the Gulf of Fonseca, just minutes by air from the Nicaraguan border. Farther east, in Olancho province, planes flew to and from the Aguacate airstrip carrying the provisions of war to Contra forces operating inside Nicaragua. At the mammoth air-force base of Palmerola, in the heart of central Comayagua province, the United States had stationed about 12,000 of its own soldiers. Since 1982 the Reagan administration has run an average of sixty military exercises per year, with the result that nearly 100,000 U.S. military personnel have trained on Honduran soil in the past five years.[4] U.S. aid to Honduras has soared from a few million dollars in 1979 to several hundred million in 1986.

"We Are . . . Only a Territory"

The brutality of war has become daily fare for tens of thousands of rural Hondurans and Nicaraguans. The reality of war also monopolizes the resources and energies of the Nicaraguan and Honduran governments. We will examine the war's impact on Nicaragua later in the chapter. For the moment, let's continue our focus on Honduras.

The citizens of this, the poorest of Central American nations, increasingly feel that they have been asked to make inordinate sacrifices in order that the United States can pursue its interests in the region. The argument made in Washington is that the war against Nicaragua is intended to protect Honduras. But becoming a base for military operations against Nicaragua may itself threaten Honduran stability. Honduran leaders seem to have little illusion that their country's needs are at the top of Washington's agenda in the Contra war. As one leader caustically put it, "For the United States we are not a nation, only a territory. We are selling them our place on the map, but not being very well paid for it."[5]

A glance at the map of Central America reveals immediately what that disillusioned Honduran leader meant. The longest territorial border in Central America joins Honduras and Nicaragua. For the most part the border region is one of the least developed areas of both countries. Historically it has been neglected by both governments. Add to this the fact that many Nicaraguans associated with the government of Anastasio Somoza, and particularly with the Nicaraguan National Guard, fled to Honduras when the Sandinista forces toppled the dictatorship, and you have an ideal setting from which to mount a counterrevolutionary war. The Contras (to be described in more detail in a subsequent section) became the weapon for waging such a war.

Ironically, the government of Honduran president Roberto Suazo-Cordova (1981-1985) resolutely pretended that there were no Contra bases in Honduras, even when their presence became an obvious, well-publicized fact by the spring of 1983. This pretense undermined the integrity and credibility of his administration. The government of José Azcona-Hoyo, which took office in December 1985, acknowledged the Contra bases, but justified its tolerance of the situation by arguing that they were inherited from Suazo-Cordova. Extending this rather odd logic, the Azcona government excused the denials of the Suazo administration about the Contras with the argument that to have admitted their presence would have been "a violation of the Constitution." As if the actual existence of the bases was not! These linguistic contortions point to the harsh reality that has confronted the Honduran government since the inception of the Contra war. The Hondurans have no reason themselves to go to war with Nicaragua, but they do not wish to lose favor with the United States either. Growing U.S. preoccupation with Nicaragua meant an opportunity for Honduras to get into the U.S. aid pipeline, possibly in a big way. If Honduras could avoid being implicated too heavily in the Contra project, it might be a good bargain. The problem was, of course, that any cooperation in the Contra war was bound to have repercussions for Honduras, as the opening scenarios of this chapter demonstrate. Other consequences were suggested in interviews with Honduran intellectuals.

Victor Meza, an outstanding sociologist and the director of the Documentation Center of Honduras, explained the country's predicament in the following terms. If the Contras were actually to win their war against the Sandinistas, the military and economic aid presently flowing into Honduras would likely be diverted to Nicaragua. In that event, the success of the U.S.-Contra project would represent a loss for Honduras. They would stand to lose U.S. aid and gain an unstable, problematic neighbor to the south. Thousands of Sandinistas would take to the mountains, and "liberated" Nicaragua would likely be snarled in further guerrilla war, perhaps for decades. That war would inevitably affect Honduras. On the other hand, if the war were to end in defeat for the Contras, the obvious fact of Honduran collaboration would leave it with a badly tarnished image. Not only might U.S. aid diminish once Honduras had lost its strategic importance, but the country would be left with weakened credibility. And this would be taking place in the Central American country that already has the most fragile sense of national identity. In addition, Honduras would have on its southern border a strongly entrenched Sandinista government against which it had cooperated in a long but unsuccessful armed aggression. On the west would be their historic enemy, El Salvador, heavily armed by the United States. According to Meza's analysis, Honduras will wind up on the short end no matter how this war turns out, if it is resolved on the battlefield.

At this point another difficulty becomes obvious, illustrating just how compromised Honduras has become by cooperating with the U.S. policy of aggressive support for the Contras. If Honduras decided to expel the Contras, how would it go about doing so? The Contras are a large military force and are well armed. They have shown little disposition to respect Honduran law. Indeed, in regions where they operate, they have become a law unto themselves. There is little reason to think they would quietly leave Honduras if they were ordered to do so by Honduran authorities. What then? Would Honduras try to force them out in armed confrontation? In that event, who would the United States support? If Honduras managed to expel the Contras, who would receive them? No country, including the United States, wants the Contras in its territory. In short, Honduras seems to have painted itself into a corner; it is stuck with the Contras until the United States decides to remove them or to wind down the war with Nicaragua.

These reflections compel us to look further into the rationale for U.S. policy in Central America today, particularly the administration's single-minded dedication to support the Contra war. Can such a policy lead to effective solutions for Honduras and the other countries of the region? If neither the Honduran government nor the Honduran people stand to gain much of enduring value from this war, why are they involved in it at all? The arguments advanced so far have already made it clear that the war taking place on Honduran soil today is not their war but ours.

UNDECLARED WAR

Today, when war in Central America is at least occasionally front-page news in U.S. newspapers, the astonishing fact is that not one of these nations has declared war on any other. It is true that each country except Costa Rica has a powerful army, and that the armies of Guatemala, El Salvador, and Nicaragua have been engaged in fighting almost continuously throughout the 1980s. But we must be clear about the fact that these armies are not fighting each other.

There are in fact two kinds of undeclared war going on simultaneously in Central America today. The first kind is the war waged by governments that face armed rebellion from within the ranks of their own population. In the past two decades Nicaragua, El Salvador, and Guatemala have all waged such wars. El Salvador is the country most openly engaged in such a war today, although Guatemala too faces sporadic armed struggle, particularly in the highland areas where the discontent of indigenous peoples is profound. Such a war ended in Nicaragua in July 1979 with the collapse of the Somoza regime. Only Honduras and Costa Rica have largely escaped such wars.

The second undeclared war, which has come to overlap with the first, is the Contra war against the Sandinista government in Nicaragua. In this second war the United States is the primary actor, while the Contras themselves are secondary actors. They are, in effect, a proxy army. Here too there has been no formal declaration of war. Indeed, the United States is in the odd position of maintaining diplomatic relations with the Sandinistas while promoting war against them.

Both wars have taken frightful tolls on the local populations, with deaths running to the tens of thousands in all three countries. The essential difference between the two kinds of war is that the second, the Contra war, depends entirely on external support for its continuance, support that comes almost exclusively from the United States. An essential similarity is that in both wars it is the Central Americans who fight and die.

The Attack on Pantasma

When the CCCS research team visited San José, Costa Rica, in January

1987, a place to meet and conduct interviews was provided by the Latin American Biblical Seminary. Our sessions were held in a sunlit room off the main inner courtyard known as the "Sala Noel Vargas." On one wall hangs the picture of the young Nicaraguan pastor for whom the room is named. His story symbolizes the hope and the tragedy that are equally associated with the present struggles for and against change in Central America.

Like the majority of his fellow Nicaraguans, Noel was born into a family living at the edge of poverty. But he was a bright, highly motivated child, and his parents struggled and sacrificed so that he could get through high school, a feat accomplished by few Nicaraguans of Noel's humble background during the Somoza era. During high school Noel underwent a religious conversion and decided that God had called him to the ministry. With both his family and his congregation backing him, Noel put together enough funds to attend the Biblical Seminary in San José.

At the seminary Noel was an outstanding student and spiritual leader, loved by all. He learned quickly, wrote with ease, and had, like so many young Nicaraguans, a gift for poetry. It seemed entirely natural that fellow students elected him president of the student body. Then, during the last two years of his studies, the uprising against the Somoza dictatorship broke out back home. Noel followed these historic events closely, identifying with the participation of Christians in the popular struggle. He wrote his graduation thesis on the meaning of Jesus Christ for the new and free Nicaragua for which he hoped and prayed so fervently. He titled it "Christology for the Dawn of a New Day."

Just a few months after the Sandinista triumph of 19 July 1979, Noel Vargas graduated from seminary and went home to Nicaragua. He returned to a country where momentous changes were taking place, and where the young had distinguished themselves with valor in the resistance to Somoza. Many of the young people in his Pentecostal church shared his sympathy for the new government and the revolutionary process. But the leadership of the church was divided over the revolution. Some leaders had their doubts not only about the Sandinistas but also about Noel, who took such a hopeful view of a future filled with change. Noel wished to avoid personal conflicts. He was also convinced that Christ was calling him to costly discipleship. So he chose to leave the relative security of the capital city. He journeyed far into the northern mountains near the Honduran border, where he joined a flourishing farming cooperative at Pantasma. He served there as a pastor and a schoolteacher, soon becoming director of the cooperative school system.

Noel knew he was risking his life by being in Pantasma, for this was a region where the Contra army frequently operated from its bases in nearby Honduras. Because it was remote, it was not easily defended by the Nicaraguan army. But Noel drew reassurance from the fact that Pantasma had no military installation and was of no strategic importance. It was, however, a good example of the successful rural cooperatives that were giving new excitement and meaning to the life of Nicaraguan campesinos in traditionally neglected areas of the country. In this respect at least, Pantasma presented an inviting target for those who wished to sabotage the programs of the revolutionary government.

And then it happened. In late September and early October of 1983, a large Contra task force was operating in the mountains of Jinotega province. They appeared to be aiming at a direct attack on the provincial capital of Jinotega. But after repeated clashes with the Sandinista army, they dispersed into smaller columns and began moving back toward Honduras. In the early hours of 18 October, a band of about 250 Contras closed in on the settlement at Pantasma. At dawn they struck, firing on the community throughout the day with automatic rifles and mortars. Greatly outmatched in firepower, the defenders were eventually overrun. According to witnesses who later discussed the events of that day, the Contra troops made straight for the buildings of the Ministry of Education. Inside were Noel Vargas, his wife, Ángela Aleman, and six other companions. Ángela, who went in search of extra munitions and reinforcements, was the only one to survive. When the others had all been killed, the Contras set fire to the buildings, destroying the Adult Education Center and all the educational materials it contained.[6]

In all, about forty-eight people died, many of them evangelical Christians. The director of the cooperative, a member of the Church of the Nazarene, was killed, as was his daughter, who worked with the Ministry of Health. Seven young people who were bringing education to the campesinos of Pantasma also died, including Noel. His wife and their young son, Noel Angel, will forever carry the scars of that horror-filled day in Pantasma. Theirs is a grief shared by countless other Nicaraguan families, and the numbers continue to grow. Their story testifies to a stark fact about the struggle for Nicaragua: the fighting and the dying take place on Nicaraguan soil.

The plaque under the picture of Noel Vargas, which hangs in the seminary room dedicated to his memory, bears these appropriate words: *Nadie tiene mayor amor que esto, que ponga su vida por sus amigos* ("Greater love hath no man than this, that a man lay down his life for his friends").

Counterinsurgency

The two kinds of war discussed in the previous section are not only united by the fact that they are waged on Central American soil and produce Central American casualties. Another common element is that their military or strategic rationale lies in a doctrine known as "counterinsurgency." This military doctrine has been embraced to some degree by all U.S. presidents since the early 1960s. One of its more enthusiastic supporters was President Kennedy, who said in his 1961 Foreign Aid Message to Congress, "The free world's security can be endangered not only by nuclear attack but also by being slowly nibbled away at the periphery, by forces of subversion, infiltration, intimidation, indirect or non-overt aggression, internal revolution, lunatic blackmail, guerrilla warfare or a series of limited wars."[7] President Kennedy proposed counterinsurgency to offset such threats, an ideal embodied in the John F. Kennedy School of Special Warfare at Fort Bragg, North Carolina.

A document prepared by the Kennedy administration in 1962 to explain "counterinsurgency" to members of Congress serves both to define the term for us and to clarify what is meant by "insurgency." Counterinsurgency, the document said, is "all military, political, economic, psychological activities directed toward preventing and suppressing resistance groups whose actions range from subversive political activity to violent actions by large guerrilla elements to overthrow a duly established government."[8]

Three important keys to the military situation in Central America today are tucked quietly away in this official statement. First, the U.S. government sets for itself the task not only of suppressing "resistance groups" in other nations but also, where possible, of *preventing* such uprisings before they can occur. This means that our armed forces may be called upon not only to perform an international policing function but also to serve as a sort of international revolution-prevention squad. Second, the United States will work to combat and suppress not only "violent resistance" in other countries but also "subversive political activity." This concept evokes images of the Monroe Doctrine, with its recipe for intervention. It presumes a right to intervene in the internal political affairs of other sovereign nations—a right that no country, including the United States, actually has. Third, the United States will intercept both political and armed opposition to friendly governments by every available means—"military, political, economic, psychological." Such means may be utilized even in countries with which we maintain diplomatic relations and whose national sovereignty we allegedly respect.

The announcement of this counterinsurgency doctrine was soon followed by the disastrous invasion of Cuba at the Bay of Pigs in April 1961. The abject failure of the CIA-trained Cuban exiles to overthrow the revolutionary government of Fidel Castro gave added momentum to the U.S. counterinsurgency program. In January 1962 the National Security Council created the "Special Group (Counterinsurgency)" in order to link the White House, the CIA, the State and Defense Departments, and other agencies in a coordinated program of worldwide action. These initiatives were eventually followed by the creation of a large network of similar special groups. Great effort was also invested in the Inter-American Security System. After 1961 the United States sponsored a "Conference of American Armies" almost every year. An ambitious program of military training and financial aid was promoted. In 1968 a high-ranking staff member of the Senate Foreign Relations Committee revealed the objective of the entire counterinsurgency project when he described it as "a policy of stop-gap measures to shore up existing governments, both democratic and dictatorial, provided they are reasonably friendly to the United States."[9]

A primary characteristic of counterinsurgency warfare is that it is undeclared and executed largely through surrogate forces. That is certainly the case in Central America today, which helps to explain why there is so much fighting even though no nation is formally at war. With heavy support from the United States, the armies and security forces of El Salvador and Guatemala are fighting against insurgent forces within their own populations. The Contras, created and sustained by Washington, are trying to overthrow the insurgents who drove the dictator and close U.S. ally Anastasio Somoza out of Nicaragua in 1979. Honduras is caught up in this latter conflict because it has assumed Nicaragua's former role as close regional ally of Washington. In that role it has served, however reluctantly and uncomfortably, as host to the Contras.

U.S.-sponsored counterinsurgency has accentuated the militarism already prevalent in every Central American country except Costa Rica. The process of militarization advanced steadily during the 1960s and 1970s, as was demonstrated in Chapter 4. Since President Reagan declared in 1981 that his administration would "draw the line in Central America," militarization has grown to an alarming new level.

MILITARISM: THE SOLUTION
OR THE PROBLEM?

If we were to survey the five countries of Central America carefully, we would discover certain groupings or pairings of these nations. A first pair would be El Salvador and Guatemala, two countries that are strikingly similar in the sense that government-instigated violence is widespread and long-standing, while guerrilla insurgency seems to have become a permanent reality. A quite different pair of countries would be Costa Rica and Honduras, despite their marked differences. Neither of these nations has experienced the repression and violence typical of El Salvador and Guatemala, and neither is presently threatened by powerful guerrilla movements. Costa Rica abolished its army in 1949, and it has had a functioning political democracy for decades. Honduras, although certainly less democratic than Costa Rica, has not been plagued by the severe political repression and social instability that characterize El Salvador and Guatemala.

Between these two groupings stands Nicaragua. Under Somoza it stood closer to El Salvador and Guatemala. Although elected (fraudulently), the government of Somoza depended on the repressive actions of the National Guard, a corrupt and brutal military force, to maintain itself in power. Yet there were significant differences distinguishing Nicaragua from the other two countries. Nicaragua did not have the same class struggle as El Salvador, nor the indigenous-rights problems of Guatemala. As a result, repression could be used more selectively in that country. Thus, during the four-and-a-half decades that the Somoza family ruled Nicaragua, there was always an appearance of civilian authority, and military repression was utilized with a measure of discretion. By contrast, in El Salvador and Guatemala the armed forces seized power, exercised it directly for long periods, and often used repressive measures indiscriminately.

What is the best explanation for the crucial differences in patterns of development displayed by these five nations? Specifically, why have El Salvador and Guatemala been plunged into such appalling violence, while Costa Rica and, to a lesser degree, Honduras have maintained more successfully the basic stability of their societies? Why, prior to the revolution, was Nicaragua more similar to El Salvador and Guatemala than it was to either Honduras or Costa Rica?

A compelling explanation offered by Central Americans themselves picks up and elaborates the theme we have already introduced. Those countries that earlier in this century tried repeatedly to impose military solutions upon their social and economic problems later suffered from chronic, seemingly uncontrollable violence.[10] By contrast, countries that sought more genuinely political solutions to those social problems suffered much less violence while they enjoyed both greater stability and increased political freedom. The two countries that stand at one extreme of the spectrum in Central American political development—El Salvador and Guatemala—have been completely dominated by the armed forces since the "military solution" was first imposed. Neither Canada nor the United States has experienced this kind of military control over political life. It is therefore undoubtedly difficult for North Americans to appreciate fully what it is like. Nevertheless, we must make some effort to understand its impact on Central American society if we are to grasp both the real roots of the present crisis and the futility of trying to resolve it by means of an escalating counterinsurgency war. A brief glance at the historical record may help.

We must first recall that the military, along with the Roman Catholic Church and the landed elite, was one of three major institutions used by the Spanish crown to subdue and govern its American colonies. Since the colonial period lasted three hundred years, the military had ample opportunity to become deeply entrenched within the political order. Moreover, throughout the colonial era the military in Central America considered itself to be "a class apart," according to Richard Millett, a well-known authority on Central America. "The possession of special privileges enhanced its sense of uniqueness and superiority, and rendered it virtually immune from civil authority." This led to a result few Central Americans would deny: "Unfortunately, power and privilege were not accompanied by a commensurate sense of responsibility"; rather, many officers "regarded military service as an opportunity for the enhancement of personal interests rather than a civil obligation."[11]

When independence came, Central America threw off the yoke of Spanish colonialism without really altering the established patterns of oligarchic and military domination. The movement for independence was not part of a wider social revolution. Independence, so goes an old quip, meant "the end of despotism and the beginning of more of the same." John J. Johnson puts it vividly: "Liberty, equality and fraternity gave way to infantry, cavalry and artillery, as the republics bled themselves in constant warfare."[12] The revolutionary rhetoric of independence was belied by the reality of *caudillismo* (dictatorship) and military rule. "Might is right"—the rule of force rather than law—became an established way of life. The political power of the military grew steadily. At first it acted as an ally of the oligarchy, but by the mid-twentieth century it had become firmly established as a formidable rival to all power groups in these societies; in fact, since the 1930s military officers have governed regularly throughout Central America.

Consider the case of Guatemala. From 1898 to 1920 the country was ruled by the notorious dictator Manuel Estrada Cabrera. Between 1920 and 1944 the country was governed by a succession of military men until the overthrow of the corrupt and ineffective General Jorge Ubico in 1944. For the next ten years the country was governed by two popularly elected presidents (one of whom was also a military man). However, as we explained in Chapter 4, a CIA intervention brought this experiment with elected government to a halt in 1954. Thereafter, only one civilian president was permitted to take office in Guatemala for the next twenty years. That president—Julio Mendez Montenegro (1966-1970)—had to promise the army not to interfere in its affairs, especially in the brutal counterinsurgency campaign that was then being waged against the Indian population in the highlands. Thus his government never represented genuine civilian rule. On the contrary, he was "a prisoner of the military establishment from the outset and [his government] maintained itself by keeping its hands off the military."[13]

When Christian Democrat Vinicio Cerezo was elected president in December 1985, he too made the usual pre-inaugural promises to the armed forces. He agreed not to bring any military personnel to trial for human rights abuses committed during their long tenure in power, a period during which tens of thousands of Guatemalans were murdered in campaigns of government-instigated violence. President Cerezo also promised not to introduce any program of land reform, thus agreeing to tie his own hands in dealing with one of Guatemala's most urgent social problems. Upon taking office, he frankly acknowledged that he possessed only a small portion of the power associated with presidential office; the rest belonged to the armed forces.

In El Salvador the historical pattern is strikingly similar. The military held the presidency from the 1931 coup of General Maximiliano Hernández Martínez until Napoleon Duarte became president of the third Junta in March 1980—almost half a century. Martínez tried to resolve the social crisis created in El Salvador by the Great Depression through an immense act of violence against peasant protest. However, the Matanza only spawned a reservoir of acute but unresolved social tensions. The unrest these tensions generated was met with ever more violent responses by a succession of military governments. The stronger the army became over the years, thanks largely to U.S. military-assistance programs, the more determined and capable it became in suppressing dissent and preventing social change. The cost of these efforts is the bitter legacy of distrust that most rural Salvadorans have for their government today.

In 1984 Napoleon Duarte became the first civilian in fifty-three years to be elected president and take office. But Duarte's election took place in a country that was engulfed by the counterinsurgency war being waged against the guerrilla movement in the countryside. He is formally commander-in-chief, but it is widely recognized that he does not directly control the prosecution of the war. The Salvadoran armed forces run the war, and that war is the central political reality facing the country. Elections and civilian presidents give the appearance of democracy and the rule of law. However, as a high-ranking U.S. embassy official candidly told the CCCS team, in El Salvador "the judicial system is dead in the water." The implications of that brute fact are all too clear. Against the backdrop of fifty years of military rule, and within the setting of counterinsurgency war, violence and militarism rather than democracy and the rule of law are still the dominant realities of Salvadoran politics. They will continue to be the dominant realities so long as the war goes on. In short, we can only agree with the conclusion of Richard Millett, who writes, "The Central American militaries have contributed significantly to the region's violence, and their current political power complicates efforts to end the crisis."[14]

The problem of militarism is aggravated in Central America by the problem of corruption in military ranks. As the political power of the armies increased, and as millions of dollars in military and economic aid began to flow through their hands, military officers became a more and more powerful economic elite. In Guatemala during the 1960s, the army established its own cement factory, and military officers ran forty-six semi-autonomous state institutions. Fortunes were accumulated in the process. The officers seized land from peasants and Indians. When oil was discovered in northern Guatemala, they built roads to the area and developed their newly acquired holdings for cattle and timber production at government expense. Thomas P. Anderson gives us a vivid account of the consequences not only in Guatemala but in El Salvador and Honduras as well:

> In Guatemala, and more recently in El Salvador and Honduras, the officers have gone beyond mere political control of the state and have become a new landed gentry and a rival to the established oligarchy. . . . The monopoly of political power and the growing concen-

tration of economic power and landholding in the hands of the officer class have caused them to be identified by those seeking to change the social order as the supreme enemy of the revolutionary process. This in part accounts for the savage ferocity of the battles that rage through much of Central America.[15]

Such abuse of authority and position has left a deep legacy of resentment in these countries, seriously eroding the integrity of the entire political system. People not only fear the repressive power of their governments; they have little or no faith in their honesty or accountability. Therefore, continued expansion of military power is probably the major obstacle to the building of genuine democracy in Central America. Until military power is effectively submitted to civilian control, which cannot happen while counterinsurgency warfare continues at its present level, triumphalistic claims about "four working democracies" in Central America cannot be more than self-deceptive propaganda. The history of "military solutions" and their sequel of accelerating militarization produce an environment of overwhelming military domination. This leaves little room for optimism that elections alone can produce genuine, functioning democracies.[16]

The Alternative Path

During the period we have been discussing something quite different was taking place in Costa Rica. We might begin by going back to the crisis of the Great Depression. In 1934 the Communist Party of Costa Rica organized a massive strike against the United Fruit Company. Smarting under the impact of the Depression, United Fruit was intent on keeping wages as low as possible. Meanwhile, workers were committed to raising salaries and improving working conditions. When the workers struck, the government could have responded by sending in the army to quell the strike. Instead, the Costa Rican government named a commission to study the problem. That commission condemned the "inhuman, unhealthful, and careless treatment" of workers by the United Fruit Company. "For the first time in its history," Walter LaFeber notes, "the company buckled and granted better wages and working conditions."[17] While the government in El Salvador was crushing worker protest, the Costa Rican government was building a basis for future social peace by insisting on negotiated compromises to political and economic grievances.

A decade later, one of Latin America's most unusual coalitions achieved the progressive social legislation that has been so instrumental in keeping Costa Rica peaceful and stable. President Rafael Ángel Calderón, elected as a fervent anti-communist, joined forces with Archbishop Victor Manuel Sanabria and Manuel Mora, founder and director of Costa Rica's Communist Party ("Vanguardia Popular"). On May Day 1943, the three men—the president, the archbishop, and the communist *caudillo*—rode dramatically into San José in the same jeep for the Workers Day parade.

Against the stubborn resistance of the oligarchy, this new-style "Triple Alliance," unprecedented in Central America, achieved a most impressive record of social legislation. In 1943, basic workers' rights became law: workers were guaranteed an eight-hour day, the right to unionize and strike, Social Security, equal pay for women and men, severance pay, collective bargaining, and labor courts. At the same time, according to Walter LaFeber, "government controls enabled the economy to remain fairly stable during the war. By the late forties the people expected the government to be active, especially as rising inflation and the lack of U.S. economic help caused deepening social and economic problems."[18]

Teodoro Picado, Calderón's successor, ran into a succession of crises due to blunders in public policy. In early 1948, when his government resorted to fraud to circumvent the electoral triumph of opposition candidate Otilio Ulate, fiery young farmer-intellectual José "Pepe" Figueres led a successful revolution, with weapons supplied by President Arévalo of Guatemala.

Despite this interruption of Costa Rica's political process, the project of peaceful change was carried forward by Figueres's transitional government. Figueres nationalized the banks, introduced progressive tax reforms, and, most importantly, eliminated the army. José Figueres, his National Liberation Party, and his progressive social-democratic program have put an indelible stamp on the last four decades of Costa Rican history.[19] Costa Ricans are justifiably proud of their impressive political achievements. In their country, civilians control political authority, and social issues are resolved through the give-and-take of the political process, not by armed force. The present war in Central America can only be seen as a threat to these achievements.

The lesson of this history is unmistakable. Countries like El Salvador and Guatemala resorted to armed force to repress their social and political problems, only to create greater long-term social turmoil and political instability. Costa Rica met its problems with social reforms and took drastic steps to forestall the curse of militarism. The risk paid off in long-term political stability. Presented with these alternatives, why should North Americans accept the argument that bullets and helicopters and more military training can bring peace or prosperity to the isthmus? After almost eight years of "military solution," thousands of U.S. advisers and other military personnel, and billions of dollars invested in solving the problems of Central America through large-scale counterinsurgency operations, the problems that gave rise to the present crisis are still unresolved.

LOW-INTENSITY CONFLICT, HIGH-INTENSITY GRIEF

The security doctrine that Washington has promoted in Central America since 1980 has a number of deeply disturbing characteristics. The failure of the United States to achieve its objectives in the Vietnam war produced a sharp debate within the government. What emerged out of that debate, and partly from military strategies experimented with in Southeast Asia, was a doctrine known as "Low-Intensity Conflict" (LIC). The name is misleading. This is a doctrine of warfare, and it is "low-intensity" only for the United States. To the populations of Central America and other regions where LIC has been carried out, there is nothing of "low-intensity" about it. In military journals it is candidly described as "total war at the grassroots level."[20] Although in some ways LIC is a more innocent-sounding synonym for "counterinsurgency," it also differs in some important respects. To understand these matters more clearly, we need to enter briefly into the obscure world of the war planners. There we confront the alien language of modern warfare. Before long the reader begins to think of the "doublespeak" made famous by George Orwell in *1984*.

Pentagon experts classify conflict situations according to a "Spectrum of Conflict." At one end is high-intensity conflict such as would be associated with an all-out nuclear holocaust or a worldwide conventional war. Next down the scale would be mid-intensity conflict, such as a conventional war limited to one area of the world. Below these two types of war on the "intensity" scale stands LIC. It is unlikely to be a declared war, one pitting two or more nations and their armies against one another. It is more likely to be undeclared and to involve guerrilla forces or proxy armies, and it is as apt to be carried out at the level of economic and political sabotage as on the battlefield. Military planners try to estimate the risk each type of conflict poses for the United States and the likelihood of its actually occurring.[21] Risk is defined as the threat to U.S. national interests and the costs of projected involvement in each type of war. The conclusion of these elaborate analyses is approximately what common sense would suggest. A low-intensity conflict is far more probable than either a nuclear holocaust or a large-scale conventional war, and incomparably less costly to the United States. Therefore—so the thinking goes—by aggressively confronting low-intensity threats wherever they occur, the United States can avert the greater risks of a "big war" later on.

Low-intensity intervention finds support in the so-called Reagan doctrine, which has become fashionable in recent years. The Reagan doctrine holds that the Soviet Union is the ultimate source of most low-intensity conflict in the Third World. The Soviets either instigate or exploit any instability that occurs in these underdeveloped nations. The United States has the right and duty to confront such communist subversion whenever and wherever it takes place. "Reagan's innovation," writes Sara Miles, "is to provide open backing for paramilitary insurgents or 'freedom fighters' against a series of established Third World governments while simultaneously waging counterinsurgency campaigns against left-wing guerrilla movements."[22] In Central America the U.S.-backed Contras waging war against Nicaragua exemplify the first case, while heavy U.S. military support for the Duarte government in El Salvador illustrates the second. In the first instance the aim is to "roll back" an established government, and in the second, to roll back a guerrilla movement. Rollback is justified on the grounds that both groups are instruments of Soviet expansionism.

Vietnam taught the painful lesson that an insurgent movement with deep popular roots cannot be defeated by simple physical annihilation of the enemy. Subsequent events have shown that in Central America, as in other places, revolutionary movements not only enjoy popular support at home but benefit from considerable international solidarity. For these reasons, according to Colonel John D. Waghelstein, a noted military analyst, U.S. policy should minimize its own direct military involvement in such conflicts. Instead it should apply the strategy of LIC. Waghelstein defines LIC as "the limited use of power for political purposes . . . to coerce, control or defend a population, to control or defend a territory or establish or defend rights. It includes military operations by or against irregular forces, peacekeeping operations, terrorism, counter-terrorism, rescue operations and military assistance under conditions of armed conflict."[23]

This definition makes it clear that LIC doctrine is a radical reformulation of the use of military power. In this strategy the purpose of military pressure is not to defeat the revolutionaries in battle but to delegitimize them and to isolate them from their social and political base so that they no longer constitute a viable or stable political alternative. It was Waghelstein who called this a doctrine of "total war at the grassroots level," using "*all* the weapons of total war, including political, economic and psychological warfare with the military aspect being a distant fourth in many cases."[24] Such an approach discourages direct U.S. invasion of a country like Nicaragua. However, it also "militarizes" all other options by incorporating them into a concept of "total war." In this sense, every dimension of reality, including religion, is subordinated to military considerations.

The LIC program, then, intends to achieve complete control over a target nation without sending in U.S. troops. "The center of gravity of such conflicts is not on the battlefield per se but in the political-social system of the indigenous state. Thus, the main battle lines are political and psychological," writes political scientist Sam C. Sarkesian. "Such conflicts require effective operations aimed at the political-social system with all of its political-psychological nuances."[25] We should notice that this approach to waging war in the Third World puts secret intelligence agencies and military units at the center of our political or ideological quarrels with other nations. We might do well to pause and consider what impact such practices have on public control over foreign policy in a democratic society. These intelligence agencies and military units function almost entirely outside the realm of public scrutiny. As the Iran-Contra hearings during the summer of 1987 demonstrated so disturbingly, such secrecy in policy-making can lead to dangerous excesses, including violation of U.S. law, deception of the public, and usurpation of congressional authority.

An important principle of LIC strategy is to work through proxy armies. Indeed, as one writer puts it, "If we must commit U.S. forces to combat in a low-intensity situation, we have lost the strategic initiative."[26] The basic U.S. role is first to finance, equip, and train the armies of friendly states, or to set up irregular counterrevolutionary forces against governments that are considered a security threat. Then, if it becomes necessary, the United States will "inject small, strategically responsive and flexible U.S. units that can meet the political and military goals of a low-intensity conflict environment."[27] When this relatively low-risk participation is integrated into the broadest possible program of psychological, political, and civic activities, so the argument goes, many objectives can be achieved without direct U.S. intervention.

Embodying this policy, the Contras are fulfilling the classic role of the mercenary as described by Machiavelli in his famous book, *The*

Prince. In Machiavelli's day, at the beginning of the sixteenth century, many states and principalities relied on mercenaries to fight their wars. After studying the effectiveness of mercenary troops, Machiavelli concluded that "the ruin of Italy is now caused by nothing else but through her having relied for many years on mercenary arms." Why are such troops unreliable? Machiavelli answered that they are in fact "useless and dangerous . . . [because] they are disunited, ambitious without discipline, faithless, bold amongst friends [and] cowardly amongst enemies."[28] It was Machiavelli's insight that such soldiers lack a key quality necessary to modern armies: loyalty to a higher cause. They are fighting not so much for "hearth and home" as for economic gain, revenge, or some other personal motive. When set against a citizen army that is fighting to defend the homeland, they are apt to fail miserably.

To see the applicability of this analysis to the Nicaraguan Contras, one only need read Christopher Dickey's eye-opening portrait of the so-called Nicaraguan Democratic Force (FDN). Dickey's book, entitled *With the Contras: A Reporter in the Wilds of Nicaragua*, describes an army cobbled together by secret intelligence agencies; trained by military officers from such countries as Argentina, where the armed forces were associated with grotesque violations of human rights; and led by some of the most violent and uncontrollable soldiers from the hated National Guard of Somoza. It is an army that could, and did, bring great destruction and hardship to the Nicaraguan countryside. But it is also an army that, according to Dickey, "could not survive without Washington."[29] It is, in short, a mercenary army that by its very nature can never live up to the extravagant claims made for it by its patrons in the U.S. government.

The Contra phenomenon is an oddity in the late twentieth century, when citizen armies have become the norm that many nations have achieved and to which others aspire. Mercenary armies such as the Contras represent a rearguard action against the movement toward decolonization and independence for smaller Third World nations. Since the very dignity and self-identity of these nations is at stake in struggles against such armies, the mercenary forces will be resisted tenaciously. That certainly has been the case in Nicaragua, and it helps to explain why the Contras have been so utterly ineffective militarily, despite their backing by the United States, their sanctuaries in Honduras and Costa Rica, and their hundreds of millions of dollars' worth of arms and equipment. In the caustic words of Costa Rican elder statesman José "Pepe" Figueres, "If the United States wishes to overthrow the government of Nicaragua, they can do it; but to do so through a mercenary army, at the end of the twentieth century, is an incredible anachronism."

It is important to stress that the ultimate target of this "total war at the grassroots level" is the populace. Adopting the view made famous by the Chinese revolutionary leader Mao Tse-tung, LIC advocates say that when a populace is supportive of insurgents, they are like "the sea in which guerrilla fish swim." The objective of counterinsurgency is to drain the sea in order to catch the fish. This explains the massive army sweeps, the creation of specialized hunter battalions, and the aerial bombardment in zones of El Salvador presumed to sympathize with the guerrillas fighting in that country. It explains why more than 20 percent of the entire Salvadoran population is displaced today. It explains why Contra forces have targeted and assassinated nurses, doctors, teachers, and literacy workers in Nicaragua. Sadly, it explains all too well the attack on Pantasma and the death of Noel Vargas.

LIC is unabashedly a strategy for war against the civilian population. The appalling number of casualties—the majority of them noncombatants—in both Nicaragua and El Salvador provides stark testimony to the sort of casualty rates that low-intensity conflict can produce. Besides the 40,000 casualties in Nicaragua and the more than 60,000 in El Salvador, hundreds of thousands of refugees have been displaced by these wars in the past seven years. This shocking toll is only occasionally newsworthy to the U.S. public. The war is remote and undeclared, and the U.S. public is not encouraged to see any direct national connection with it. Consequently, the citizenry does not develop a sense of responsibility for the war's consequences.

Finally, we would do well to ask what impact LIC has on the truth. Since LIC involves a "struggle to win the hearts and minds" of Third World peoples—not to mention of the U.S. public—great importance is given to propaganda and other forms of opinion management. The public must be persuaded, by whatever means, that these low-intensity conflicts represent high-intensity threats to U.S. national security, to democracy, or to some other cherished value. "Because of the strong political constraints imposed upon U.S.-sponsored counterinsurgency operations," writes Third World specialist Richard Alan White, "it is imperative to confer international legitimacy upon client governments, while at the same time discrediting the insurgent forces."[30]

The Pentagon analysts who promote LIC are convinced that the Vietnam war was lost not on the battlefields but on the television screens. The U.S. government and the Pentagon failed to win adequate support for the war in national public opinion; that mistake must not be repeated in Central America. Therefore, every available method of opinion management must be utilized to "win the hearts and minds" of the U.S. public today. At a seminar on LIC, Air Force Deputy Assistant Secretary J. Michael Kelly put it bluntly: "I think the most critical special operations mission we have today is to persuade the American people that the communists are out to get us. If we can win this war of ideas, we can win everywhere else."[31] In short, our own people have become the battlefield for a "special operation," and anti-communist propaganda is the primary ideological weapon. The question of truth becomes secondary in these calculations.

LIC strategy and ideology cannot but clash with basic values both of the Judeo-Christian tradition and of the democratic political heritage North Americans treasure so much. A noted LIC specialist states the case clearly:

> If American involvement is justified and necessary, then national leaders and the public must understand that low-intensity conflicts do not conform to democratic notions of strategy or tactics. Revolution and counterrevolution develop their own morality and ethics that justify any means to achieve success. Survival is the ultimate morality. . . . Americans must understand that not all of these factors may be in accord with the democratic norms and with the American political system in morality and ethics.[32]

These comments again recall the name of Machiavelli, who is notorious in the tradition of political thought because he argued that in statecraft "the end justifies the means." Machiavelli saw quite clearly where such a political morality leads, and he endorsed it as a necessary element of statecraft. Ruling authorities, he wrote with characteristic candor, "cannot observe all those things which are considered good in men, being often obliged, in order to maintain the state, to act against faith, against charity, against humanity, and against religion."[33]

This perspective has been condemned by ethicists and by partisans of free government ever since it was first put forward. No U.S. leader would openly advocate such a political morality. Yet, because LIC strategists think that political instability or social revolution in Central America threatens U.S. security, the citizens of the United States are in effect being asked to accept a foreign policy based on just such a morality. But must we wage an LIC war against Nicaragua in order to assure our own survival? Does it not make more sense that our government pursue our legitimate national interests using means that are morally defensible and compatible with the norms of a democratic society?

What, then, is the right thing for the United States to do in Central America today? In order to respond to this question, we will briefly examine the justifications that have been given for waging the present war against Nicaragua, a war that has become the centerpiece of U.S. policy in the region.

The Nicaraguan Threat

On 1 May 1985, President Reagan sent to Congress an "Executive Order Prohibiting Trade and Certain Other Transactions Involving Nicaragua." In fulfillment of the requirements of law, he began the document as follows:

> By the authority vested in me as President by the Constitution and laws of the United States of America . . . I, RONALD REAGAN, President of the United States of America, find that the policies and actions of the Government of Nicaragua constitute an unusual and extraordinary threat to the national security and foreign policy of the United States and hereby declare a national emergency to deal with that threat.[34]

The United States has about seventy-five times the population of Nicaragua. The value of economic production in a single medium-sized U.S. city would easily eclipse that of the entire Nicaraguan nation. Nicaragua has no natural resources vital to the United States. Despite the war of words that has raged between the two countries, and even despite the bitter toll in Nicaraguan lives taken by the Contra war, Nicaraguans have repeatedly expressed their desire for friendship and mutual respect between our two countries. Why, then, is tiny Nicaragua "an unusual and extraordinary threat" to the richest nation in history? Europeans, Canadians, and above all Latin Americans repeatedly express their amazement at such an implausible idea. Yet the president appears to take his own words seriously, and they have been reinforced by the steady parade of high U.S. officials over the past six years who have ceaselessly proclaimed Nicaragua a threat to U.S. security.

The U.S. public has, in fact, been subjected to such a persistent drumbeat of accusations against Nicaragua that it has become difficult even to approach the matter rationally. U.S. officials have so aggressively portrayed Nicaragua as a communist dictatorship and as a tool of Soviet expansionism in the Western Hemisphere that an East-West framework of interpretation has penetrated every aspect of public dialogue on Central America. The air reverberates with Orwellian buzz-words—on the one hand, terms such as "totalitarian," "Marxist-Lenin-ist," and "communist dungeon," and, on the other hand, phrases like "Freedom Fighters" and "democratic resistance." Such words convey strong emotion but little meaning—precisely the intention. Let us strive to cut through them to the essential grounds upon which U.S. policy toward Nicaragua rests according to the arguments of our public officials.

Arming the Salvadoran Guerrillas

In February 1981 the U.S. Department of State issued a sensational white paper entitled *Communist Interference in El Salvador.* This white paper attempted to link the Salvadoran insurgency to a vast arms net-work stretching from Moscow and Vietnam to El Salvador by way of Cuba and Nicaragua. However, the document met with widespread skepticism. According to Wayne Smith, chief of the U.S. interests sec-tion in Havana at the time, the white paper

> became a source of acute embarrassment to the administration, pri-marily revealing shoddy research and a fierce determination to advo-cate the new policy, whether or not the evidence sustained it. Some of the supporting documents turned out to be forgeries. Others were of such vague origin as to be worthless. None of the documents linked the USSR to the supply of guerrilla forces in El Salvador or demon-strated that the violence there was a case of external aggression rather than an internal conflict.[35]

Less than two weeks after the State Department white paper was issued, the Reagan administration—less than two months after assuming office—took the first step in its war against Nicaragua. On 9 March 1981, the White House sent Congress a "Presidential Find-ing on Central America" that authorized the CIA to engage in covert operations in that country. The authorization gave the CIA almost $20 million and encouraged it to provide assistance to groups within Nic-aragua who would oppose the new Sandinista government, including private business groups and the press. It also "called for a covert arms interdiction program" to halt weapons Reagan claimed were "flow-ing from Nicaragua to leftist guerrillas in El Salvador, Honduras, and Guatemala."[36]

By May, anti-Sandinista Nicaraguans were training in paramil-itary camps in Texas, California, and Florida. In August the CIA began drawing up contingency plans for military operations inside Nicaragua. By November the National Security Council was recommending creation of a 500-person paramilitary force to interdict those alleged arms shipments. The president approved these recommendations, including nearly $20 million more in CIA funding on 23 November 1981. Already the covert program was large and growing larger, but to Congress and the public it was portrayed as limited to the defensive goal of interdicting arms. At the very moment these plans were approved, U.S. diplomats in Havana and Managua were advising Washington that Nicaragua had "drastically reduced support to the guerrillas and signalled a desire for improved relations with the United States."[37] However, the expanded covert operation was a significant boost to the ex–National Guardsmen in Honduras and other anti-Sandinista groups who coveted a return to power. Almost immediately CIA operatives set about creating the Contra army.

Among the seven directors of the newly formed Nicaraguan Democratic Force was a former Jesuit priest named Edgar Chamorro. Chamorro, who later resigned from the Contra directorate, reported that when the CIA formed the FDN, CIA officials never talked to FDN leaders about the objective of interrupting arms traffic to El Salvador. From the beginning the actions of the FDN had nothing to do with intercepting arms but were instead aimed at overthrowing the Nicaraguan government—by Christmas of 1983, according to an internal CIA memorandum.[38] The arms-traffic accusations were only a pretext for a different objective, one that was already decided upon but not fully shared with Congress or the American people.

It is important to realize that Nicaragua shares no common land border with El Salvador. Its entire northern border connects it with Honduras. The border area is a militarized zone dominated by U.S., Honduran, and Contra soldiers. It is therefore remarkable that in the more than six years since the initial white paper was issued, no significant arms shipments have ever been captured. The U.S. government has utilized impressive instruments of modern technology to monitor arms traffic into El Salvador, including helicopters, reconnaissance aircraft, radar, and modern ships in the Gulf of Fonseca. Yet this effort has produced no solid evidence of the alleged arms traffic that was the pretext for the Contra operation. Two conclusions seem inescapable. First, the charges of Sandinista gun-running to the rebels after 1981 were false or severely exaggerated. Second, stopping arms traffic was never Washington's primary objective in creating the Contra army.

"Revolution without Frontiers"

A second argument used to justify the Contra war is essentially an extension of the first, pointing to tendencies alleged to be inherent in the very nature of the Sandinista regime. According to this view, the revolutionary government is by definition expansionistic and therefore is necessarily a threat to all of its neighbors. Washington has made repeated attempts to root this accusation in the words of the Sandinistas themselves. Thus the president, the secretary of state, and other leading officials have quoted Sandinista leaders as proclaiming that the Nicaraguan revolution is a "revolution without frontiers." However, when Secretary Shultz repeated the quotation in testimony before the Senate Foreign Relations Committee in August 1984, Congressman Edward J. Markey of Massachusetts challenged him to identify the exact source of the quote. The State Department was unable to do so. "Nobody could find a citation outside the Beltway [Washington]," Markey concluded. "We're positive it did not originate in Nicaragua," he noted, but was invented "to lend credibility to the administration position that you can only deal by force with these people."[39]

In September 1985 the State Department published a white paper on alleged Sandinista expansionism entitled *Revolution beyond Our Borders,* thus highlighting the quotation once more. The white paper claimed to have located the elusive quotation in a speech that had been given by Tomás Borge, Nicaragua's interior minister, on 19 July 1981. Borge's words were "This revolution goes beyond our borders." This seemed to be the solid proof that Congressman Markey had demanded the year before. However, the State Department had taken the phrase completely out of context. In the speech Borge emphasized that "Nicaragua . . . is a country with *moral authority* not just in Central America, or Latin America, but throughout the entire world." He pointedly added, "This does not mean that we export our revolution. It is sufficient—and we cannot avoid this—that they take our example"[40] (emphasis added). In effect, Borge was arguing publicly to a huge crowd of Sandinista supporters that Nicaragua could not export its revolution, except by the force of example it could set at home.

Nicaragua Must Become Democratic

As the years passed and the Contra war expanded, these early justifications for Washington's aggressive support of the Contras were abandoned. Increasingly, the United States insisted that the purpose of supporting the Contras was to force the Sandinistas to create a more democratic government and society. Meanwhile, the Sandinista government mobilized the populace for national defense. Not only did the Sandinista army grow, but so did the militia forces. With war at its doorstep, Nicaragua underwent a predictable remilitization. As acts of sabotage and attacks on the civilian population began to mount, the Nicaraguan government declared a state of emergency in March 1982. The Sandinistas, blocked from receiving military aid from the United States, sought it in Western Europe. When they were frustrated in Western Europe by U.S. pressures, they turned to East Bloc countries, including the Soviet Union. The level of Soviet aid steadily increased, and U.S. leaders pointed to that aid as proof that Nicaragua always intended to create a "Cuba-style regime."

What ensued was a tragic spiral of initiative and response in which the United States now justified its support for the Contras on the basis of Nicaraguan ties to East Bloc countries, especially Cuba and the Soviet Union. Nicaragua in turn justified these ties as necessary to its very survival, while continuing to cultivate ties with Western countries and doggedly pursuing negotiations with the United States. At the same time that it coped with a widening war, the Sandinista government sought to carry out the elementary tasks of nation-building that lay before it after forty-six years of dictatorship. Building a new sense of political community in Nicaragua was among the most important of these basic tasks. To that end it was necessary to overcome the legacy of Somoza, which meant redefining Nicaragua's relationship with the United States.

But how could that relationship be redefined in the face of the Contra war? The new U.S. administration taking office in 1981 showed no interest in Nicaragua's tragic history with Somoza, including what his own countrymen saw as his complete identification with the United States. The Reagan administration saw Nicaragua not as a country with its own history and its own desperate need for "national reconstruction" but as a strategic location on a geopolitical chessboard. It saw the Sandinista movement not as a group of nationalists emerging from the unique and unrepeatable circumstances of political struggle in Nicaragua but as mere cogs in the machine of Soviet expansionism. By severing the Sandinistas from their own roots in Nicaraguan history, Washington forsook the possibility of dealing with the Nicaraguan revolution on its own terms and on a Central American scale. Only by disassociating the Sandinistas from Nicaraguan history could it seem reasonable to take remnants of the National Guard, which symbolize everything hateful and oppressive about the Somoza dictatorship, re-arm them, re-baptize them as "Freedom Fighters," and send them back into Nicaragua to sow destruction and death. Yet that is precisely what Washington did.

In retrospect the results of such a policy seem inevitable. Nicaraguan mistrust of the United States deepened. Actions taken by the Sandinista government to assure order in the face of widening sabotage were readily interpreted in Washington as "proof" that their presuppositions about the Sandinistas were correct. Henceforth, no action the Sandinistas could take—whether it was the holding of elections, the writing of a new constitution, or the agreement to sign international treaties guaranteeing that U.S. security interests would be protected—could satisfy Washington's demand for "reform" in Managua. Unwilling to negotiate their own sovereignty, the Sandinistas had no choice but to mobilize for a long war.

This radical estrangement between Nicaragua and the United States has been extremely harmful to both countries. It has created painful division and turmoil in the body politic of each. A towering irony is that in Washington the Contra war has been justified on the grounds that it is the best available means to promote freedom and democratic government not only in Nicaragua but throughout Central America. In holding to this view, Washington has come to stand increasingly alone. Other nations, including close U.S. allies in Europe and Latin America, have long viewed the Contra war as an inappropriate means to the ends the United States professes to seek. In their view, LIC warfare is profoundly antidemocratic; a far more democratic method is the diplomatic process of negotiation. Let us turn now to the peace process that other friendly nations have struggled so hard to make available to us.

THE SEARCH FOR PEACE

The territory of a state is inviolable; it may not be the object, even temporarily, of military occupation or of other measures of force taken by another state, *directly or indirectly,* on any grounds whatever. . . . (emphasis added)

Article 20, Charter of the Organization of American States

No State or Group of States has the right to intervene, *directly or indirectly, for any reason whatever,* in the internal or external affairs of any other State. The foregoing principle prohibits not only armed force, but also any other form of interference or attempted threat against the personality of the State or against its political, economic and cultural elements. (emphasis added)

Article 18, Charter of the Organization of the American States

This OAS pact, signed by the U.S. government and the governments of our Latin American neighbors, was enacted in 1948 to safeguard the sovereignty and stability of all the nations in the Western Hemisphere and to promote peaceful relations among them. Judged by these standards, the Contra war stands in clear violation of this agreement. Curiously, however, this war has produced a hopeful consequence: the determined and sustained effort toward a negotiated peace in Latin America. This result has no doubt taken Washington by surprise, for the United States is accustomed to having its way in Latin America, above all in Central America. When the United States chose to isolate Cuba in the early 1960s, most Latin American states cooperated with U.S. policy, even to the point of breaking diplomatic relations with Cuba.[41] Washington mobilized similar support for its invasion of the Dominican Republic in 1965.

The Latin American response in the 1980s has been quite different, however. Not only have Latin nations not closed ranks behind the U.S. policy of promoting LIC warfare in Central America, but they have actively mobilized against it. Perhaps for the first time in inter-American relations, Latin Americans themselves have seized the initiative in a multilateral diplomatic process aimed at securing a just and lasting peace in Central America. As they see it, they are pursuing the best means available to secure not only their own interests and those of the Central American countries, including Nicaragua, but also the interests of the United States. The basic vehicle of this remarkable diplomatic initiative is the Contadora peace process, which has enabled Latin Americans to advance their own definition of the collective security of the Americas.

Contadora Peace Process

The Contadora initiative grew out of early efforts, first by Mexico and then by Venezuela, to defuse the growing hostilities between the United States and Nicaragua before they escalated into a major war. The immediate source of that growing hostility in 1981 was Washington's alarm over the strength of the armed guerrilla movement in El Salvador. The FMLN guerrillas launched a strong offensive against the Salvadoran army in October 1981, throwing that government on the defensive. Suddenly Washington foresaw the prospect of another successful revolution in Central America. U.S. policymakers insisted that the FMLN's success could only be attributable to Sandinista support. Thus events in El Salvador during 1981 fueled the tension between the United States and Nicaragua, and in November U.S. officials hinted publicly that a direct military action against Nicaragua was under consideration. These threats prompted the first diplomatic intervention from Latin America, which came from Mexican president José López Portillo.

It was no accident that Mexico was deeply preoccupied by the growing regional crisis. Mexico is the only country to share a border with both the United States and Central America. It literally stands between the protagonists. Moreover, Mexico shares with all of Central America a common history of U.S. intervention in its internal affairs, which makes it particularly sensitive to the sovereignty issue. Finally, Mexico too underwent a long and painful revolution in the early decades of this century. Out of that revolution came the nation-building efforts that produced the stability Mexico enjoys today. From the vantage point of its own recent history, Mexico can appreciate both the causes of revolution in Central America and the necessity to allow Central Americans themselves to resolve revolutionary crises. At the same time, Mexico has a strong interest in regional stability. All these factors have made Mexico an interested and important party to the conflicts.

Through the efforts of López Portillo, high-level contacts were established between the United States and Nicaragua in December 1981. In early 1982 Mexico put forward a "three point plan for reducing tensions: (1) an end to U.S. threats of military action against Nicaragua; (2) a mutual reduction of military posturing, and (3) a nonaggression pact between the two countries."[42] The Nicaraguan response was enthusiastic. But the Reagan administration greeted the Mexican proposal with silence. The reception in Congress was decidedly warmer, however, with more than one hundred members signing a letter to the president urging him to accept the Mexican offer. The administration took steps that gave the appearance of doing so, but behind the scenes it was vigorously mobilizing the Contras for direct attacks inside Nicaragua, attacks that spread rapidly in the summer of 1982, once again heightening the threat of a more generalized war.

At that point Venezuela entered the fray as a partner to Mexico in promoting negotiations to end the crisis. In this respect it is important to recognize that Venezuela has for decades been one of the United States' closest allies in Latin America. For thirty years it has been one of the more democratic countries in the region, and it is a country with impressive anti-communist credentials. In short, Venezuela is a country that has much in common with the United States and is sympathetic to U.S. interests in Latin America. Venezuela also lies on the southern border of Central America. By the summer of 1982, Venezuelan president Luis Herrera Campíns felt obliged to join the efforts of Mexico's López Portillo in promoting a diplomatic alternative to war.

In January 1983 the foreign ministers of Mexico and Venezuela—as well as those of Colombia and Panama, the two other countries situated closest to Central America—met on the Panamanian island of Contadora to launch the formal peace process that has since been known by that name. At Contadora each of these nations made a major commitment of their own prestige and political capital to the promotion of a negotiated resolution to conflicts within Central America, including those between the United States and Nicaragua. Throughout the spring and summer of 1983 the Contadora nations labored to create a diplomatic framework in which negotiations could succeed. At one point the four nations together "had over one hundred technical advisors and diplomats working on the draft."[43]

A first breakthrough came in July, when Nicaragua agreed to accept a multilateral negotiating framework in which all major regional issues were to be discussed simultaneously. Then, in September, the Central American nations signed the Document of Objectives, a twenty-one-part document that specified the major political and security issues to be resolved. By September 1984 the Document of Objectives had been elaborated into a series of draft treaties. The essential thrust of these treaties was to encourage demilitarization and nonintervention in Central America. In other words, they spoke directly to the security issues that underlay U.S. fears of Nicaragua and that justified aggressive U.S. support of such countries as El Salvador and Honduras.[44] The treaties proposed strict limits on weapons and weapons systems, the size of armies, and the number of military bases, and they set up a verification procedure to enforce the limits. They also called for the elimination of foreign military bases and exercises. Finally, the treaties called for a halt to all external assistance for rebel groups fighting against governments within any Central American nation.

On the day the draft treaties were first made public, Secretary of State George Shultz applauded them warmly, declaring them to be "an important step forward" on the road to peace. Shultz was quick to point out that U.S. allies in Central America conditionally accepted the treaties as proposed, but that "Nicaragua, on the other hand, has rejected key elements of the draft."⁴⁵ Imagine the surprise in Washington, then, when Nicaragua announced two weeks later that it accepted the treaties and was prepared to sign them as they stood. Suddenly U.S. enthusiasm for the treaties plummeted. Within a month, U.S. allies in Central America proposed a "counterdraft" that permitted the United States to keep its military bases and to continue to conduct military maneuvers, and that excused the United States from being bound by the treaties' provisions. This version of Contadora was so skewed against Nicaragua, which was now suffering severely from the Contra war, that it effectively stalled the entire negotiating process.

Despite these obstacles and frustrations, the Contadora initiative was kept alive by the determined efforts of Latin American leaders. During the spring and summer of 1985, Latin heads of state from nations that Washington was generously praising for their commitment to democracy in the Americas began to speak out more and more forcefully on Central America. Arguing for the renewal of negotiations and urging the cooperation of the United States, Argentine president Raul Alfonsín said, "Our view is based on the principle of self-determination, non-intervention and support for the work of the Contadora group. . . . We cannot cast aside the security of the region for the security of the U.S. . . . We must avoid the idea that anyone can interfere in any given country." President Belisario Betancur of Colombia added, "A military response is a non-policy. Central America requires political and diplomatic solutions, not military ones."⁴⁶

In order to give weight to these words and to reinforce the peace process, the nations of Argentina, Brazil, Uruguay, and Peru formed the Contadora Support Group in July 1985. Now Contadora had the open support of eight Latin American nations that were home to 85 percent of Latin America's total population. Their appeals were increasingly directed at Washington and centered on two related issues: that the United States should lend its support to Contadora and cease its support of the Contras. However, this appeal continued to be rejected in Washington, as Secretary of State Shultz made clear in December 1985 when he declared that the United States would go on supporting the Contras even if a Contadora treaty were signed.⁴⁷

In an effort to break the deadlock produced by Washington's determination to keep the Contra war going and Nicaragua's unwillingness to continue making concessions that were not reciprocated in this crucial respect, the Contadora nations and support-group countries issued the Caraballeda Declaration in January 1986. This declaration "called for work on signing the Contadora treaty to go forward simultaneously with work on ending aid to the Contras."⁴⁸ It was this decision that led the eight Latin American foreign ministers to meet with Secretary of State Shultz in February 1986, a meeting described in the preceding chapter. As we saw there, the ministers left Washington empty-handed because at that time the president of the United States was ardently pursuing additional support for the Contras. President Reagan's efforts were finally rewarded, after bitterly divisive debates within the Congress, with the passage of $100 million in military aid to the Contras in July.[49]

Thus in mid-1986 the Contra war was generously stoked up by renewed U.S. funding, while the Contadora peace process was delivered a serious blow. Nicaraguans dug in to confront the grim reality of renewed fighting throughout their country. Then in November came the first of startling revelations about the National Security Council's efforts to circumvent congressional restrictions on Contra aid prior to the July approval of the $100 million. As the scandal unfolded, it became clear just how desperate the administration's commitment to the Contra cause had been. Officials running the Contra program had defied the congressional ban on aid to the Contras, secretly solicited funds from other sources, and deceived or misled the congressional committees charged with oversight of such programs. In the months that it took for this story to emerge fully, new life was breathed into the peace process. This time the initiative came from Central America itself.

Arias Peace Plan

On 5 February 1987, President Oscar Arias of Costa Rica hosted his counterparts from El Salvador, Honduras, and Guatemala in San José to unveil a new peace initiative for Central America. The initiative soon became known as the Arias Peace Plan. Immediate reaction to the Arias proposal was probably more enthusiastic in the U.S. Congress than anywhere else, as reflected in the Senate's passage on 13 March (by a vote of 97 to 1) of a resolution urging the Reagan administration to treat the proposal seriously. The Senate's action was a good measure of the repercussions that the Iran-Contra scandal had had on U.S. policy in Central America.

Within the region itself, early reactions were cautious, but the proposal did make headway. It offered something to everyone: a ceasefire, arms reductions, and amnesty for groups fighting against existing governments. These measures aimed at immediate de-escalation of military conflict. In addition, the proposal offered a calendar for democratization within Central American countries, including the restoration of political liberties and the scheduling of elections according to the constitutional provisions of each nation. Perhaps most important, the proposal broke sharply with U.S. policy by calling for suspension of aid to the Contras. In short, the Arias Peace Plan was a diplomatic initiative that aimed to achieve goals espoused by all parties, including the United States. But it committed all parties to work toward those goals through negotiations and compromises achieved at the bargaining table rather than through military actions on the battlefield.

Throughout the spring and summer of 1987, the Central American leaders struggled toward a summit meeting to confront the Arias plan. President Arias himself toured Europe to promote the plan and received strong encouragement. In June he visited Washington, where he addressed the National Press Club, insisting in his speech that Contra aid was incompatible with his peace plan. At the same time, presidents Alfonsin of Argentina and de la Madrid of Mexico announced that the Contadora initiative and support-group countries were planning to provide economic aid to Nicaragua to make up for some of the deficit created by declining Soviet aid. Their actions demonstrated the depth of Latin American commitment to remove Central America from the grip of East-West hostilities.[50] They also demonstrated Latin American determination to find regional solutions to regional problems. Finally, these actions revealed how profoundly Latin America disagrees with Washington in its assessment that the only problem in Central America is Nicaragua, and that the only solution is military pressure against that country.

The summit of Central American presidents was finally scheduled for 7 August 1987. On 5 August the Reagan administration announced that it would propose its own peace plan for Central America, one that included a cease-fire and direct negotiations between Washington and Managua. The announcement cast sudden doubt over the impending summit in Guatemala City. Observers waited and watched to see if this move would disrupt or abort discussion of the Arias plan by the Central American leaders. It did not. On 8 August the five Central American presidents faced television cameras to announce the signing of the Arias Peace Plan. After five years of unstinting labors, the peace process had achieved a first important victory in the long-term struggle to build trust and political community in Central America.

At this writing, hopes run high throughout Latin America that the Gordian knot of fear and hostility has been cut through. Huge challenges remain, of course, because many of the details of the peace treaty still need to be worked out. Through the autumn months of 1987 and into the spring of 1988, Central Americans labored to make the peace process work. The awarding of the Nobel Peace Prize to President Arias signaled the support of the international community for diplomatic solutions to Central America's conflicts. In the face of such widely held sentiment for peace, Secretary Shultz's announcement in mid-September 1987 that the administration intended to seek an unprecedented $270 million in Contra aid could only be viewed with dismay and alarm. He told the Senate Foreign Relations Committee that such aid would "enhance, not diminish, chances of a peace accord in Central America."[51]

In January and February 1988 the administration, perceiving that it lacked support in Congress for anything approaching the $270 million figure that Secretary Shultz had mentioned the previous September, scaled back its Contra aid request to $36.2 million, including $3 million in military aid. However, Congress rejected this aid request, and formal U.S. funding for the Contras expired on 29 February 1988. Nevertheless, the administration was still pressing for renewed Contra aid in March 1988. Neither Latin American nor Central American leaders agree with such a policy. Even the request for such aid puts the United States on a collision course not only with Nicaragua but with the very Central American nations—such as Costa Rica—that we claim to be defending. With the lines so clearly drawn, and with many lives and much human dignity at stake, are we not compelled now to take a stand as Christians and as citizens, declaring to our governments whether we are for peace or for war? Whatever the outcome of the current peace initiatives, we must be ready, with our Central American neighbors, in the words of President Arias, to "give peace a chance."

6. THEY CRY "DEMOCRACY, DEMOCRACY!" BUT THERE IS NO DEMOCRACY

And afterward, I will pour out my Spirit on all people. Your sons and your daughters will prophesy, your old men will dream dreams, your young men will see visions. Even on my servants, both men and women, I will pour out my Spirit in those days.

Joel 2:28-29

President Ortega and the Nicaraguan Baptists

Nicaragua, which is predominantly Roman Catholic, has a sizeable and growing evangelical presence. The Nicaraguan Baptist Church, the oldest Protestant denomination working in the country, was founded the year after the historic Panama Conference of 1916, in which Protestant churches in North America divided the mission fields of Central America among themselves. In 1987 the Baptists celebrated their seventieth anniversary in Nicaragua. They are now an important fixture on the Nicaraguan religious scene.

On the evening of 30 January 1987, the Baptists held the concluding celebration of their week-long annual assembly. One hundred seventy delegates plus a number of guests (including members of the CCCS team) crowded into the simple auditorium of the Baptist Seminary in Managua. Coming from far and wide, they represented all regions of the country. They had participated for five full days in discussion and debate, Bible study, and prayer; now they were about to conclude their meetings with a historic event in the life of their church. The president of the republic, Daniel Ortega, would arrive at any moment to address the assembly and engage in dialogue with the delegates.

Last-minute items of business were attended to as the hour of

171

the president's scheduled arrival came and then slipped by. The heat was stifling, as it usually is in the late afternoon in Managua. The excitement and tension in the air deepened. Suddenly, without fanfare, the president strode into the hall and embraced the members of the welcoming party. Except for two or three unarmed young men who appeared to be bodyguards, he was alone. He had driven himself in a Toyota jeep from the *Casa de Gobierno* (the government house), visible in the distance across Managua's desolate city center, still in ruins from the earthquake of 1972. Flanked by the presiding officers of the convention, President Ortega walked briskly up to the small stage accompanied by an exuberant rendition of "Valiant Baptists" sung by the assembled delegates.

What followed would have taken most North Americans by surprise, accustomed as they are to hearing that the Sandinista government is atheistic and hostile to the church, and that there is widespread religious persecution in Nicaragua. The deeply moving and affirmative dialogue that took place over the next three-and-a-half hours makes little sense from that perspective.

The proceedings began with the reading of Scripture. The chosen text was Psalm 72: "Give the King thy justice, O God. . . . May he defend the cause of the poor of the people, give deliverance to the needy, and crush the oppressor! . . . In his days may righteousness flourish, and peace abound. . . . He has pity on the weak and the needy. . . . From oppression and violence he redeems their life; and precious is their blood in his sight." These words resonated deeply in the ears and hearts of these people, who live in a desperately poor society that has recently thrown off the yoke of oppression and set about rebuilding—only to have a war of counter-revolution launched against it.

The tiny figure of Antonia Gonzalez rose to give the prayer of invocation. She gave thanks for God's loving presence, which enabled these humble people, for the first time in their history, to hold a dialogue with the president of their nation. She prayed for the youth of Nicaragua and their anguished families. Having barely begun to build the revolution, these young people were being called into battle to defend it. A lengthy report followed on the labors and achievements of the Baptist convention, highlighting the pastoral commitments and the civic contributions of Baptist congregations all across Nicaragua.

Finally President Ortega himself took the microphone. Quietly, simply he spoke, and without notes. He touched on the important influence of Christianity in Nicaraguan life: "There is a common denominator among our peoples˙ Christianity. It is this affirmation that transcends what is merely individual or materialist and the power of gold or weapons. This force is what makes it possible for people anywhere to have a common language, a language of solidarity, of fraternity, of peace and of love." He spoke of the struggle to build a new and better society. "We are doing something that is truly new. . . . We have undertaken a struggle against egotism, robbery, individualism, . . . all those deeds that diminish the spiritual power of humanity. This people is fighting for its spiritual and material rights." Although it is not an easy struggle, he said, it is one that "corresponds to the principles of Christianity, of love, solidarity, and fraternity, that of giving oneself for others."

Inevitably, President Ortega also spoke of the war that holds Nicaragua in its grip. "This war is a terrible thing, but we must face it. The alternative is to go back to the situation that existed before July 1979. . . . You yourselves have had to offer your quota of blood, of suffering, of martyrdom. Pray! Mobilize yourselves for peace!" He looked to the future, to the ongoing process of rebuilding this tiny impoverished nation. He spoke of the role that Christian citizens would play. "The revolution continues with the participation of the Nicaraguan people, with you who are celebrating this convention in the midst of war. . . . We are in agreement with the participation of Christians. . . . There is much to be done, but we need a participation that is critical and constructive."

By the time the president had finished speaking, the program had already run an hour and a half. It was about 7:30 in the evening. Many delegates had been in the meeting hall since early that morning. But Daniel, as he is known to all Nicaraguans, announced that there was time for questions. Hands were thrust in the air immediately. What happened next would have astonished anyone familiar with presidential news conferences in the United States. The microphone was passed around the audience. Delegate after delegate stood to ask a question of the president. Ordinary people expressed in their own words the problems they faced and the issues that troubled them. Daniel took questions for nearly an hour, patiently writing them down on a notepad. Then he proceeded to answer each one in detail, responding to inquiries about former National Guardsmen serving prison terms. He explained the government's negotiations with Miskito Indians over regional autonomy, and answered practical questions about land, housing, the cost of living, and military service. Another hour flew by.

Finally the president reached the end of the questions. Officials on the platform prepared to present him with two gifts—a beautiful Bible and a Baptist T-shirt. Suddenly the diminutive figure of Antonia

Gonzalez stepped back up on the stage. Taking the president's hand, she peered up at him, wagged her finger vigorously back and forth in his face like a zealous schoolteacher, and told him a story from the days of the popular insurrection. "I used to hide the *muchachos* (the affectionate term for young men and women who fought against the Somoza dictatorship) in my home. When the National Guard came looking for them, I would say, 'These are all my children!' Of course, they weren't. Today I want to tell you, Daniel, what I told the *muchachos* during the revolution. Never go into battle without first praying to God!" With that Antonia returned to her seat amidst the laughter and thunderous applause of everyone present. The gifts were then presented to the president.

At that point a veteran pastor read from chapter four of 2 Corinthians: "We are afflicted in every way, but not crushed; perplexed, but not driven to despair; persecuted, but not forsaken; struck down, but not destroyed; always carrying in the body the death of Jesus so that the life of Jesus may also be manifested." He offered a biblical reflection entitled "Pastoral Words to the President and His Government." The meeting closed with an intercessory prayer for the president, his family, and his government. Then Ortega and the others marched out, stopping to embrace dozens of delegates along the way—to the accompaniment, once again, of "Valiant Baptists."

Grass-roots Participation by Christians in Nicaragua

Such an event is not at all unusual in Nicaragua today. It is increasingly commonplace for political leaders to reach out in diverse ways to maintain contact with rank-and-file citizens. Various groups—whether churches, labor unions, campesino organizations, or women's associations—seek out political leaders and press their concerns or demands upon these officials. In North America today, Nicaragua is shrouded by polemical debate and propaganda, but there is a vital and renewing political dialogue going on inside the country. That long and spirited meeting between Daniel Ortega and the Baptists was televised and rebroadcast to the nation the following Tuesday evening. Every Friday night the president and other high government officials visit a community somewhere in Nicaragua for a dialogue of this kind. It is called *De cara al pueblo* (Facing the People). Every Tuesday that dialogue is shared with the rest of the public on national television. President Ortega's visit to the Baptist convention was unusual only in that he came alone. Normally at least half-a-dozen cabinet-level ministers are present to answer specific questions about government policy and to hear the views of the Nicaraguan people. This is one of the ways the Nicaraguan government is providing opportunities for political expression to a people that has never before enjoyed such freedom.

The meeting at the Baptist assembly also revealed the vibrance of religious faith in Nicaragua today. Throughout the country Christians have taken up their social and political roles as citizens, girded by a strong consciousness of their spiritual heritage. The church is speaking to the state in a complex and multifaceted dialogue. We in the United States tend to hear only those Christian voices that are critical of the Nicaraguan revolution. There is, however, a wide range of Christian voices. At the grass-roots level especially, many of these voices speak critically to the government, but from a position of basic trust in the goodwill of their political leaders and of hope for the future.

In Nicaragua today, many theologically conservative Protestant churches have opted to work prophetically within a revolutionary society. Baptists and other Nicaraguan evangelicals (as well as many Catholics) pursue this option at a time when their country is being attacked by forces that profess to be defending Christian and democratic values. For them it is a claim that rings hollow. Meanwhile, the Sandinista government, despite its imperfections and the considerable obstacles that are thrown in its path by the war, is striving to draw these various popular elements of Nicaraguan society into meaningful participation in the political process. The resulting dialogue suggests a new way of seeing the crisis in Central America—one that starts from the bottom, rather than at the top, as it does in the United States.

DEMOCRATIC BEDLAM

If one starts with what might be called a "Washington's eye view" of Central America, a curiously clear-cut picture emerges. In President Reagan's unusual speech to a joint session of Congress in April 1983, he made a bold and unequivocal claim. Democracy, he said, was on the march in Central America: "I can tell you tonight [that] democracy is beginning to take root in El Salvador, which until only a short time ago knew only dictatorship. The new government is now delivering on its promises of democracy, reforms, and free elections." Since that claim was made more than four years ago, it has been repeated countless times by the president himself and by other high officials. Much the same thing has been said about Honduras and Guatemala. Until recently these countries were governed by dictatorships. But now, on the basis of elections that Washington judges to be democratic, they are confidently proclaimed to be democracies.

On the other side of the ledger stands Nicaragua. Much of President Reagan's joint-session speech was an angry attack on that country. It was described as a threat to its neighbors and to the United States. In the ensuing years, high-ranking U.S. officials have incessantly repeated this theme, describing Nicaragua as a "festering sore," a totalitarian country bent on destroying democracy throughout the Western Hemisphere. Let's take a look at several recent examples.

In Chapter 4 we mentioned the visit that representatives of the Contadora nations made to Washington in early February 1986. During that visit they appealed to Secretary of State George Shultz to promote U.S. cooperation with the diplomatic peace process in Central America. They urged negotiations with Nicaragua and an end to aid for the U.S.-supported Contra army. However, just two weeks earlier, on 28 January, Secretary Shultz had met with several Contra leaders. Following that meeting he issued a statement praising the Contras as representing a "program for democratic reform in Nicaragua, the only one of the five countries in Central America whose people do not enjoy the benefit of a government freely chosen in fair elections."[1] He sharply contrasted Nicaragua with these four alleged democracies by asserting that it labors "under a severely repressive communist regime with no claim to a popular mandate." This point of view has enabled Secretary Shultz and other members of the Reagan administration to refer to the Contras as the "democratic resistance."

Just one week later Secretary Shultz appeared before the Foreign Affairs Committee of the U.S. House of Representatives to explain and defend administration policy in Central America. Again he referred to the march of democracy in Latin America, claiming that over 90 percent of Latin Americans "now enjoy democratic government, as opposed to less than one-third in the early 1980s."

We can marvel at this swift and decisive turn in the political tide. But we can also judge this trend more cautiously. It is true that in many Latin American countries the army has returned to the barracks and elections have been held. These are positive steps. But it remains to be seen whether genuinely democratic governments will now be consolidated, since the power and independence of the Central American militaries have not yet been curbed. At any rate, Secretary Shultz followed this exceedingly optimistic view of democratic reforms with a dire warning about Nicaragua: "The most immediate danger to democracy in Central America, of course, is the assault on it from communist Nicaragua." On 26 February, two weeks after the foreign ministers of the

Contadora nations had visited with Secretary Shultz, President Reagan addressed the nation on television. In that speech he ignored the advice of our Contadora allies and repeated verbatim what the secretary of state had told Congress.

These official pronouncements from Washington suggest several things that need to be examined more closely. First, it is apparent that the promotion of democracy has been set forth as an essential goal of U.S. policy in Central America. Therefore, as citizens we are invited to judge the success of our present policy on such grounds. At the same time, we might ask ourselves a simple question: Should our nation—or, indeed, any nation—be in the business of deciding which governments meet our democratic litmus test? If so, what do we do when our elected officials decide that the government of some other nation does not pass that test? Are we then entitled to try to overthrow that government? Would such actions be consistent with the rule of law, which is so vital to the integrity of a democratic nation? Second, we should ask whether Washington's rosy view of the spread of democracy in Central America is shared by the Central American people themselves. Who in Central America agrees with Washington's assessment? Third, what are the criteria that enable U.S. officials, or anyone else, to say that one country is democratic while another is not? Are the criteria used by U.S. officials applied consistently throughout Central America? The CCCS team spoke about these matters with dozens of people in Central America. What they had to say certainly shed light on these issues. Here is a sampling.

A well-known Central American sociologist interviewed in San José, Costa Rica, captured succinctly what our research team itself observed. He said, "Today all groups in Central America talk of democracy." And so they do. From the most reactionary groups on the right to the most radical guerrilla groups on the left, there is much talk of bringing authentic democracy to the region. No one whom we interviewed spoke against democracy, even in a qualified way. Yet across this spectrum of society are groups who not only disagree among themselves but who are engaged in armed hostilities against one another. If they don't disagree about the virtues of democracy, they certainly disagree about what democracy is. They have very different visions of what democratizing Central America means. What the elites generally mean by democracy, the sociologist told us, is elections in which only political parties they control play a decisive role. Such elections contribute little to a real sharing of power and authority.

Moreover, elections must be set against the background of the past forty years. In that period of time, the sociologist told us, there have been ninety changes of government among the five Central American nations. Exactly one-third of these changes were openly unconstitutional because they were imposed by the military through force or the threat of force. Another forty-six, or just over half, were achieved through elections. However, as was shown in Chapter 4, many of those elections were marred by fraud. Four changes of regime came about through popular uprisings, and ten were temporary (interim) governments, appointed to serve until elections could be held. Throughout this period there were often no open channels for political participation by ordinary people. For at least half of that period the governments of several Central American countries were conducting counterinsurgency wars of the sort described in Chapter 5. For varying periods of time this included Guatemala, El Salvador, and Nicaragua. Such tactics resulted in the internal suspension of the rule of law and, in some instances, the creation of a state of terror. Politics became a cruel "zero sum game"—one group's gain could be had only at the cost of another group's loss. This train of events virtually destroyed the social climate necessary for democracy. It seriously undermined what one scholar that we interviewed called the "culture of tolerance," the only context in which democratic institutions can truly flourish. Such an atmosphere of oppression and fear, however, was precisely the setting in which the elections that Washington has praised so highly took place.[2]

"El Salvador Is a Success Story"

Let us take the case of El Salvador, which has been so carefully cultivated by Washington as the democratic showcase for Central America in the 1980s. That country held a presidential election in 1984 that was lavishly praised in Washington. Yet, when the CCCS team first visited El Salvador on 9 January 1987, thirty-six people had already been assassinated in political violence that year. Members of a Salvadoran Protestant church spoke to us of the climate in which they seek to carry out their pastoral work. Movements that do not coordinate their work with the government are classified as suspect, they told us, and are subjected to campaigns of intimidation. Since 1981 the government has been determined to suppress or co-opt all movements that work with the poor. "We work in a very insecure climate," the church members noted, "in a nation that talks of democracy but does not respect human rights."

Another organization at the grass-roots level that provided testimony on this issue was *Comadres,* the Committee of Mothers and Relatives of Prisoners, Disappeared, and Politically Assassinated.

Originally founded under the sponsorship of the archdiocese of San Salvador, its members are women whose husbands or children have suffered at the hands of government security forces the inhumanities that the group's name denounces. Some of the mothers themselves have been arrested and tortured, acts facilitated by the State of Emergency Law that has been in effect throughout this entire "democratic" period. Decree 50 of the State of Emergency Law allows the security forces to seize any citizen on suspicion of "subversion" and to hold such individuals under arrest for fifteen days (eight days without notice to anyone). While they are in custody, their arrest is entirely a military matter. This means, in effect, that in El Salvador the military is a law unto itself. Elections have had no impact upon this cruel situation.

One member of *Comadres* described being picked up under the provisions of this law. She was subjected to torture for fourteen days and then sent to prison for five months. Never presented for trial, she was finally released. Why was she treated this way? "Because we say that here there is only the word democracy—there is no real democracy. Our president may be a democratic man, but there is no democratic system in El Salvador." She paused and then added, "We have taken our message to many countries. Only the United States has refused to admit us." When human rights groups attempt to investigate these incidents, they too run the risk of being arrested under Decree 50. As of January 1987, five members of the independent Salvadoran human rights commission were in Mariona prison, the penitentiary where those charged with political offenses are incarcerated.

Views such as these were echoed over and over again in other countries hailed by Washington as democratic. In Honduras, North American missionaries working with the poor said, "Here there is no democracy. We need to build a community of trust. It is utterly lacking here—on all levels." Another person told us, "Votes do not make democracy, but rather democracy makes votes meaningful." He went on to suggest that Honduran workers do not blame their unemployment on Nicaragua, nor do Honduran peasants think they are without land because of the Sandinistas. Nicaragua is a long-run threat, he said, only because the common people of Central America "have never had a voice in their most important political decisions. Now the Nicaraguan people do seem to have it."

In the same vein, Indian pastors of a Guatemalan Protestant church said of the 1985 elections that brought Christian Democrat Vinicio Cerezo to the presidency, "Only the right wing participated . . . and these elections were held after a long period of persecution during which most of the leaders of Indian communities were eliminated."

When the question of democracy was discussed with the U.S. ambassador in Guatemala, he told the CCCS team that there was an authentic democratic opening in the country. The evidence he offered was the fact that "no active-duty military men are in the ministries now—except the head of the police." He added that the new government sympathized with land reform, perhaps the most pressing issue facing the country. But, he noted, the government could not undertake such reform because it had promised the army before the elections that it would not do so. After his election, President Cerezo himself stated that he possessed perhaps 30 percent of the power associated with his office. The remainder, he implied, still rests with the army, which has controlled the country for thirty years.

When the CCCS team returned to El Salvador and visited the U.S. Embassy, we were told unequivocally by a leading political officer that "El Salvador is a success story." In 1979 the country was run by the oligarchy and the military. People were so disgusted with the government that they were joining the guerrillas in large numbers. But the situation has been turned around decisively in the past several years. The officer compared El Salvador to Venezuela. What he did not say was that Venezuela—a Contadora nation whose foreign minister was among those urging George Shultz to stop aid to the Contras and negotiate with Nicaragua—has enjoyed relatively free and honest elections for more than twenty years. This achievement was greatly facilitated by the relative prosperity produced by the oil boom of the 1970s, which allowed Venezuelans to build up some of that community of trust that is essential in maintaining a stable democracy.

But what about El Salvador? The same embassy official went on to describe the atmosphere in which this "democratic" government functions and how the administration of President Duarte utilizes its legislative majority in the Salvadoran National Assembly. "The right wing here sees Duarte as a communist. He ignores them in the Assembly. His party often suspends the rules and just passes whatever legislation they want to on the day it is introduced. There is no debate with the right wing parties." Yet these are the only parties represented in the assembly. No party to the left of the center-right Christian Democrats even ran any candidates for office in the 1984 presidential election. Moderate and leftist parties either were crushed during the repression of earlier decades, or broke up and reformed as part of the armed opposition that is presently fighting a guerrilla war against the Duarte government.

The embassy officer's own account suggests that the elected government of El Salvador today is neither very representative nor very democratic in its internal functioning. It operates in an environment in which the majority of the people, the poor and powerless, lack trust in the government. To make matters worse, there is the whole question of the rule of law. Having described El Salvador as a democratic success story, the embassy official went on to say that there was one area in which reform had been difficult to carry out: the judicial system. "It's dead in the water," he said.

"The Only Note You Ever Strike Is 'Elections'"

We must now ask the obvious question: Under the circumstances just described, how can the rights of Salvadoran citizens be guaranteed? The answer is that they cannot. The rule of law does not prevail in El Salvador. That is why government-instigated violence has been so tragically widespread and systematic in recent years, and why it continues to this day even under a "democratically elected" government. This situation lends a large measure of credibility and force to the testimony of grass-roots groups in El Salvador. They are the ones victimized by ongoing government repression at the hands of armed forces over which the elected government has little control. Mute but eloquent testimony to this reality is the fact that not one military officer has been brought to justice in El Salvador during the past seven years, despite the fact that tens of thousands of citizens have been murdered by security forces.

This scenario was put in perspective by a Salvadoran Catholic bishop who said that the recent elections were different from those of the past in that Salvadorans really did not know in advance who would win. This was a step forward. As he put it, El Salvador may now have achieved "the formal part of democracy." But, he asked, what does that really mean for the average person? "It's like having a musical score in front of you marked 'democracy.' Whenever you start to play the music, the only note you ever strike is 'elections,' 'elections,' 'elections.'" This, he said, is what U.S. policy looks like in Central America. It is one-dimensional. It considers only one important facet of a multifaceted process. All the rest is forgotten or lost in a preoccupation with security. Those who question the sufficiency of the U.S.-sponsored elections are all too easily grouped under the labels "subversive" and "communist." But these words have an Orwellian quality. They are arbitrary. They fail to discriminate. The result is that in countries like El Salvador, elections do not in themselves make government more responsive to the people. Indeed, they may only provide a mantle of legitimacy to the outside world beneath which the armed forces continue to wage war against a segment of the populace.

A QUESTION OF TRUST

As this book was being written, the United States was celebrating the two-hundredth anniversary of a historic event: the drafting of the U.S. Constitution. The Constitutional Convention that met in Philadelphia during the summer of 1787 was probably one of the great historic events of the modern age. The constitution that it produced has been widely admired and often copied. It has come to symbolize the rule of law, protecting the rights of individuals. Citizens of the United States are justifiably proud of their constitution. This is all the more reason to feel dismay over the Iran-Contra hearings during the summer months of 1987, which coincided with a special celebration of the U.S. Constitution in which fifty-five legislators traveled to Philadelphia to re-enact completion of that original document. Those hearings revealed that in the name of promoting democracy in Central America, officials of the National Security Council and the CIA had knowingly and systematically violated both the letter and the spirit of that Constitution. These actions were shocking because the American public does not expect such deception on the part of its government officials. The basic core of trust that U.S. citizens normally put in their government is something that was slowly and carefully built up through a long historical process.

Trust: The Making of the U.S. Constitution

The United States was founded upon a mutual agreement among thirteen states of unequal size and resources, with considerable rivalry and mistrust among them. A great deal of discussion and good old-fashioned horse-trading went on before the Constitution gained the approval of the fifty-five delegates sent to Philadelphia in 1787. In fact, it was because of these disagreements, and because the delegates at the convention were uncertain whether they would gain popular support for what they were doing, that they closed their meetings to the press and to the public. Once they had written a constitution, they set about to win public acceptance for it. This was achieved by adding the first ten amendments to the Constitution, which we call the Bill of Rights. That the American public would accept the Constitution and then be governed successfully under it bespeaks their long colonial experience of self-government and their shared tradition of English common law.

Despite the fact that the Constitution was hammered out by a small group of men—property owners and intellectuals—without benefit of consultation with the people that they represented, it has endured. This came about, first of all, because the Constitution is itself a product of the rule of law. Second, by reinforcing the tradition that government is under the law, not above it, the U.S. Constitution nurtured a large measure of trust between the government and the people. In U.S. history the Civil War stands as a painful reminder of what can happen when the climate of trust breaks down in the face of vested interests and deep social antagonisms.

Trust is the result of mutual faith and concern. On the part of the government it calls for faith in and concern for all citizens, including the poor and the powerless. It also requires that the people have faith in their leaders and in their nation's political institutions. The rule of law and the fairness of public policy help to guarantee mutual trust. These attributes contribute to a general atmosphere in which citizens in all stations of life find, in the words of a familiar Latin American expression, *espacio para ser hombres* (space to be human).

Trust: The Missing Ingredient in Central America

With the possible exception of modern Costa Rica, the nations of Central America were not built upon a foundation of such trust. This has been made amply clear in the preceding chapters. The seeds of mistrust were sown in the colonial period. The plant was cultivated with economic greed, and watered by the shortsighted policies of local rulers and of successive U.S. administrations. Thus it has borne the bitter fruit of living death and outright warfare. The necessary ingredients for political dialogue based upon some measure of mutual acceptance were never present, as is evident, for example, in the inhuman treatment of the Guatemalan Indians. Mistrust, fueled by deep-seated fear, has exacted the heavy toll of thousands of dead and disappeared in El Salvador. Whatever space for dialogue was present in Honduras is rapidly disappearing beneath the onslaught of a war that is not of Honduran making. Even the consensus upon which the model democracy of tiny Costa Rica is based is in danger of coming apart under the strain of economic pressures and ideological polarization. By contrast, for the first time in their history, the people of Nicaragua have an opportunity to develop, however imperfectly, the reservoir of trust necessary for creating a democratic society. But this opportunity is in jeopardy because of internal polarizations that are fueled by fear and mistrust. Whatever chance the Nicaraguan people may have to work out their own future is now being impeded through the frequent attacks and acts of sabotage by Contra forces.

In times of war, existing democratic institutions stand in great peril, as the recent Iran-Contra scandal has made abundantly clear. During World War II the U.S. government felt compelled to set aside such important constitutional guarantees as freedom of speech and freedom of movement for citizens of Japanese descent. This, the government said, was in the interest of national security. These events make us aware of the fragility of democracy. To build up democratic institutions where they have never before existed—especially in a setting of ongoing war, which is the ultimate expression of mistrust—is exceedingly difficult, perhaps impossible. Yet this is precisely what we claim to be imposing, by force of arms, upon the peoples of Central America.

The yearning for room to be fully human among the Central American peoples is so great that they continue to struggle to achieve it, even against the greatest odds. Traditionally passive people have been galvanized by the Spirit of God into movements of social transformation. These movements have their roots in the history of the 1960s, 1970s, and 1980s. During this period the Roman Catholic Church played a vital role in these movements. We need to know something about the recent history of that church in order to understand what is taking place in Central America today. As we reflect upon it, we find that it is making its own deep and authentic contributions within the larger history of the Christian church.

UPSIDE DOWN IN A TOP-DOWN CHURCH

In the past it was common for North American Protestants to blame much of the backwardness of Latin American societies on the Roman Catholic Church. In fact, it is a rationale that the CCCS team heard several times during interviews with national leaders and missionaries in Central America. Roman Catholicism, we were told, is an authoritarian, superstitious, and backward religion that for centuries has slept in the same bed with the national oligarchies and corrupt governments. It is therefore unable or unwilling to challenge the social and political status quo. Although there is a large element of historical truth in such statements, today a remarkable change is under way in the Catholic Church.[3]

The Second Vatican Council

Over the past fifteen years a veritable revolution in religious consciousness has taken place in the Catholic Church of Central America. Using the word "revolution" to describe this transformation does not seem excessive. Before 1968 this church was extremely hierarchical and traditional, weak in resources, and closely allied with social elites and national rulers. It lacked significant contact with the mass of ordinary citizens. But, as the church redefined its pastoral and social role among the people, things began to change. What happened within the church to cause this change? What were the historical circumstances in Latin America—and throughout the world—that set the stage for these momentous stirrings?

John XXIII, supposedly a caretaker pope, set in motion a series of events that shook the church to its foundations. "Good Pope John" was particularly moved by the cries of the poor; indeed, he is often credited with coining the phrase "the church of the poor." In 1958 he issued a call for the first worldwide church council in almost a century. It convened in 1962, addressing the issue of the role of the church in the modern world. Although a concern for the poor was not paramount on its agenda, the pope was able to express his global concern for alleviating poverty. The council, which concluded its work in 1965, paved the way for the questions that bishops from Latin America soon began to address to their own social and ecclesial reality. It not only encouraged Catholics to take a hard look at their faith and pastoral practice, but also urged them to take a more critical posture toward elementary issues of justice in their societies. The council also promoted more active lay participation in carrying out the mission of the church. This emphasis was reinforced by a new stress on Bible study.[4]

The foundation was now laid for the premiere event in the recent history of the Latin American church. Pope Paul VI inaugurated the Second Latin American Conference of Bishops in Medellín, Colombia, in 1968. The time was ripe for change in the Latin American church. Breaking out of their long-standing habits of isolation, bishops had begun to interact pastorally with their flocks. They were gradually and painfully becoming aware of the masses of displaced and dehumanized people to which their church had previously offered only heaven as a way of escape. So what came out of Medellín was a shock to many people. For others it was a clarion call for change. In remarkably specific and compelling language, the bishops at Medellín pledged to put the weight of the church on the side of the poor in their struggle for liberation.

See—Judge—Act

Vatican II had used a top-down deductive method to study the problems of the world: first defining church doctrine, then seeking to apply these teachings to concrete situations. But, as we saw in Chapter 1, the "Medellín methodology" turned the tables on this approach. It chose to use an inductive (from the bottom up) method of societal analysis: see, judge, act. The practical result of this decision was to turn a top-down church upside down. Medellín observed the depth of the crisis in Latin America and called for "an order where man is not an object, but an agent of his own history."[5] The foundation for the social transformations that Medellín envisioned was evangelization. The church, the bishops insisted, must become the evangelizer of the poor.[6] It is unlikely that the Medellín bishops foresaw how deeply the established church was itself to become evangelized through its own renewed evangelizing ministry among the church of the poor. For a major instrument to be used by God for this evangelization project was already in place: the Ecclesial Base Communities—in Spanish, *Comunidades Eclesiales de Base,* or CEBs in shorthand. Medellín calls them "the focus of evangelization" and "the most important source of human advancement and development."[7] We shall have more to say about them presently.

The 1970s was a turbulent decade of accelerating change and deteriorating social conditions. In 1979 the Bishops Conference reassembled at Puebla, Mexico, under Pope John Paul II. Despite some rearguard opposition, Puebla basically reaffirmed Medellín's commitment to the poor. The conference reasserted the church's "preferential option for the poor" and called the CEBs communities "of faith, hope and charity."[8] The bishops also defended the right of the peasants to organize.[9]

In Central America these new expressions of pastoral concern for the poor have had to struggle to win recognition from a hierarchy that jealously guarded its episcopal authority. Many bishops viewed the CEBs with caution, fearful that their own authority might be threatened. Thus the so-called popular church in Nicaragua experienced almost constant conflict with the archbishop of Managua, Cardinal Miguel Obando y Bravo, because many grass-roots Catholics are supportive of the Sandinista revolution. He has been very cool to grass-roots initiatives that are not under his direct supervision and control. Archbishop Oscar Romero represented the other end of the spectrum in terms of hierarchical openness to grass-roots initiatives by laypeople. He placed a concern for his people above his episcopal prerogatives. Most Central American bishops stand somewhere between these two clear options. Few have come close to identifying with the cause of the poor as Romero did in his ministry. Consequently, leadership in renewal movements among the poor has fallen to the clergy, religious sisters, Delegates of the Word, and the poor themselves. The poor are now passing from one calloused hand to another the torch that Medellín lit.

THE CHURCH: "SPACE TO BE HUMAN"

All over Central America there are clusters of small grass-roots communities struggling to create spaces in which people can live more fully human lives as creatures of God. Chapter 1 introduced us to one such gathering: Christ the Saviour Church in the Zacamil barrio of San Salvador. Hundreds of other parishes and a handful of Protestant churches are signaling the emergence of this kind of church in Central America, a church of the men, women, young people, and children that make up the popular movement in Central America.

After attending a worship service in Zacamil, the CCCS team was invited to join a meeting of small-group leaders in the garage of the parish house. A middle-aged couple, peasants, were being introduced to the group. They had traveled from their remote village to the capital by a roundabout way to tell their story to the Zacamil pastoral team. Only two days before, Salvadoran helicopter gunships had fired upon four neighboring villages. Although the military chief of staff had assured the CCCS team a few days earlier that this low-intensity war tactic was no longer being employed, these humble Christians told us in their thick peasant brogue that innocent people had been killed and many more left homeless.

During the discussion that followed, a small-group leader gave her testimony. She told us that her twenty-two-year-old son, a university student, had been assassinated on 7 August 1980. "But I wasn't able to pick up his body for fear of being killed," she commented gently. Three years later she was dragged out of her house at midnight with her husband and other children and brutally beaten while her tormentors yelled, "Where have you hidden the arms?" Miraculously saved, her children escaped to Mexico. "But I have remained here," she concluded, "because I'm needed. We are working for the kingdom of God." This mother's vision is a theological key to understanding what is happening in the grass-roots churches in Central America today. We shall return to this in Chapter 7.

The "Church of the Poor"

The people we met in Zacamil were leaders in one of those small groups of Catholics called CEBs. The majority of the participants are poor, disenfranchised peasants and the displaced inhabitants of the festering shantytowns that surround most of the capitals of Central America. They meet to pray, sing Christian songs, study the Word, and discover what Scripture is saying to their own particular situations. But in the explosive sociopolitical reality of Central America, these seemingly innocuous acts by poor people are very threatening to those in power. Such grass-roots communities are viewed with profound suspicion by our own government as well. As a result, in Guatemala and El Salvador the CEBs have been hounded to death and many of their members forced into hiding.

During the 1960s and 1970s, these CEBs began to make their presence felt in the slums of the big cities of Latin America, among the highland Indians of the Andean region, and in all the countries of the Central American region.[10] They were initiated in Panama City, Managua, and San Salvador even before the Catholic bishops met at Medellín. That conference then opened up the institutional spaces that the common people needed to create new and authentic communities of Christians. During the next decade the pace accelerated, so that by the mid-1970s the CEBs had become a significant force throughout the region.

The Ecclesial Base Communities are part of a much larger religious phenomenon often called "the church of the poor." This movement includes such popular organizations as human rights groups, peasant and labor unions, and the lay liturgists called *Delegados de la Palabra*—Delegates of the Word. Giving their support to these interrelated movements is a small core of dedicated priests, sisters, theologians, and middle-class people who have identified with the cause of the poor.[11]

Delegates of the Word

In countries where any kind of a grass-roots community is viewed with official suspicion, the Delegates of the Word have a special significance. They often provide a less visible way than the CEBs of encouraging struggling Christian groups, though they function somewhat differently in each of the countries of Central America. In Guatemala and El Salvador these delegates are often leaders of the CEBs. According to T. S. Montgomery, over 15,000 lay leaders were trained in El

Salvador alone during the 1970s.[12] But in Honduras, where there are some 10,000 delegates today, they serve small and isolated groups of peasants that have not developed into full-fledged CEBs. During its twenty-year history, this movement has developed an identity to fit the religious and social reality of Honduras.[13] Over the years the Honduran Delegates of the Word have become more involved with the endemic problems of poverty and injustice. Since 1982 they have found themselves challenged to deal compassionately with the high-intensity suffering of the Honduran peasants—the result of the low-intensity proxy war that the United States is waging against Nicaragua.

A Passionist priest who coordinates a team of delegates in one region of Honduras told the CCCS team that the problem in his country is hunger. "It is not a problem of faith," he noted. He went on to explain that the common people have a strong religious faith. But how should they understand their faith? Should they accept their misery and wait passively for something better in the next life? Or should they assert their own dignity as God's children and work to create something better in this life? The priest answered his own questions, suggesting the kind of approach that delegates in his parish might take in their Christian communities. "Christ became incarnate. He didn't ask us to disincarnate!"

In Honduras such historical incarnation takes the form of small communities called "houses of prayer." Delegates, most of whom have only a second- or third-grade education, are usually chosen by the communities themselves. Prayer rather than scriptural reflection is the initial focus of these communities. The goal of the delegates is "to change the way people pray"—to help them communicate more freely with God even as they relate more incarnationally with the problems of their communities. In the process of praying and discussing personal and community problems, they will turn increasingly to Scripture. At some point the groups may come to see themselves as Ecclesial Base Communities.

As they move out into society with a "prophetic proclamation of salvation," the delegates are elected to key positions in the peasant organizations. This has sometimes gotten them into trouble with the authorities. The priests who work with them have been accused of training leftists. The priests disagree. Their role, they point out, is to prepare Christians to become conscious of the reality in which they live. This awareness, together with their desire to incarnate the gospel in their own reality, is what motivates the Delegates of the Word and the CEBs.

Ecclesial Base Communities

The CEBs are loosely organized local groups of impoverished Christians who have acquired a sense of identity and purpose. They foster the spiritual growth of their members, but they also serve as vehicles to pursue community interests. Most begin through the efforts of church representatives. But since there is an acute shortage of priests, lay members often lead in the celebration of the Word. Scripture is central to the outlook of the CEBs. In these small groups, writes a Spanish priest, "the everyday life of the members, the church, and the world are read, prayed over, and reflected upon in relation to the Word of God."[14] As the CEBs function under indigenous leadership, the poor in Central America begin to study the Bible for the first time, interpreting its message in light of their own life experiences. The Bible becomes a focal point and resource for social and political criticism. Its message sounds radical: the social and political order under which these people live is seen as deeply unjust. The Christian freedom promised in the Bible includes a liberation from the very conditions under which these people are living.

This momentous discovery prompts one writer to observe that the CEBs may well be "the most subversive institution the Latin American church has developed."[15] It is important that we be clear about why this is so. It is not because these groups were created to undermine existing political institutions. Their original inspiration had little to do with politics as such. Rather, it is because the leaven of the Word is acting in the lives of a people that live in dehumanizing poverty, under unremittent oppression, in a twilight zone of "violent peace." When driven by the Word, they take it upon themselves to change that violent situation, even if by adopting peaceful means they are regarded as a threat by those who hold power.

The transforming power of Scripture in the lives of peasants can show itself in unexpected ways. This is poignantly illustrated by an event that took place during a CEB Bible study in Guatemala. During group discussion a prominent Central American theologian asked an elderly Indian to share his viewpoint on the Scripture. As he prepared to formulate his reply, the old man suddenly began to weep. Troubled, the leader asked the man what he had said to embarrass him. The Indian replied, "No, I'm not embarrassed. It is just that never before has anyone asked me for my opinion!" When a downtrodden peasant learns that his opinion counts in a body of Christian believers, he will begin to lift his head high and to defy those that would take this newfound sense of dignity from him.

Within the framework of the CEBs, everyone has an equal voice, and decisions are made after they have been talked out at great length in an atmosphere of mutual trust. The grass-roots communities have therefore been called "schools for democracy." They are in fact the spiritual motor of a revolutionary process in which the poor of Central America, who have never had a voice or a meaningful vote, are now participating in political decisions through numerous popular organizations. When we talked to Indians and other peasants (both Protestant and Catholic) in the remote reaches of Guatemala, El Salvador, Honduras, and Nicaragua, we were struck most forcibly by their indomitable spirit and by their long view of history. No matter how violently their traditional masters are rejecting their demands, one gets the impression that these people will not be stopped. As one Salvadoran peasant put it to us, "We may not live to be free, and perhaps our children won't either, but our grandchildren will."

This church of the poor—not Marxist agitators or Cuban infiltrators—is in great measure responsible for the Christian-based hope that keeps the struggle for democracy alive in the hearts of countless Central Americans. The church of the poor turns to a much higher authority than Marx: their appeal is to the Word of God for the prophetic space they need to combat injustice. In fact, most Central American Indians have never heard of any other "Marx" but the Gospel of "Mark"—these two names sound much the same in their native dialects. It should not surprise us that this kind of church causes considerable uneasiness among church hierarchies; it is a phenomenon beyond their control. As an army general admitted to us, the church of the poor is viewed with profound distrust. It is feared by the oligarchs, by the U.S. government, and by all those who do not want to see their world of privilege changed. Strenuous efforts have therefore been put forth in Central America to wipe out the CEBs.

Still, these popular movements are growing, despite the Vatican's guarded attitude toward them and the ruthless persecution by death squads. After being decimated by the brutal repression of the early 1980s, the CEBs are once more on the rise in El Salvador and Guatemala. Religious awareness and political commitment have become integrated and mutually reinforcing in the church of the poor. The intense and unifying experience of poor peoples throughout Central America—studying the Bible, worshiping together, making decisions in common, and selecting their own leaders—provides a rich base from which the church has contributed to the development of the popular organizations.

FIRST STEPS TOWARD
SELF-DETERMINATION

Out of the mobilization taking place in the CEBs has grown a broad range of popular organizations. They were created with the active participation of the poor and belong to them. Together with the grass-roots Christian communities to which they are so closely united, the popular organizations are one of the most important examples of the struggle to create more democratic societies in Central America. They represent an important dimension of democracy that is not guaranteed by elections alone. Let us look for a moment at the specific cases of El Salvador and Nicaragua, which have been portrayed so negatively by government officials.

Popular Organizations in El Salvador

The popular organizations in El Salvador are readily labeled by U.S. policymakers as communist or communist controlled. There is a strong tendency to lump them all together. If they are independent of the government that Washington has worked so hard to see elected, and critical of that government, they are viewed as part and parcel of what are called "professional guerrilla movements." This label suggests that these groups prefer armed conflict to peaceful civic participation. It also gives the impression that these organizations represent only a small minority on the violent left, which is extremely misleading. Actually these groups have tens of thousands of members. They are part of the "broad popular fronts" of political opposition that grew up in response to electoral fraud and political repression. As Archbishop Romero put it in his pastoral letter of August 1978, "Organizations that voice dissent from the government—political parties, trade unions, rural organizations—find themselves hindered and even prevented from exercising their right to organize legally and to work for their aims." He reminded his countrymen that "the meaning of the Greek word *demos* is the totality of the citizens." Yet in El Salvador "groups among the mass of the people meet only difficulties and repression when they try . . . to defend the interests of the majority."[16]

It was the failure of formal democratic reforms during the years of the Alliance for Progress that led to the creation of popular organizations in El Salvador. As was suggested previously, their initial formation was richly stimulated by reforms within the Catholic Church. A closer look reveals a startling fact: the original nucleus of the broad opposition front against which the Duarte government is fighting today was composed of Christian organizations. It is worth taking a moment to look at that history.

In the mid-1960s, under the stimulus of the Alliance for Progress and Vatican II, leaders of several political parties and university-student groups set about to train peasant leaders and establish rural self-help associations. Four separate organizations sprang up: two were based in the universities, and two were based in mainstream but progressive political parties. The Social Christian Party established the Center for Social Studies and Popular Promotion, known by the initials CESPROP. This center was dedicated to Christian reflection on the problems of rural El Salvador. Its primary answer to these problems was to promote small-scale local development projects—building schools, digging wells, marketing crops, seeking secure title to land. The Christian Democratic Party followed suit, creating *Accion Comunitaria,* the Office of Community Action. The Christian Democrats who worked in *Accion Comunitaria* were deeply influenced by the CESPROP program. They were also influenced by the teaching methods of Paulo Freire, the renowned Brazilian educator, and sought to practice these methods in the Salvadoran countryside. The emphasis was on encouraging peasants to cultivate a critical self-awareness.

On the university side, two other organizations appeared. Students in the National University established the Social Christian Revolutionary Federation of University Students, or FRUSC. Despite its ponderous, radical-sounding title, this student movement was set up to compete with the student organization sponsored by the Communist Party. FRUSC engaged in spirited theological competition with the communist-influenced student group. In the Catholic University a second student group was formed called the Salvadoran Catholic University Association, or ACUS. This movement was initially guided by Belgian priests. Its members went into the countryside, into such areas as Aguilares and Suchitoto in eastern El Salvador, which are today associated with the guerrilla struggle.

In 1966 there was no guerrilla struggle in El Salvador. There was only the presence of these four urban-based groups reaching out to promote healthy and needed change among desperately poor rural peoples. Their focus was human development, in the form of education, medical care, and economic development. To that end they promoted peasant organizations. There was nothing at all in the program of any of these groups about overthrowing the government. To the contrary, their activities were legal and legitimate in the fullest sense of the word. They aimed at improving society by enabling peasants to help themselves.

But consider their fate. These organizations made some headway in the late 1960s. They succeeded in encouraging widespread peasant involvement and hope. But those hopes were not to be fulfilled. The election of 1972, discussed in Chapter 4, was a decisive turning point for these groups and their peasant members. After Napoleon Duarte, the Christian Democrat who won the election, was arrested and sent into exile, the Salvadoran army launched a fierce campaign of repression against such groups. Eventually three of these organizations were crushed and disappeared. Their leaders were either killed, forced into exile, or pushed into the ranks of newly forming guerrilla movements.

Only ACUS survived, but it was effectively driven out of the functioning political arena. What was left for it to do? As a Christian organization it still had its original commitments. So, in a low-key, semiclandestine way, it continued to pursue its goals. Its surviving members went on working to establish CEBs and training Delegates of the Word. From the ranks of these peasant communities, rooted in the study of the Bible and the practice of the Christian faith, came the founders of the new popular organizations of the late 1970s. One of the most prominent of these was the Popular Revolutionary Bloc (BPR), commonly known as the *Bloque*. A major affiliate of the BPR was the Christian Federation of Salvadoran Peasants (FECCAS). Another key popular organization was the United Front of Popular Action (FAPU). Each of these popular organizations eventually became associated with the mounting armed resistance to the repressive dictatorships that governed the country. Far from being "professional guerrillas" sent by Cuba or some other revolutionary state, these were organizations with deep Christian inspiration that had tried all peaceful avenues of change, only to find them closed by terror and violence.[17]

All of these events, we must note, took place *before* the Nicaraguan revolution. As we turn our attention now to Nicaragua, we should bear in mind that popular organizations grew up in that country in much the same way that they did in El Salvador, but independent of the Salvadoran process. In order to appreciate the dynamics of the Nicaraguan revolution, it is important to grasp the relationship between the popular organizations and the FSLN, the Sandinista Front for National Liberation.

Popular Organizations in Nicaragua

U.S. officials acknowledge that the FSLN in Nicaragua came to power as part of a broad popular movement of national resistance against Somoza. They insist, however, that the FSLN has emerged as a despotic minority, betraying and ousting the truly democratic elements in the movement, while co-opting the popular organizations or creating new ones in order to consolidate the party's hold on power and to further its own interests. The true democrats are said to be the Contras, who are now fighting the Sandinistas.

This account of Nicaraguan history is inaccurate. A very broad cross-section of the Nicaraguan people participated actively in the struggle against Somoza, particularly after the assassination of Pedro Joaquin Chamorro, the famous publisher of *La Prensa,* in January 1978. After the insurrection broke out in September 1978, the FSLN had to advance its own timetable in the military struggle because armed citizens in neighborhoods and villages were taking the lead in clashes with the National Guard. But those who actually fought in the insurrection were not the leaders of the established political parties or members of such private-sector associations as the Superior Council of Private Enterprise (COSEP). The fighting was done by the grass-roots rank-and-file citizenry. They saw the Sandinista Front as the legitimate leaders of the uprising. Therefore, when the dictatorship of Somoza fell, the FSLN was widely popular among the peasants and working-class people who make up the majority of Nicaragua's population. Many of these people had already begun to organize before the revolution succeeded. After victory came, the FSLN did create some new organizations, such as the Sandinista Youth Movement. But much of its energy was devoted to consolidating and strengthening existing organizations. Those are groups that fight for their own interests, giving Nicaragua a truly popular participation that it has never known before.

The popular organizations in Nicaragua developed in response to the specific conditions of the Somoza regime. They included organizations of women, landless peasants, urban workers, neighborhood youth groups, and others, as well as the more traditional interest-group organizations such as those for teachers, ranchers, clergy, and the like. Some of the popular organizations—such as the Luis Amanda Espinoza Women's Association (AMNLAE) and the Association of Rural Workers (ATC)—were created prior to the popular insurrection and enabled these groups to play an important role in overthrowing the dictatorship. Others, such as the July 19th Sandinista Youth and the Sandinista Defense Committees (CDS), although created after the revolution under FSLN sponsorship, drew together elements of pre-existing organizations. In short, these groups had identities of their own, independent of the FSLN, though they accepted the FSLN's legitimacy in leading the revolution.[18]

These popular organizations have been closely and actively involved in tasks of national reconstruction. Besides promoting the interests of their members, they cooperate in various ways in national defense, in educational and health campaigns, and in food distribution and neighborhood improvement. Thus these organizations provide opportunities for the poor to participate directly in political life. Prior to the 1984 elections these organizations expressed their interests through a legislative body known as the Council of State. Originally composed of thirty-three seats and later expanded to forty-seven, the council made provision for both political parties and popular organizations to elect representatives.

Since the 1984 election, Nicaraguans have been at work writing a new constitution and, more recently, preparing for municipal elections. All manner of popular organizations have played an active and central role in drafting the constitution. In this respect the Nicaraguan constitution is the product of a much more democratic process of participation by the citizenry than was the U.S. Constitution, which was drafted in secret by delegates who greatly exceeded their original mandate. In addition, the 1984 election placed many members of popular organizations in the new National Assembly. For these reasons popular organizations in Nicaragua have considerable influence on the legislative process. Through them the people are empowered in ways they never were under the Somoza dictatorship. Members of these popular organizations bitterly oppose the Contras, whom they associate with that cruel regime.

In short, for tens of thousands of poor people in Central America, the popular organizations offer hope for a genuine democratic alternative. Christians are playing an important role both in creating and in sustaining these organizations. These Christians, one of them explained to our CCCS team, have found enough space to be *duenos de su propia historia* ("responsible actors in their own history").

THE REFORMATIONAL SPIRIT OF CHANGE IN CENTRAL AMERICA

The events taking place in Central America today have important historical precedents. This is not the first time Christians have participated in struggles for human rights while living in societies plagued by injustice. Although the experience of Central American Christians is in many ways unique, there are also points of contact between their experiments in democratic participation and our own North American Protestant heritage.

The Pilgrims who came to North American shores and the countless other immigrant groups that followed them were impelled by a dream. They wanted to be free from a top-down world where autocratic monarchs and church hierarchs imposed religious and political decisions upon them. They sought freedom to worship God and to chart their own destiny. A similar dream, based upon solid biblical convictions, moved the Reformers of the sixteenth century to defy the religious and political powers of their day. As that dream spread, it inspired small groups of common people throughout Europe to question the established churches and to gather themselves into various kinds of alternative Christian communities. This is a dream that has not died, as the experience of the church of the poor in Central America testifies so vividly.

Ironically, those following this dream today are often not Protestants but Catholics. Small groups of Protestants in El Salvador and Guatemala and a larger number of evangelicals in Nicaragua are exceptions to the rule. Many of today's Protestants have chosen not to protest, perhaps out of a lack of understanding of the richness of grassroots Protestant movements in their own heritage. Richard Shaull, a Presbyterian theologian who has worked for many years in Latin America, calls the emergence of the CEBs in the Catholic Church "a new reformation."[19] It is perhaps more accurate to speak of a reformational spirit in these CEBs than to try to straitjacket them into some clearly defined Reformation model. At the same time, concerned Protestants have noted the absence of this reformational dream and of its reformational roots among many evangelicals in Central America. We shall have occasion to address this issue in the next chapter. Meanwhile, it is useful to consider the church of the poor in Central America through reformational eyes. Our purpose is to ask whether or not the CEBs can point the way for us to "a reformed approach to the Central American crisis."

Within the CEBs it is the Bible, and not some Protestant model of the church, that serves as a guide to pastoral practice. Thus motivated, a small but growing number of evangelical Protestants are becoming a part of this ecclesiogenesis—the birth of a new kind of church.[20] It is the way the CEBs respond to biblical concerns more than to any "reformational signs" that is attracting these grass-roots Protestants to the CEBs. Displaced peasants and refugees comprise one group of people strongly attracted to the CEBs. Among them are theologically conservative, even fundamentalist Protestants who are making common cause with their Catholic sisters and brothers in popular organizations and in nonsectarian CEBs. Especially in the war zones, beleaguered campesinos have found in grass-roots evangelical churches "spaces of life" in situations where death abounds. Where everything seems to be hopeless, they offer hope. It is "a hope so great," a peasant pastor testifies, "that for the first time we can feel it profoundly. This people which . . . had been silent and bent over . . . [have] overcome this situation to rise up proudly amidst the pain, with hope."[21]

What does the Protestant Reformation have to do with the search for democracy in Central America? And do the CEBs have anything to say to Protestant churches in North America? To find answers to these questions, let us look at three biblical themes highlighted by the Reformers that bear directly upon the theme of this chapter.

As the Reformation message spread, it kindled hope in the hearts of long-oppressed people. It opened up the necessary room for peasants and artisans in a closed hierarchical and feudal society—not unlike that of colonial Central America—to become the protagonists of their own history. This result was probably not foreseen by the Reformers. Nor was the impact of Scripture upon Central American peasants expected, either by Protestant leaders or by the Catholic hierarchy. The doctrine of the priesthood (or holy office) of every Christian and the "protestant principle" of ongoing reformation encouraged the demand among poor and oppressed Christians to create space in which they could pursue their own life callings freely. Let us develop this important idea a bit further in order to appreciate its relevance to the Central American crisis.

The Holy Office of Every Christian

The so-called universal priesthood of believers was a basic premise of the Reformation. It opened up the churches to greater participation by the laity at every level of ecclesial life, except the altar and the pulpit. For centuries after the Reformation, ecclesial offices in many of the dominant churches continued to be restricted to a privileged few. From time to time, however, grass-roots movements appeared to challenge this monopoly. Many of them developed into closed sects, with little concern for the problems of the larger society. But a few moved on to open up wider spaces where ordinary Christians could begin to develop their gifts more fully as children of God. Despite the repression that was often inflicted upon them, most of them made important contributions to our common heritage that mainline Protestantism gradually absorbed.

There are striking parallels between those earlier grass-roots movements and the CEBs in Central America today. In each case, peoples on "the underside of history" discovered experientially through their study of the Bible the implications of the threefold office of our Lord. The earthly ministry of Jesus Christ spoke in new and exciting ways to those who fed on the crumbs of the Reformation. Jesus taught that, by the grace of God, Christians are not only priests; they are called to be prophets and kings as well (1 Pet. 2:9-10). But how can oppressed peoples today appropriate the prophetic, kingly, and priestly ministries in ways that speak directly to their situation? For them, prophetic witness becomes complete when the Word of God is incarnated (John 1:14) in concrete historical situations. Kingly, suffering service, not absolute monarchy, is the model for pastoral ministry (Mark 10:42-45). Because of our Lord's work of redemption, priestly sacrifices have no meaning unless the priests are willing to validate them with their lives (Heb. 7:26-27).

The functions of the biblical idea of office—prophetic incarnation, pastoral service, and priestly sacrifice—are the privilege of every Christian. This was the Reformation message to which common people responded eagerly. For simple peasants and artisans in the sixteenth century, this truth became a freeing and empowering discovery. Emboldened by the same conviction, lowly Central American campesinos are also discovering and appropriating the space—the space that is rightfully theirs as children of God—in which to fully exercise the gifts the Holy Spirit has given them.

Speaking as prophets, long-muted Indians have accepted the risk of announcing the whole counsel of God in situations of rank injustice. As servant-kings, the lowliest peasants have accepted from God the right to participate actively in the re-creation of their world. Acceptance of the prophetic, priestly, and kingly office by the poor in Central America leads inevitably to a rupture in the traditional pattern of elite control and mass submission. Within the grass-roots Christian communities of the poor, the doctrine of the holy office of every Christian stimulates an explosion of spiritual gifts and services. In Central America today it has made possible the creation of numerous ministries that are dedicated to the service of the oppressed. This proliferation of creative opportunities for ministry is what is known as voluntarism.

The Freedom to Choose

Voluntarism is usually defined as exercising the right to support the religious and civic institutions of one's own choice. It is an outgrowth of the biblical idea of free choice and personal responsibility working itself out in the everyday relationships of human beings. After centuries of Constantinian Christianity,[22] the grass-roots Reformation of the sixteenth century opened the way for common, ordinary people to make religious and political choices without pressure from priest or magistrate. In our day the proliferation of voluntary societies has become one of the characteristics of religious and political pluralism. However, we often forget the historical source of this freedom. Thanks to those dissident communities in Europe (some of which became the churches in which we worship today), we can now choose the particular church and the specific groups with which we wish to associate.[23] We need to be reminded, however, that this is a right that was never granted to the poor in Central America. This is what makes the contemporary movements of the base communities so significant. In the CEBs people are creating small spaces where they are free to make fundamental choices, usually for the first time in their lives—indeed, for the first time in generations.

At the same time, we must understand that the biblical idea of free choice is intended for the common good. Voluntarism became a force for good when common people *together* began to create enough room to make fundamental decisions that affected their communal lives and ultimately the welfare of entire nations. Voluntary decisions can, however, be either life-giving or death-dealing, depending on the values that govern such choices. We must not forget that the Salvadoran and Guatemalan death squads are also voluntary societies. Nor must we confuse the biblical right of free choice with the rugged individualism of certain mainstreams in North American Christianity. The privilege of making choices and decisions requires a fundamental attitude of trust among all participating parties. It demands vulnerability and the willingness to take risks. That is why the church of the poor is playing such an important role in the development of democratic institutions in Central America. Impoverished Central American Christians are acting in concert to assert their right to life, land, labor, and community within small voluntarist communities. They are exercising the same privilege as the grass-roots churches in the Reformation. That they should be doing this in Central America, where it had never been done before, should be hailed by Christians everywhere.

Open-Ended Reformations

The Reformers recognized that no human institution is static, that there is no such thing as a once-and-for-all reformation of the church. The church is always in need of new reformations. So important is this reformational insight that it has been called the "Protestant principle."[24] Ongoing reformation requires that churches encourage a "spirit of prophetic criticism, of creative protest."[25] The genius of the Christian movement has been its capacity to incarnate itself into the cultures and societies of the peoples that it wins to its cause. This has been both a bane and a blessing. For over the centuries Protestant churches have often fallen prey to social conformity and self-centeredness. But in their contact with the world, and through openness to the promptings of the Holy Spirit, they have also found the inspiration for new societal reformations. Reformations breathe outward and inward. Protestants, by their very name, are called upon to speak out against every claim to absolutism, whether religious or social or political. But their protest must be creative, in response to the demands of each new historical challenge. The creative protest of the CEBs is a challenge to our un-Protestant societal conformity. Ongoing reformation requires also that a Protestant critique be turned inward upon Protestantism itself, just as the CEBs are a response to self-criticism within Roman Catholicism. We must become self-critical, because "no religious pattern or form can be exempt from criticism in the light of fresh apprehensions of truth."[26]

Thus the Reformation left us a legacy of social involvement, even though all too often it was not expressed in concern for the plight of the poor and disenfranchised. In the continuing social upheavals that this lack of concern generated, grass-roots dissident churches exerted quiet pressure or expressed themselves in more radical ways.[27] They asked, even demanded, that they be allowed "a piece of the action." These movements are part of the heritage of our North American churches, many of which now carry on work in Central America as well. They are also part of the heritage of many Protestant churches in Central America.

REFORMATIONAL CHALLENGES TO NORTH AMERICAN CHURCHES

These two visions of the church—the "top-down" institutional church and the "bottom-up" dissident groups—exemplify two radically dif-

ferent perceptions of the Christian faith and, consequently, two opposing understandings of the way people participate in the political
processes of nations. This same polarity of theological and political
perceptions is at the root of much of the conflict in Central America
today. It is a polarization that affects not only public institutions but
also the Catholic and Protestant churches in Central and North America. We need to recognize this fact, seek to understand it, and then confront it with the kingdom vision found in Scripture.

"If One Member Suffers,
Every Member Suffers with It"

Perhaps the best place to start is with our own reformational heritage.
The "holy office of every Christian" is based upon the Pauline doctrine of the body of Christ. For centuries Paul's teachings have been
used by some to defend a "top-down" ideology. This interpretation
must be challenged and corrected by the "bottom-up" metaphors that
Paul himself uses to describe the participation of every member in the
body. Can we put ourselves for a moment in the place of oppressed
Christians who hear the words of the apostle for the first time? "Those
parts of the body that seem to be weaker are indispensable, and the
parts that we think are less honorable we treat with special honor. . . .
If one part suffers, every part suffers with it; if one part is honored,
every part rejoices with it" (1 Cor. 12:22-23, 26-27).[28]

Can we now participate in a dialogue with our Nicaraguan Baptist sisters and brothers, and with the church of the poor throughout
Central America, keeping in mind the apostle's exhortation? What do
Paul's words say to us who may unconsciously have fallen into the trap
of ignoring, patronizing, demeaning, and discriminating against the
peasants of Central America? The apostolic words call us today to a
greater degree of acceptance of powerless people, of those who are
weaker and darker-skinned than many of us. The Bible enjoins us to
identify with their sufferings and to rejoice with them when they are
blessed with true peace and begin to enjoy fuller freedom of religious
and political expression. For, as Paul reminds us, "You are the body of
Christ, and each one of you is a part of it" (1 Cor. 12:27).

Making Choices and
Allowing Others to Choose

One form of voluntarism in Central America is the choice that Christians are making in identifying with the struggles of the poor. Is this a

viable option for North American Christians as well? Such participation in the church of the poor requires a voluntary choice for kingdom values. The poor themselves must make that choice. For they too are often seduced by the materialist values of our affluent society. This difficult choice can liberate all of us from a narrowly focused and self-centered Christianity. It will force us to deal with the agonizing problems and demonic structures of our world. This new, upside-down—actually right-side-up—approach to Christian commitment forces us to ask searching political questions. Do the impoverished peoples of Central America, the overwhelming majority of the population, have as much right to shape their future as we have to shape ours? When the parishioners of Zacamil engage in pastoral work at the grass-roots level in El Salvador, and when the assembly of Nicaraguan Baptists engages in dialogue with its president, are those not valid expressions of democratic participation? And if so, how can we accept a foreign policy based on LIC, which repudiates and undercuts such healthy practices?

A major stumbling block in accepting the popular movements in Central America is our suspicion that they may be naive tools of international communism. This makes us fearful of initiatives that come "from below." These fears cause us to negate the most cherished tenets of our democratic ideals as well as the fundamental premises of the Reformation and the biblical faith upon which they rest. The erroneous perception that the new self-awareness of the poor has been insinuated upon them by ill-intentioned infiltrators reflects a contemptuous and condescending attitude. It suggests that "we know best what is good for them," that these poor people are incapable of thinking for themselves, that they are dependent upon either malevolent Marxist agitators or altruistic capitalist benefactors to address their basic problems—as if these were the only alternatives available. In fact, it is commitment to the kingdom of God in a crisis situation—not some international conspiracy—that drives the poor in Central America.

Once we have dealt with these basic issues, we must then decide what to do as North American Christians to support the poor in their struggles. Can we, as committed Christians, citizens of a nation that prides itself on its democratic ideals, take the risk of putting this reformational vision into practice? More concretely, can we risk accepting the profound social and ecclesial transformations that the popular movements in Central America are demanding? If so, then we will have taken a long step toward helping them resolve their crisis.

Conversion from the Poor to the Poor

The church in North America also needs daily conversion. Central America could be a stimulus toward such renewal if we were to allow the church there to speak to us. This renewal could mean a changed outlook. We tend to think of Catholics in Central America as the objects of our missionary witness. But this is only partially true, because many grass-roots Catholics are being converted in the CEBs. Former nominal Catholics in Central America testify to a "profound transformation" in their lives as a result of their study and practice of Scripture. The same is happening to some nominal Protestants. They are being evangelized by the poor. As they identify with the reality of the poor, they experience a Christian conversion in which God's Word and the agonizing crises of Central American life are brought together.[29]

We too must be converted to the the world of the poor. We need to step down from our rich banquet tables and learn from Christians who are feeding on the Word as they huddle around a fire on a dirt floor in Central America. Too often when we proclaim the message to them, we ask them to turn their backs abruptly upon the world. In the CEBs, however, conversion is not a break with the world in which they live. It is rather a sanctified re-entry into it. This is an ongoing process of maturation, a continuous renewal, in which the followers of Jesus Christ are always being called to turn their backs upon the death-dealing values of a materialist and idolatrous world. At the same time, true Christian conversion also returns us to the world with a message of hope and service. This way of undergoing Christian conversion can become a profound experience in which Central and North American Christians can participate together. Such cooperation might have more significance for ongoing societal transformation and the furthering of God's kingdom in both of our cultures than any other conceivable action.

7. WHEN JUBILEE AND KINGDOM EMBRACE

Nothing matters but the kingdom of God, but because of the kingdom, everything matters.

THE TWO ARE ONE

The land shall have a jubilee! This divine imperative is the abiding will of God for all his people living in their lands of promise. It is a command, but even more, it is a benediction. "You shall . . . proclaim liberty throughout the land to all its inhabitants; it shall be a jubilee for you" (Lev. 25:10).

The Liberty Bell in Philadelphia is inscribed with these words. They express the spirit of independence marking the liberation of thirteen struggling colonies from British rule. Originally this message of emancipation came to twelve harried tribes of ex-slaves, only recently delivered from the house of bondage in Egypt. In recent years this call to jubilee has taken on renewed urgency for oppressed bands of Christians scattered across the face of Central America. Although often silenced—not only in ancient Israel but among modern Christians as well—the trumpet of jubilee *(jobel)* continues to sound forth its powerful message of down-to-earth renewal, communal righteousness, and peace, instilling among downtrodden peoples the hope of a new way of life.

Echoes of the jubilee proclamation are meant to resonate through every part of life. In the crisis situation of Central America, these reverberations strike a responsive chord in the call for a more equitable distribution and use of land, for meaningful and gainful employment, for a renewal of communal living, for the better development of creational resources, for relief from alien interventions, for the cessation of hostilities, for a more aggressive pursuit of peace, and for greater participation in the democratic decision-making processes of society at large. This listing summarizes the basic themes running through the preceding chapters. With it we have come full circle. It is time now to look ahead. Is there hope for Central America? for a more promising future? Are there prospects for a measure of all-embracing shalom? for a new day dawning? What would it take to make such dreams come true? And what can we as North American Christian communities do about it?

In addressing these crucial questions, we open this concluding chapter by reflecting on the fundamental and comprehensive meaning of the biblical call to jubilee. It embraces such urgently important aspirations as freedom, peoplehood, justice, servanthood, and peace. The promises of jubilee were to be a lasting legacy in Israel.[1] Its norms hold today as well. But how? Originally they were couched in cultural forms suited to the agrarian and pastoral life of Israel. As such they still tug insistently at the heartstrings of the millions of campesinos and urban poor who inhabit the five small countries of Central America. At the same time, however, they reach out to all of us. For while the *forms* of our jubilee obedience must change with changing times, as biblical *norms* they still lay their abiding claim upon us.

Israel, it seems, never dared to take the risk of keeping jubilee. Yet the summons to jubilee does not get lost in the flow of biblical history. When at last the time had fully come, Jesus "went about all Galilee . . . preaching the gospel of the kingdom" (Matt. 4:23). And what stands out in his kingdom proclamation? Early in his ministry, there in the despised northern province of Galilee, Jesus faced his hometown people gathered in the synagogue at Nazareth. Choosing the text for his sabbath sermon, Jesus opened the book of Isaiah, turned to its jubilee prophecy, and found the place (61:1-3) where the following is written:

> The Spirit of the Lord is upon me, because he has anointed me to preach good news to the poor. He has sent me to proclaim release to the captives and recovering of sight to the blind, to set at liberty those who are oppressed, to proclaim the acceptable year of the Lord. (Luke 4:18-19)

In a word, Jesus preached a jubilee sermon. It was at the same time a kingdom sermon. The two converge. In updating the Messianic proclamation of jubilee, Jesus also fulfilled it—that is, he "filled it to the full." He thereby confirmed it as a perennial norm for kingdom living, lending it a permanent reformational, revolutionary power.

"ALREADY" / "NOT YET"

A "Christendom" model of society, forcibly imposed by bearers of the sword and the crucifix, has long dominated the countries of Central America. The biblical idea of the kingdom was squeezed into the mold of a medieval model of society, a system that continued throughout the eras of British imperialism and U.S. domination. Now fresh winds of reformational change are blowing across the isthmus. There is pressure for a reconstruction of the old order. Christians in many quarters envision reshaping their culture to fit more closely the norms for kingdom living. Eagerly they seize upon Jesus' jubilee proclamation: "The time is fulfilled: the kingdom of God is at hand; repent, and believe in the gospel" (Mark 1:15).

"At hand"—what does that mean? That the kingdom has come near, is waiting just around the corner, about to arrive? Or that it has already arrived and is present among us here and now? The conviction is growing among grass-roots believers that it is wrong to pose this as an either/or option. The gospel points simultaneously in both directions. Christians are therefore called to work for renewal within the biblical tension of the "already so" and the "not yet fully so," between kingdom pressure as a present reality and the eschatological pull toward its future consummation. For the church of the past, the beatific vision was an almost exclusively future hope. Now the church of the poor, while not losing sight of the ultimate victory, is at the same time, and with renewed vigor, staking its claims on its experience of the presence of the King among its members today. The final ushering in of God's new order still hovers on the horizon. But its irreversible beginnings are now already theirs to have and to hold both now and forever. In the midst of death they cling to the standing offer of life. This is both a gift to be received and a mandate to be worked out.

In the base communities Christians are wrestling with this mystery of Christ's royal presence—"already" and at the same time "not yet." How is this to be understood? Surely this cannot mean that the kingdom is partly present and partly future. For where the King is, there is his kingdom, and Christ is never so divided. Kingdom reality is therefore never a half-and-half equation. Its presence is always holistic, just as the King is always wholly present. Someday Christ will be "all in all." These simple believers cling firmly to this hope. But they also know the comfort of sharing his undivided presence today. Neither the King nor his kingdom can be partly present and partly future. How then are these believers, and we with them, to understand Jesus' word that the kingdom is "at hand"? Reading the Bible in the light of their situation, and their situation in the light of the Bible, this is what they sense: the struggle for life in Central America is caught up in the biblical tension between the kingdom long *veiled* and *hidden* but now at last becoming *manifest* and *visible*. For this reason only those with "ears to hear" really catch its message, and only those with "eyes to see" really perceive its wonder.

For generations the presence of the King and the reality of his kingdom lay hidden, obscured, veiled beneath thick layers of ecclesiastical, social, political, and economic neglect and malpractice. Now the veil is being swept aside. The already and ever-present kingdom, long concealed, is breaking through in many circles and challenging the old order of rival kingdoms. At a very profound level, this is at the very center of the crisis of Central America. Such spiritual eruptions always create decisive moments in history.

Therefore, only a superficial analysis of the crisis sweeping these five nations will locate the rock-bottom cause of the crisis in a confrontation between East and West, between capitalism and communism, or between the Contras and the Sandinistas. These are at most the tip of an iceberg. A more fundamental struggle is taking place, that between emerging signs of the coming kingdom, long obstructed, and the deeply entrenched oppressive rule of the idols of death. Their legions, threatened by the mysterious power of the kingdom, rise up in self-defense, clinging desperately to their kingdoms of privilege and power.

From beginning to end and from various viewpoints, we have been addressing the crisis situation in Central America. That reality called "crisis" involves a combination of old habits and new departures that, as historically formative influences, are now converging to bring this course of events to a head. Embedded in this unfolding drama are a number of key indicators of the new directions in which Central American societies appear to be moving. Ambiguities abound. Yet there are also clear signs of hope. In evaluating these factors, often as mixed blessings, our criterion is the biblical message of the kingdom of jubilee. Accordingly, the basic question we face is this: These factors, these signs of hope, these key indicators to which we now turn—what and how are they contributing to a potentially better future for the peoples of Central America?

A NEW WAY OF READING THE BIBLE

"When you pass through the waters . . ."

Esperanza had been a Delegate of the Word in a northeastern province of her own country, El Salvador. But when members of the CCCS team talked with her in February 1987 in the Mesa Grande refugee camp (near San Marcos) in western Honduras, she had already been in exile there for six years.

As a Delegate of the Word, first in El Salvador and now in the refugee camp, she was active in organizing and leading inductive Bible study groups. The delegates call it "celebrating the Word." In the Mesa Grande camp, Esperanza is one of over eighty Delegates of the Word who in turn train and mobilize a larger group of lay leaders to meet the spiritual needs of the more than 11,000 resident refugees.

As we sat in her unadorned, dirt-floor "living room" in the refugee camp, Esperanza told her story. She came to Honduras in the aftermath of the Lempa River massacre of March 1981. In the eyes of Salvadoran authorities, Esperanza and other members of the grass-roots communities were "subversives." Bloody persecutions broke out. So Esperanza and her company were forced to flee their homeland. The Salvadoran army was pursuing them from behind, driving them to the river. From above, helicopters were strafing them. Before them lay the Lempa River, and it was quite possible that hostile Honduran soldiers were waiting for them on the other side.

As Esperanza and her family fled from the pursuing army toward the equally threatening river, her thoughts turned to the Exodus of the Israelites from Egypt. Years of group Bible study had saturated her mind with biblical episodes, biblical truths, and biblical language. Her immediate circumstances could hardly have been more similar to those of the biblical narrative.

"Although we were filled with terror," she told us, "we knew that God was with us, just like when the Israelites crossed the Red Sea." Her face radiated a deep, joyful faith. Through her testimony the presence of God also became real for us. She continued her story.

As she and her family neared the river, a terrible act of vengeance compounded their problems. People upstream (almost certainly military personnel) opened the sluices of the dam and released a raging torrent of water. "Lord, what's going on here?" she groaned. "When Israel went through the river, you stopped the waters. But now, just the opposite. Somebody has opened the dam, and this current will kill us!"

Not strong swimmers themselves, Esperanza and her husband

tried desperately to keep their children together. They grabbed a loose slab of wood, put their infant son on it, and somehow managed to push him to the other side. ("That's him over there," she told us, pointing to a young boy seated nearby.)

Although many drowned or were killed by the army, Esperanza's whole family made it across the river. But in the turbulent passage, most of their clothes were torn from their bodies. "We walked several days, practically naked, through the jungles," she told us. "But we remembered Adam and Eve, how they weren't ashamed when they were walking with God. So that whole thing of being ashamed of our bodies, we just forgot all about it. We had such tremendous joy in our hearts because God had saved our lives. And we felt hope."

As Esperanza shared this experience with us almost six years after it had happened, we could sense the sinewy faith that sustained her family. "God is with us, we're sure of that." That faith has kept them busily at work with the other Delegates of the Word and the catechists, "celebrating the Word" that for them is life itself.

> Fear not, for I have redeemed you;
> I have called you by name; you are mine.
> When you pass through the waters,
> I will be with you;
> and when you pass through the rivers,
> they will not sweep over you.
> When you walk through the fire,
> you will not be burned;
> the flames will not set you ablaze.
> For I am the Lord, your God,
> the Holy One of Israel, your Savior.
>
> Isaiah 43:1-3

Esperanza did not mention this text hidden away in the book of Isaiah. Perhaps she didn't even know about it. Generally, her mind grabbed onto the *events* of Scripture, the great divine acts of salvation, rather than the word promises that tend to excite and strengthen the minds of more sophisticated believers. Yet the prophet's word was literally appropriate to her own experience when she "passed through the waters."

If Esperanza were to reflect on Isaiah 43:2, how would she understand its meaning? By contrast, when we meditate on the same text, how do we read its promise? Does it ever even occur to us that someday *we* might have to cross a river other than the symbolic "river Jordan"? Or has any of us ever gone "through the fire"—the fire of bullets, grenades, and strafing helicopters? Crossing rivers and walking through fire seem utterly remote to our world of experience. We have other problems to bring to God: marital tensions, bankruptcy, cancer.

Could anyone possibly expect Esperanza to understand these words the same way we would, or expect us to understand these words the same way she would?

And what about the prophet Isaiah himself, and the people of Israel? What did this "water and fire" promise mean to them? Who is closer to the original meaning—Esperanza or us, or each of us in our own way? Can Esperanza and her Delegates of the Word also help *us* to interpret Scripture more faithfully?

The Hermeneutic Bridge

Esperanza's story reveals several important things about the use of the Bible in Central America today. Bible reading and study is on the move. This remarkable phenomenon is reflected in the record sales of Bibles and New Testaments throughout the region.

Many Central Americans are finding the message of the Bible intensely relevant to their own situation. To them it is often as if they themselves were living the events of the biblical narrative all over again. Looking into the pages of Scripture is very much like looking into a mirror.

In hermeneutical terms, the "fusion of horizons"—that of ours today with that of Bible readers two thousand years ago and half a world away—which is so difficult for sophisticated North Americans is often a very natural process for readers like Esperanza. Their "hermeneutical camera" seems to have a kind of built-in automatic lens-focus. This is apparently an exegetical privilege of those who read the Bible "from the underside of history."

Reflecting on the interpretation of Scripture in the thousands of base communities, Carlos Mesters offers the following graphic comment:

> Biblical exegetes, using their heads and their studies, can come fairly close to Abraham; but their feet are a long way from Abraham. The common people are very close to Abraham with their feet. They are living the same sort of situation. Their life-process is of the same nature and they can identify with him. When they read his history in the Bible, it becomes a mirror for them. They look in that mirror, see their own faces, and say: "We are Abraham!" In a real sense they are reading their own history, and this becomes a source of much inspiration and encouragement. One time a farm worker said to me: "Now I get

it. We are Abraham, and if he got there then we will too!" From the history of Abraham he and his people are drawing the motives for their courage today.[2]

In a vast network of Bible study cells all across Central America, such feet-on-the-ground *realism* is what best characterizes their interpretation of Scripture. It is easy to single out for criticism the relatively few statements about Jesus as a revolutionary or socialism as the kingdom of God. Even these expressions must be interpreted in context, with an open mind and a healthy dose of Christian charity and empathy, as well as subjected to the most rigorous exegetical analysis. But to accentuate these few quotations gives a distorted impression of the overall process of grass-roots biblical reflection going on there. Actually, for good or ill, much of it is very conservative, often literalist, sometimes even fundamentalist.

However, in the wide variety of viewpoints and expressions that arise from such an extended process of inductive group reflection, the one consistent common denominator is a strong sense of historical realism. Scripture reading in the base communities moves very naturally back and forth between the biblical world and the people's own. It does not enunciate any definitive or uniform doctrine of Scripture, nor is it obsessed with technical questions of historical criticism. Yet it regularly treats the biblical narratives as real history. The saving acts of liberation history in Scripture are "germinal events" or "archetypes." As such they are to be taken with utmost seriousness.

The Real Jesus in a Real World

For many Central American readers of the Bible, Jesus is as real as their own brother, and Palestine as vivid and concrete as their own countryside. This comes through dramatically in the Bible studies of the Solentiname community of Nicaragua, founded and led by poet-priest Ernesto Cardenal.[3] Solentiname's peasants, who live on a group of small islands in the southern extreme of Lake Nicaragua, respond instinctively to all the Galilean lake scenes of the Gospels. When they compare the miraculous catch with the fish they themselves pull out of their own lake every day ("haddock and shad and *mojarras*"), one can almost smell the fish. They happened to be studying Jesus' calming the sea just three days after three of them—Ivan, Bosco, and Chalia—had capsized in the middle of Lake Nicaragua and had spent two hours waiting to be rescued. The biblical account became so real that Chalia wept during the study.

Their comments on the calling of Jesus' first disciples, coming shortly after the miraculous catch, are linked to their own island life, including a missionary outreach to neighboring islands and to San Carlos, the nearest mainland port:

NATALIA: "Then they abandoned their belongings. Yes, they left the boats right there and the nets."

RODOLFO: "Probably a rotten boat like the one that belongs to the Cooperative."

NATALIA: "They were poor, but they had their few things. The way poor people do. And they left their things right there and followed Jesus."

DONA ANGELA: "They let themselves be caught by him." Another of the boys said: "That was the miraculous catch, and not the haddock and shad and *mojarras* and all the other different fish they caught with the net. And they caught us and that's why we're gathered here. . . ."

MARCELINO: "Because they left their belongings right there, the word of God came to these islands. Perhaps later we can carry the word to the other side of the lake too. To Papaturro, or maybe San Carlos, San Miguelito."[4]

Inevitably, the Solentiname community senses keenly the dramatic correlations between the political circumstances of Jesus' time and their own. They have something in common with Jesus of Nazareth, with which we, as comfortable, affluent Christians, can scarcely empathize: the experience of living in a vortex of political violence and repression. This "hermeneutic bridge" binds them existentially to many facets of the biblical world into which their historical experience gives them privileged insight. Naturally the Herods spoke to them of the Somoza dynasty and the Roman soldiers of Somoza's dreaded National Guard. One participant, not inappropriately, compares Pilate to the "gringo ambassador" in Managua and impishly makes him speak broken Spanish: "Me not know nothin. . . . Me innocent." In discussing Herod's slaughter of the innocents, they could not possibly miss the fact that Somoza was committing similar crimes against Nicaraguan children.[5]

The Cross: Violent Death in a Violent Society

When Central Americans today read the Passion narratives, they find themselves on familiar terrain. They too live in a society riddled by violence and injustice, run by corrupt oligarchies and ruthless armies under the shadow of an imperial world power.

Hundreds of their own brothers and sisters, including their

beloved archbishop, Oscar Romero, have been slain by methods fright-fully similar to the sufferings and death of Jesus. Thus they read the Gospel accounts the way they themselves have experienced comparable events. They look for the powers and agents at work and how each conspires to destroy "the Just One." They easily understand the man with the water jug (Mark 14:13) and Judas's kiss of betrayal (Mark 14:44) as similar to the secret passwords and code signs that have also been part of their own experience. When the Gospel text decries the shedding of innocent blood (Matt. 27:4) and depicts the awkward dilemma of national leaders who are stuck with some "blood money" (Matt. 27:5-6), this is all chillingly familiar to them. Their firsthand experience of religiopolitical murders gives them an immediate insight into the dynamics of how Jesus died to redeem us. The Gospels tell them that Jesus died for their sins. Their own experience tells them a great deal about how that could have happened. The Gospel narratives also let us in on the response of the chief priests and elders to the embarrassing problem of that blood money: "What is that to us? That's your responsibility" (Matt. 27:4). Such words these Christians have also heard before, in one way or another, from their own "Christian" national leaders. They recognize from their own sufferings this sin of indifference and silence over the shedding of innocent blood. In many respects these grass-roots Christians in Central America are certainly much closer to the source than we are, and we should be humble enough to listen to their witness.

Underlying all these interpretations of the gospel is the completely real and living Jesus of Nazareth, Son of God, but also wholly Son of Man. These believers are his disciples. So when they speak about Christ's violent death, they are also talking about the risk of their own death. Some of them have heard Bonhoeffer's moving words from Nazi Germany: "When Christ calls us, He bids us come and die."

Human Beings as Imagers of God

Permeating the life of the base communities is a profound respect for all human beings as individuals who bear God's likeness and receive his gifts. They simply assume that each person brings undiscovered talents to the community, that God's Word speaks to everyone, and that all will contribute to the community's faithful hearing of its message. Educational disadvantage, even illiteracy, is a major obstacle to such personal development. But the experience of inductive Bible study and dynamic group discussion often triggers astounding learning processes among these formally uneducated people. They usually achieve great improvement in reading skills, becoming more or less functionally literate. They learn the play of ideas and the give-and-take of argument. They develop leadership abilities and learn to solve interpersonal problems. All of these learning processes reveal to them the greatest truth about themselves: they are God's images.

Among the peasants of Solentiname, the communal process of discovering their own true worth was dramatic. "Before the poet came with the Word," they often said, "we really lived more like animals than human beings." But when they began meeting with Ernesto Cardenal in "the little huts of the Family of God" to study *Good News for Modern Man,* amazing things began to happen. In very concrete, creative ways they were led to discover God's image in themselves. Then they began asking questions. Can only people from Grenada and Managua be poets? Does God distribute the gift of song and verse only among the well-born? They began holding poetry workshops. Thus a school of peasant poetry arose, which still sings its own unique songs. People who had never seen a painting before began to produce paintings themselves. They built a studio, formed a common-purse cooperative, and became a world-famous school of primitive painting.

The Kingdom of God and the Struggle for Justice

Some base communities opt to withdraw from society rather than struggle to change it. But the majority turn toward the world around them as the place to demonstrate the love they have learned from Christ through the Word. They discover that the biblical vision of the kingdom of God compels them to take responsible action against the evils of their society. In these actions they usually build on two basic truths of the New Testament. First, God's kingdom is a kingdom of justice (Matt. 6:33), reconciliation (2 Cor. 5:18-20), equality (2 Cor. 8:13-15), and abundance (Rev. 22:1-5). The kingdom brings the blessings of shalom, jubilee, and life abundant. Second, in Christ the kingdom has already come. Christ has risen and broken the powers of evil. "He must reign until he has put all his enemies under his feet" (1 Cor. 15:25). This is the reason Jesus taught us to pray for the kingdom to come in this world and God's will to be done on this earth. The most revolutionary conviction of these Christians can be simply stated: things *can* change. Through faith they have broken the chains of fatalism and resignation.

Marcelino, never having lived in a city, reflects on what a city would be like. He draws language from Solentiname island life. He envisions the city as light. Perhaps someday, he dreams, "we may even get to be a city, too, because then we won't be in scattered huts the way we are now, and we'll have electric light, and when somebody goes by in a boat he'll see those lights of our union. But the thing that will shine most, and that's what Christ is talking about, is love."[6]

Central Americans find such world-transforming visions throughout the Bible. In the Exodus account, which they take with great historical realism, they see a compelling paradigm of faith's march toward victory. The jubilee "manifesto" of Jesus (Luke 4:18-20) and the communal life-style of the early church[7] also inspire this very strong commitment to societal change. Its deepest roots lie in the affirmation of a good creation, to be consummated by what is still better, the "new heavens and new earth." Believing in Christ means believing in the God who "makes all things new" (Rev. 21:5)—beginning now.

Shortly before his death, Oscar Romero said, with admirable honesty and humility, "The poor have taught me to read the Bible." Central America's poor also have much to teach North American Christians about what the Spirit is saying to the church today.

THE ROLE OF EVANGELICAL CHURCHES

To look at the Protestant churches[8] in Central America, one would hardly guess that the region is in crisis. They are growing dramatically,[9] much to the alarm of the Catholic hierarchy. Innumerable small congregations—and a handful of very large ones—can be found everywhere. Some church leaders and missionaries we talked with saw no crisis other than that caused by the prevalent sins of drunkenness and sloth. Others talked in glowing terms about successful evangelism programs and growing congregations, and of unprecedented government support of the evangelical churches. They thanked God for religious freedom, despite the ever-present fear of a communist takeover.

On a memorable Sunday in Guatemala the CCCS team visited a Pentecostal church where 14,000 people gather regularly for worship. The same day, in a large charismatic church, we listened to a North American family of gospel singers thank God for the blessing of designer clothing. Not all the Protestant churches we visited were consumed by success, however. A few weeks later we worshiped with both struggling peasant congregations and a large middle-class church. They had one thing in common: their leaders have suffered persecution, exile, and death because of their prophetic preaching and active involvement in works of mercy and justice.

These diametrically opposed conceptions of what it means to be an evangelical church have their roots in the earliest history of Protestantism in Central America. The first Protestants to settle in the region arrived around the beginning of the nineteenth century. They came not as missionaries but as representatives of British colonial interests—as coffee planters, railroad builders, and traders. By right of treaty, they built Anglican chapels, despite rigid laws that prohibited the practice of any religion except official Roman Catholicism.[10] A few years later, courageous Bible distributors worked their way through the isthmus, taking advantage of new opportunities that governments, controlled by Liberal Party politics, afforded them.

The efforts of two early missionaries to Guatemala dramatize the two main approaches to missionary work that were to characterize Central American Protestantism for years to come.

The first approach attempted to change social structures by converting political and intellectual leaders. In 1882 General Justo Rufino Barrios, the president of Guatemala and a Liberal reformer, persuaded the Northern Presbyterian Church in New York to appoint Reverend John Hill as their pioneer missionary to Central America. Hill's strategy was to socialize with the Liberal elite in order to win the nation to Jesus Christ through them. He founded the "American College," pastored an English-language congregation, and also founded the first Spanish-speaking Protestant church in Central America. For a time Hill's approach seemed to be working. As a dramatic sign of his support for the Protestants, Barrios donated land for a church building. The result is the Central Presbyterian Church in downtown Guatemala City, which stands surrounded on four sides by the national palace, the presidential residence, and the barracks of the presidential guard.

Hill's evangelistic strategy unraveled when his benefactor died in battle. Hill's successor, Edward Haymaker, had a different vision. With the support of the Presbyterian board, he founded rural churches and converted the "college" into a school for poor children. He translated portions of the Bible into an Indian dialect. Moreover, his vision was not limited to Guatemala or to the building of Protestant churches. Entering the debate over the infiltration of "Bolshevism" into Central America, he pointed out that the real problem was not an East-West conflict but a North-South conflict. When the United States intervened militarily in the internal affairs of Nicaragua in the late 1920s, Haymaker argued that this policy had "hopelessly failed to bring peace." Instead it was sowing the seeds of suspicion and hatred.[11] His published views were shared by two Scottish missionaries, Harry and Susan Strachan, who had recently settled in Costa Rica and launched mass evangelistic programs throughout Latin America. They became the founders of a variety of church, educational, and social ministries that would become known as the Latin America Mission. Haymaker and the Strachans openly addressed the political problems of Latin America, especially Nicaragua. They were fundamentalists. Yet in the heyday of fundamentalism, they and other missionary and national colleagues sent a cablegram to President Coolidge downplaying the danger of communism in Central America. Susan Strachan later lamented "the nervous fear" that the United States had of "the subtle growth of Communism," and suggested that, instead of intervention, "a better way might be found" to combat this menace.[12]

Such political awareness among missionaries and national pastors represented a minority opinion and was short-lived. In general, the identity of the evangelical churches in Central America has been molded not by social and political concerns but by their inordinate fear of three great "diabolical isms": Catholicism, liberalism, and communism. The latter two enemies are often so confused in the minds of evangelicals that anyone who speaks of the kingdom message of justice and jubilee may quickly be labeled both a liberal and a communist. The attitude of evangelicals toward Catholicism is often ambiguous, at times even contradictory. They are deeply suspicious of what the hierarchy "may be up to." They consign the Church of Rome to the kingdom of Satan. Yet, at the same time, many evangelicals approve when Rome censures a liberation theologian or the local hierarchy clamps down on the CEBs. They take this as one more evidence that the church of the poor is indeed the work of the devil.

However, one should avoid generalizing about Protestantism in Central America. Early missionaries from both the historical churches and the independent "faith missions" were motivated by a deep compassion for the social and economic needs of the people. They founded hospitals, clinics, and orphanages, and they were generous with their material resources. Such "works of mercy" were primarily used as means to attract people to the gospel and to evangelical churches. But politics was generally proscribed.

Today, however, Protestantism in Central America is much more complex. It is made up of at least four overlapping streams that represent competing responses to the Central American crisis.

Mainline evangelicalism. This stream of faith is characterized by what has been called "a world-affirming view."[13] It is aware of societal ills, although it is not always able to explain them and is sometimes hesitant to confront them. It is concerned about a "balanced" mission approach in which evangelism is foremost, but compassionate social involvement is a key component in its holistic evangelism strategy. This was especially so during the late sixties and early seventies, the era of the Alliance for Progress, a time of optimism in Latin America. The Central American crisis had not yet bubbled to the surface. During the same period a small group of young evangelical scholars founded the Latin American Theological Fraternity. This informal fellowship now provides a much-needed forum where evangelicals of various theological persuasions can meet around the Bible to discuss the critical issues that face the church. Its members are concerned to provide creative Protestant responses to the growing crisis. Three of the authors of this book are members of this fraternity.

Classical Pentecostalism. The first Pentecostals arrived in Central America in the mid-1930s, at a time when popular suspicion of Protestantism was ebbing rapidly. They brought a message which accented a "world-denying apocalyptic vision"[14] that promoted a radical divorce between the religious and the secular realms. For many Pentecostals even today, the church offers a place of spiritual refuge where they can escape, at least in their minds, from the evils of society.

The CCCS team met with many Christians who see no hope in the Central American crisis except the imminent return of Christ. Most pathetic are the materially destitute Christians who find their only solace in this belief. In La Lucha, a poor barrio outside an industrial town in Honduras, Pentecostal Christians told us of their problems when we talked with them in February 1987: "Before, we picked coffee. Now there is no more work. Now we sew bits of cloth to make mop rags. Then we walk the streets trying to sell one or two to buy food for the children. Often we can sell none, so we do not eat. What can we do? Only Christ is the way. He will give us the better life; we long for it, our eternal home."

We are too easily tempted to discount the Pentecostal message because of its escapist tendencies. But we may not forget that the hope of heaven is very real to evangelical Christians, that it is often the only thing that keeps people (even more radical Christians) alive in Central America. Even a radical liberationist such as Hugo Assmann has in a recent book urged his colleagues to be more sensitive to popular beliefs in the miraculous as well as to grass-roots Pentecostal spirituality. Until "progressive" Christians are able to offer genuine spiritual release along with their social analysis, he says, they need to humbly recognize that something may be missing in their pastoral action.[15] Liberationists have yet to take seriously the existence of real demonic forces at the personal as well as the institutional level. In lands where people take the spirit world for granted, any liberation that overlooks bondage to demonic spirits can be only partial at best.[16]

The Charismatic Renewal. Since the early 1970s the charismatic movement has had a strong influence among the middle class and the elite of Central America. Catholics and Protestants alike have found new life in its emphasis on the renewing work of the Holy Spirit. Introduced by priests and missionaries from North America, "the renewal" has become a source of hope and security for many in the midst of terrifying instability. Small fellowships of Christians have grown rapidly into the megachurches we visited in Guatemala. Large urban Pentecostal churches, which appeal to middle-class people, have begun to look and sound increasingly like charismatic churches. Even more staid traditional churches have become charismatic, and their membership has swelled dramatically. Some, like the Verbo Community (the "Church of the Word") in Guatemala City, have attempted to avoid being labeled Protestant in order to attract Catholics, while at the same time keeping a discreet distance from the Catholic Church.

General Efrain Rios-Montt, an ex-president of Guatemala and a lay leader in the Verbo Community, represents a new twist on the tensions between church and society among Central American evangelicals. His is a "world-changing" vision,[17] but the vantage point is top-down. On 5 January 1987 the CCCS team listened at length to the general as he expounded his faith and politics in a room of the Verbo Church.

Breaking with traditional Protestant views in Central America, Rios-Montt believes that Christians should be active in society in order to change it. He views the church as a Guatemalan-style military campaign. As a soldier the Christian must know how to follow orders. He marches, he salutes, he shoots. Order must be maintained. When there are uprisings, those caught need justice, not mercy. Execute them! That's what God wants, and what the people want. Such exercise of authority destroys communism and brings peace.[18] But Rios-Montt is not only a general; he is above all a Christian. Therefore, he believes that the answers to human need are not found in society, no matter how high a stake he has in preserving a particular social order. Only Jesus Christ is the answer. His program for the future is to pray and pray and pray. Our security lies not in the United States, not in Russia, not in Europe, but only in Christ Jesus.

Although the mix of earthly and spiritual kingdoms may differ, the two basic constituents of this duality are constant in most neo-Pentecostal churches in Central America. The political sphere, the economic sphere, the material sphere—each has its vertically structured place in the divine order of things. Society is to be ordered on Old Testament principles of inflexible law and implacable retribution. Body and soul, the earthly and the heavenly, the present and the hereafter, the kingdom of man and the kingdom of God—each is right in its own time and place. Variations on this theme are present in many charismatic communities and wherever this doctrine has been absorbed by other churches in Central America.

Thanks to the almost omnipresent TV evangelists, this radical dualism is now being rapidly superceded by a more deadening heresy. It comes with a powerful appeal to people, both rich and poor, whose materialistic values are threatened by the demands of the popular movements. These broadcasters declare that the children of light do have a role to fulfill in the world. It is to conquer the kingdom of darkness, which now has a name—Marxism—and if need be to use arms. In some extreme cases this gospel of anti-communism has become the ideology that legitimates the violence perpetrated against large segments of the population of Central America.[19]

The Church of the Poor. Ironically, this militant Christianity is lending added impetus precisely to the movement it is attempting to destroy: the growing church of the poor among conservative Protestants in Central America. There a deepening commitment to the renewal of society is being nurtured. Such social awareness appeared in Central America in the early 1970s among young Protestant intellectuals who were attracted to the ideas of liberation theology. They were viewed with suspicion, if not outright hostility, by a majority of the churches. For a while debates on this subject remained largely at the level of academic inquiry. However, with the worsening economic crisis and the escalation of systemic violence in the 1980s, a radical change of attitude took place among pockets of impoverished evangelicals. If the vaunted upward mobility of Protestantism ever worked for many of the poor in Latin America, it was no longer helping them. The new and practical message of hope that the CEBs are announcing has turned out to be more convincing than ivory-tower liberation theologies or the otherworldly, two-kingdom gospel that other churches preach. More recently the escalation of violence has pushed entire congregations, even from fundamentalist churches, into the church of the poor. In Guatemala alone there are reportedly some two hundred Protestant and ecumenical CEBs.[20]

This turn of events is something entirely new. It offers the only authentic alternative to traditional Protestant positions. But it is often badly misunderstood. Only by drawing close to those who are suffering can we begin to understand this emergent Protestant church of the poor. An evangelical pastor in Guatemala testified to the way in which "the Holy Spirit is moving his people down unforeseen but certain paths":

> What God is doing amidst his people really escapes our theological comprehension, . . . especially among the base of the Christian community. . . . This eagerness for liberty, this enthusiasm for building a new society, this revolution, is evangelizing the church. . . . Never before have we seen how evangelical Christians and Catholics can meet together in a village of the highlands to celebrate their faith, because there are no longer ministers or priests in this zone.[21]

Indeed, one overlooked dimension of the unusual growth of Protestantism in Guatemala is the rapid influx of Indians and other peasants into the dissident church. Protestant and Catholic pastoral training teams have their hands full coping with this new phenomenon. They are preparing Catholic Delegates of the Word, CEB leaders, and lay Protestant pastors throughout Central America. This is a situation, a lay pastor confesses, which "for those of us who have worked in the service of the Lord as Protestants . . . is a miracle . . . of God."[22]

HALLMARKS OF A NEW REFORMATION

"Protestantism has been here now for over a century," an evangelical missionary told the CCCS team in January 1987, "but reformation has not yet come to Central America." Now at last, however, strong reformational impulses are arising from the loosely knit but widespread network of Christian base communities. Haltingly so in most evangelical circles, despite what some describe as "the Protestantizing of Central America." Notably so—of all places—among Roman Catholics. Some Roman Catholics are more Protestant, more reformational than many evangelicals.

What a strangely familiar turn of events. Echoes from the past can be heard in Central America. "By faith alone," "by grace alone," "by Scripture alone," "through Christ alone"—these often-forgotten hallmarks of the sixteenth-century reformation are reverberating anew in the church of the poor. What does this recovery of the heartbeat of the gospel mean for grass-roots Christians in a revolutionary situation? One thing is clear: it means being not less evangelical or less biblical, but immensely more so. Let us try to walk a mile or so further in their sandals, tuning in to their reformational reflections.

Sola fide: "by faith alone." Throughout Central America in much of traditional Protestantism as well as Catholicism, faith came to expression primarily in a highly personalized holiness ethic that left structural sin and institutionalized injustice untouched. But now, through the contemporary renewal movements that have sprung up in these five small countries, faith has come alive as heartfelt trust in the Word of God, as personal and communal commitment to the lordship of Christ, and as concrete, outgoing obedience to the gospel of the kingdom and its jubilee projects. Salvation is indeed by faith alone. But faith never remains alone. The reality and relevance of this justified faith is itself justified in acts of justice. It issues in works of righteousness and compassion on behalf of the poor and needy, the outcasts and the powerless (Jer. 22:16; James 1:22-27, 2:1-26).

Such a justified faith, seeking justice, calls for a threefold commitment. First, there is *commitment to life*. The diabolical setting of death and destruction as it has long prevailed in Central America calls Christians to be radically and comprehensively pro-life. Second, there is *commitment to truth*. Central America today is caught in a whirlwind war of raging propaganda. In the midst of this informational disaster zone, a major casualty is truth. The Christian community is summoned to stand up as a witness to the truth. Finally, as always, there remains an abiding *commitment to the poor*. In nearly every country in the region a small minority, the elites of society, continue to monopolize a shamefully disproportionate share of the resources of creation, while the vast majority of the people remain desperately poor. This calls for two actions: not only ministering to the church of the poor in their misery but also joining them in their struggle for a better way of life.

Sola gratia: "by grace alone." As the creeds of the Reformation era testify so eloquently, the heart of the gospel is salvation by the free and sovereign grace of God alone. By this catholic confession the Christian church everywhere stands or falls. All too often, however, while we routinely repeat the "saved by grace" formulas, the way we live our lives and the demands we place on the lives of others speak instead the pragmatic language of works-righteousness. Let others pull themselves up by their own bootstraps, we say, as we have done!

Another factor adds to their struggles: these grass-roots Christians feel betrayed in part by the very gospel to which they are so deeply indebted. They have come to sense keenly that much of past missionary practice, transported to their world by Western Christianity, has left them with a religiosity that ignores their unbearable load of suffering. The submissive piety that it inculcated, its crass legalisms and cheap grace—these emphases elicited little in the way of active obedience. They sold the gospel short.

Still, the gracious offer of new life, although long obstructed by incorrigible powers, remains a standing hope for these expectant Christians. They, more deeply perhaps than we, are often surprised by the sheer joy of God's grace. It is a free gift. But it is not cheap: in their crisis situation it is a costly gift. For the free flow of grace meets with stubborn resistance by the graceless powers that be. Yet, in the face of overwhelming odds, the key to responsible Christian living is the same: grateful service. We are saved to serve. God's grace is both free and freeing. It liberates. It shatters the power of the idols of death. It opens up new and unforeseen possibilities for self-sacrificing, and also for self-asserting obedience to the kingdom call for jubilee.

Sola Scriptura: "by Scripture alone." Bible study in the base communities is infinitely more than an enjoyable spiritual exercise. Scripture is their staff of life as they face the idols of death. It is their supreme standard for faith in action. Church traditions, religious practices, social-economic-political systems—none of these are on a par with God's Word. They must instead be judged by it. Scripture's liberating message is also the final court of appeal in seeking to offset the insidiously unreformational impact of television evangelists, who use the media to verbally slay their tens of thousands with a reactionary version of the gospel.

These grass-roots Christians have learned that biblical reflection may no longer remain the exclusive province of a privileged few. The dramatic word-pictures and vivid imagery of the gospel speak volumes to Central American peasants today, just as they did to the common people of Palestine in Jesus' day. The gospel's message is far richer than that of the weightiest theological tomes. In fact, theology, including liberation theology, is not the foundation of church life but one of its by-products. As in sixteenth-century Europe, so in twentieth-century Central America, *sola Scriptura* is proving to be a radically iconoclastic principle of reformation. It fosters the "exegetical suspicion" needed to re-examine generally held, apparently self-evident readings of the Bible that often turn out to be misreadings. It also nurtures the "cultural suspicion" needed to call into question conventional practices and long-standing ideologies that masquerade as Christian options but are in actuality opposed to the jubilee spirit of God's kingdom.

Listening perceptually to the witness of the prophets and apostles, the church of the poor, gathered in the CEBs, insists that sensitive Christians cannot rest content with the status quo. To the dismay of many outsiders, however, they are reading the Word in very innovative ways—upside down, it seems, from the bottom up. "Upside down is," however, "a relative concept," according to author Christopher Hill. "The assumption that it means the wrong way up is itself an expression of the view from the top."[23] However wrong it may seem to many people, such a re-reading of Scripture is very conceivably much closer to the original slant of the Bible writers than to the upwardly mobile slant of Western readers. For the faithful in Israel and the early church were also largely down-and-out communities, looking up to God for deliverance from hostile forces. The kingdom vision of these Central American Christians, with its reformational, revolutionary call for constructive change, strikes fear into the hearts of oligarchies and hierarchies. It often puzzles and incenses Marxists too, who are driven by a different view of reality. It even upsets some North American church people, who have so privatized the Bible that they fail to grasp the full-orbed dynamics of the gospel.

Solo Christo: "through Christ alone." These reflections on faith, grace, and Scripture reach their crowded climax in the centrality of Jesus Christ. He is the "all in all" of Christian commitment: the personal and communal focal point of faith, the ground of God's proffered grace, the key to the meaning of the entire biblical drama.

The reformational principle of *solo Christo* expresses the central biblical teaching that Christ's mission in and for the world is an absolutely unique, once-and-for-all event. However, it did not end abruptly and completely on the Mount of Ascension. Christ sent his disciples into the world with the promise of accomplishing "greater works," precisely in view of his return to the Father (John 14:12). With this, Christ opened a new phase in his ongoing world mission, summoning his followers, now as in the first century, to a "costly discipleship" in his name (John 15:18-27). This mandate, which flows from the linkage between Christ's decisive mission and our follow-up mission, forms the basic agenda for the church of the poor in Central America today—a kingdom mission aimed at bringing the fruits of jubilee to their troubled world.

THEOLOGY IN THE SERVICE OF LIBERATION

This is not the time or the place for a general discussion of liberation theologies. We shall instead consider this movement from a single viewpoint, asking only questions related to the central concern of the book as a whole. The basic question is this: What contributions are liberation theologians making to a better understanding of the kingdom of God and its message of jubilee, and how are their views helping

Central Americans reach out beyond the present crisis toward a better future?

A New Way of Doing Theology

Liberation theologians see themselves engaged in an ongoing process of doing theology "along the way" and "on the move." They therefore prefer to think of their works in the tentative format of looseleaf notebooks, with older pages replaced readily by newer ones born of continuing reflection.[24] From this point of view it is possible to appreciate this theology-in-the-making as a latter-day expression of the time-honored reformational principle *semper reformanda*—"always reforming."

This fledgling movement carries with it substantial continuities with the basic themes of the Judeo-Christian tradition, but also significant discontinuities, especially in its methodology. Only in a generic sense can we speak of liberation *theology*. Actually what we find is a cluster of liberation *theologies*. But the rich variations are bound together by a common project—namely, vigorous engagement with Latin American reality from the perspective of the poor. Approaching life from the underside of history, liberation theologians are taking advantage of the inductive methods hinted at by Vatican II (1962-1965) and legitimized by Medellín (1968). Exercising these options leads to redefining *who* does theology, *why, where,* and *how* it is done, and *what* its agenda is.

These Latin American theologies are thus led to distance themselves from traditional Western theologies. The pressing concern of the latter in our times is the challenge of post-Christian "unbelievers," while that of liberation theologians is the plight of Christianized "nonpersons." Moreover, the philosophical mind-set of much of Western theology keeps it from giving serious consideration to alternative methodologies that are demanded by the Latin American crisis situation—the use of social, economic, and political tools of analysis. Liberation thinkers also look askance at the tendency of Western theologians to seek to accommodate modern secularizing trends that are as yet largely foreign to the Southern world. Again, because of its acceptance of the Enlightenment dichotomy between dogma (theory) and ethics (praxis), Western scholarship tends to be abstract, lacking down-to-earth relevance; it therefore fails repeatedly to translate its often penetrating critique of the glaring injustices of modern societies into a concrete and active commitment to the struggle for constructive change.

From the Bottom Up

Liberation theology is not a self-generating, self-sustaining school of thought. Its basic impulses arise from the biblical reflections of Christian grass-roots communities. As theological reflection it is of only secondary importance, adding a theoretical dimension to the deeply religious voices of protest and renewal that emanate from the church of the poor. A Lutheran national pastor in Central America that the CCCS team talked to in January 1987 put it this way:

> Liberation ideas arose in the Christian base communities, not among liberation theologians. The latter have even distorted them a bit. Liberation is a product of the people of God. Theologians tend to add some dubious things, leaving it open to criticism. Actually it should be called a theology of *life*. For we find the God of life in every aspect of life, including politics. If this theology does not liberate, it is not of God, for the gospel is liberating.

Liberation movements gained ground in several other countries of Latin America more readily than in Central American countries. This delayed response was due to a general lack of support on the part of the Central American hierarchy. Base communities were therefore often compelled to cloak their activities in secrecy. Eventually, however, liberation projects were successfully launched throughout Central America, prompted by the desperate conditions of the people. They took hold most naturally in countries that were most ripe for revolution—El Salvador, Guatemala, and Nicaragua. There they often earned the title "quarries of the revolution." Resistance to liberation movements by traditional authorities meant that the church of the poor had to find its own way, living strictly from the bottom up, developing its own leadership. In this situation many drew inspiration from Dietrich Bonhoeffer's struggles against the oppressive regime of his day, as captured in these words:

> There remains an experience of incomparable value. We have for once learned to see the great events of world history from below, from the perspective of the outcast, the suspects, the maltreated, the powerless, the oppressed, the reviled—in short from the perspective of those who suffer. . . . We will have to learn that personal suffering is a more effective key, a more rewarding principle for exploring the world in thought and action than personal good fortune.[25]

Basic Motifs of Liberation

Let us now look briefly at a set of distinctive themes elaborated by a few Central American theologians that express the jubilee hopes and kingdom expectations of the church of the poor.

Pablo Richard, a Chilean now residing in San José, Costa Rica, where he teaches at the National University, is making a significant contribution to liberation hermeneutics. To capture the prophetic witness of the church of the poor, Richard draws upon the analogy of a tree as a hermeneutic model to illustrate the relationship between the primacy of grass-roots spirituality and the second-order value of theological exposition. Accordingly, Richard paints word pictures of a tree with its roots, trunk, and branches.

The roots represent "the original and originating experience . . . of God in the history of the oppressed." The trunk symbolizes the need for "such an experience to be acknowledged and shared with others" in the base communities, and then "communicated and spread within the popular movement." The branches, which draw life from the roots and through the trunk, point to liberation theology as "a theoretical confrontation with the total rationality of the practice of liberation," by which "the church of the poor thus reaffirms its identity and prophetic mission within the popular movement."[26]

Elsa Tamez, an evangelical from Mexico, also carries on her work as a biblical theologian in San José, Costa Rica. A distinctive emphasis in her writing is the call to exercise a preferential option for the poor. In a careful study of the concepts "oppression," "oppressors," and "oppressed" in Scripture, Tamez demonstrates God's predilection for "the poor and needy," which issues in the divine imperative for doing justice in society. For "God identifies himself with the poor to such an extent that their rights become the rights of God himself: he who oppresses a poor man insults his Maker, but he who is kind to the needy honors him (Proverbs 14:31)." Across the pages of Scripture "God's self-revelation occurs in the context of a history of conflict; it is also clear that in this history God is on the side of the subjugated. This experience of God . . . finds expression today in the religious life of oppressed peoples who are seeking their liberation." For "poverty is a challenge to God the Creator; because of the insufferable conditions under which the poor live, God is obliged to fight at their side."[27]

Pointing the way to reconciliation, Tamez turns to Proverbs 29:13: "The poor man and the oppressor meet together; the Lord gives light to the eyes of both." Commenting on this passage, she concludes that "the oppressors are oppressors to the extent that they become rich, and that they are rich to the extent that they oppress the poor. Yahweh gives both the poor and the oppressor the opportunity to build a just society."[28]

What are we to make of Scripture's consistent advocacy of the poor? Is poverty a condition for salvation? Are the rich excluded from entry into the kingdom of God? Rich Christians like ourselves are inclined to argue that wealth and poverty are not decisive criteria. Accordingly, the Bible's insistent concern for the poor is hardly felt as a serious challenge to the status quo in which the vast majority of our brothers and sisters in Central America suffer the debilitating effects of abject poverty. But this way of reading Scripture and reality misses the thrust of biblical teaching on this issue.

We must be clear on this point. God sides with the poor, but not because they are "better" or holier than the rich. Poverty is not a means of grace any more than riches are. When God defends the weak and needy, this choice is not a declaration of their salvific status.

God takes the side of the poor because he is the God of righteousness and justice. He favors the poor and needy because in the Bible they are regularly identified as the victims of unrighteous discrimination. They are the ones who embody privation, oppression, powerlessness, and exploitation—all that God opposes in human relationships. In the name of justice, therefore, he intervenes as the Helper of the helpless and the Defender of the defenseless. In the words of the sixteenth-century reformer John Calvin,

> God Himself, looking on men as formed in His own image, regards them with such love and honour that He Himself feels wounded and outraged in the persons of those who are the victims of human cruelty and wickedness. . . . We cannot but behold our own face, as it were in a glass, in the person that is poor and despised, who is not able to hold out any longer, but lies groaning under his burden, though he were the furthest stranger in the world.[29]

In Scripture we see God opting for the poor because they are poorly treated. So we too are called to oppose those "principalities and powers" that obstruct justice, those forms of institutionalized violence that dehumanize, disinherit, enslave, and rob the poor of their life and livelihood. Around the turn of the century the Dutch theologian and statesman Abraham Kuyper sounded a similar note:

> When rich and poor stand opposed to each other, God never takes His place with the wealthier, but always stands with the poorer. . . . God has not willed that one should drudge hard and yet have no bread for himself and his family. . . . We shall not be satisfied with the struc-

ture of society until it offers all human beings an existence worthy of man. Until then, the structure must remain the object of our criticism.[30]

This preferential option finds an echo in the words of the modern Swiss theologian Karl Barth:

> The human righteousness required by God and established in obedience—the righteousness which according to Amos 5 should pour down as a mighty stream—has necessarily the character of a vindication of right in favour of the threatened innocent, the oppressed poor, widows, orphans and aliens. For this reason, in the relations and events in the life of His people, God always takes His stand unconditionally and passionately on this side alone: against the lofty and on behalf of the lowly; against those who already enjoy right and privilege and on behalf of those who are denied and deprived of it.[31]

When people in positions of power and authority cooperate in taking up the cause of public justice, when they too exercise a preferential option for marginalized peoples, then they too find God on their side. The kingdom remains closed to the rich who, in the biblical sense, act like the rich. But when rich and poor together embrace the hopes of the poor, then we begin to see jubilee signs of the coming of the kingdom. These signs are the last best hope of the poor.

In Chapter 1 we met Jon Sobrino, a colleague of Archbishop Romero. In speaking to a Lutheran group in the United States, he explained that the "striking poverty of a very, very large number of people is the most decisive reality in Latin America and in El Salvador." This is a matter of ultimate concern. For "in El Salvador, poverty has to do with death." Poverty is "so contrary to the will of God" because it "means eternally to be near to death." Sobrino brings together real poverty, real death, and real violation of God's will in these words: "The poor ones are those who are destined to die before their time. This is what cries out to heaven. At least this much we know about the will of God: He does not want this situation. Why? Because it vitiates, threatens God's own creation."[32]

Systemic poverty erects a most terrible antithesis between true religion and idolatry, between serving the God of life and rendering self-serving homage to the idols of death. Sobrino elaborates the point:

> What do we mean by idols? By idols I mean historical realities, things that exist which demand victims to survive. . . . At times we Christians, at least some of us, have thought that the opposite of God is the non-existence of God, and the opposite of faith would be unbelief.

But I don't think this is quite exact. The opposite of God are the idols, and they do exist. And the opposite of faith is not simply unbelief, but idolatry, and that does exist.[33]

This life-and-death crisis is so agonizingly real to members of the body of Christ in Central America that it must also be a matter of deep concern to the body of believers as a whole. Accordingly, in a recent work entitled *Theology of Christian Solidarity,* Sobrino and his co-author, Juan Hernandez Pico, reach out across national boundaries to open up ecumenical horizons that bridge the barriers separating Christians in different countries. Older models of the church, pluriformity as well as uniformity models, no longer answer the needs of our times. The critical demands of our day call for a solidarity model. Moved by this vision of the catholicity of the church, Sobrino and Pico warn against pressing Christian solidarity into the ideologies of either the West or the East. They advocate instead a two-way mission bringing brothers and sisters in the North and South closer together. In this light Sobrino and Pico issue "a call for solidarity from the churches that confess their faith in the God and Father of our Lord Jesus Christ. Like any call, like any vocation in the church, these processes test ecclesial faith, force it to exercise discernment, and expose it to critical risk."[34]

"Testing All Things . . ."

"Theology as usual" is out of place in crisis-ridden Central America. To engage in traditional "theologies of noninvolvement" would be the height of irrelevance. These are deep-seated convictions among theologians of liberation. A revolutionary situation calls for new ways of doing theology. One may quarrel with the scope of things in liberation theology, or call it social philosophy instead of theology. But, if it is taken at face value, as Emilio Núñez points out in his evangelical critique, its "emphasis falls on action, on praxis, not on knowledge for its own sake. It is a philosophy of the transforming action of society. It strives to change the situation of poverty and underdevelopment."[35] One need not be a card-carrying liberation theologian to give such thinkers an honest hearing. As theologians of liberation have paid traditional Western theologies the honor of earnest critique, so we are obliged to return the favor. With Paul, we must "test everything, [and] hold fast what is good" (1 Thess. 5:21). We may be rightly critical of certain troublesome views held by some liberation theologians.[36] But we can criticize them fairly only by seeking to follow in their footsteps a mile or two as they, in their own way, open up a jubilee vision of the coming kingdom.

What about Marxism?

Some critics lay the entire "problem" of Central America at the doorstep of liberation theology, which in turn is simply equated with Marxism. In the attempt to come to terms with this most frequent and severe criticism, it is important to keep in mind a couple of considerations. Not all liberation thought is equally committed to conventional Marxist ideas. Nor do all liberation theologians lend them the same status or use them in the same way.

Moreover, in any critical analysis of the relationship between Marxism and liberation theology, it is important to bear in mind the following threefold distinction with respect to what Marxism means. In the first place, Marxism often appears as a religio-philosophical movement based on an atheistic ideology. Few if any liberation theologians appeal to Marxism in this sense. Second, Marxism offers a political strategy for revolution designed to overcome glaring class discrepancies. In general, liberation theologians advocate revolutionary action only in view of unyielding systemic injustice and only after exhausting whatever peaceful means are available to disenfranchised people. Third, Marxism brings with it a set of tools for societal analysis based on the principle of class conflict. Those involved in the liberation movement have reached the conclusion that such methodologies offer the best hope for making sense out of Central American reality and for proposing a way of escape for exploited peoples condemned to looking at the world from the bottom up. It is primarily in this third sense that Marxism plays a significant role in many liberation theologies.

Such reliance upon Marxist tools of analysis raises the question, quite naturally, of whether such methods can ever be cleanly detached from the materialist and dialectical principles upon which they rest. Methodologies are never ideologically neutral. But that holds for capitalism as well as communism. In thus forcing liberation theologians to reflect critically upon their chosen tools of societal analysis, Western critics of liberation thought must subject their methods to like scrutiny. As Western Christians living in the Northern Hemisphere, we are conditioned to view capitalism and communism as mutually exclusive systems, and to think that these two social philosophies exhaust the viable options. All thinking people are therefore compelled—so it is argued—to choose between the collectivism of the East and the individualism of the West, between socialism and free enterprise. Through the long history of past and present foreign domination and intervention, this dubious and often very cruel choice has been foisted upon our neighbors to the South. Traditionally the peoples of Central America have been held captive by the politics of free market economies. In recent decades Marxist influences have entered the region. This leads many to view the crisis in Central America fundamentally, though we believe wrongly, as an East-West confrontation. But if it be granted for the sake of argument that this allegedly inescapable choice exhausts all the real possibilities for ordering society, then, after nearly half a millennium of devastating experience with colonial, capitalist domination, one can hardly blame those seeking liberation for turning to Marxist tools of societal analysis as the only promising way out of their crisis.

That the crisis in Central America is terribly real is indisputable. It is not necessary to be a Marxist or to be committed to Marxist tools of analysis to recognize the desperate plight of these countries. All it takes to rouse one to righteous indignation is a good reading of Isaiah and Amos. In the words of Oscar Romero,

> The terrible words spoken by the prophets of Israel continue to be verified among us. . . . Amos and Isaiah are not just voices from distant centuries; their writings are not merely texts that we reverently read in the liturgy. They are everyday realities. Day by day we live out the cruelty and ferocity they excoriate. We live them out when there come to us the mothers and the wives of those who have been arrested or who have disappeared, when mutilated bodies turn up in secret cemeteries, when those who fight for justice and peace are assassinated.[37]

On the basis of such appeals to Scripture, Romero repudiated as a false dilemma the choice between capitalism and Marxism. What the right-wing elites in El Salvador called a "communist conspiracy" he called "the cause of the people." Commenting on this issue, Robert McAfee Brown says,

> The fact that "Marxists say it" must not preclude the right of others to reach similar conclusions, perhaps by very different routes. The cry for social justice considerably antedates Karl Marx; the promise of "liberty for the oppressed" was not only enunciated by Jesus, but borrowed by him from the prophet Isaiah. Christians cannot be asked to disavow or be suspicious of a position of their own simply because close to two millennia later Karl Marx happened to offer his own version of the same truth.[38]

"Holding Fast to What Is Good"

Liberation theologians are recovering a number of biblical perspectives—deeply embedded though often forgotten—in the reformational tradition. Giving renewed expression to these insights, they are contributing to the reactivation of a kingdom vision of jubilee in Central America today. Let us look briefly at a few of these breakthroughs.

Recovering a Holistic Way of Life

In the process of "liberating theology," these theologians are disentangling themselves from scholastic patterns of thinking and living that, through generations of missionary activity and theological training, have been transmitted to Latin America. Now, reflecting on their reality in the light of the Word, they are concluding that these traditional ideas, Catholic and Protestant alike, fail to account for their life experience. This new departure comes to forceful expression in their rejection of deeply entrenched dualisms. Gutiérrez states the case clearly in his criticism of "the distinction of planes" model. He describes the traditional "two storey" outlook in terms familiar to us all: "the temporal-spiritual and profane-sacred antithesis," which is "based on the natural-supernatural distinction." This model, which "distinguishes faith and temporal realities, church and world, leads to the perception of two missions in the church and to a sharp differentiation between the roles of the priest and the layman." This dichotomy touches all of life. For a long time it has stood in the way of true liberation. For "until a few years ago it was defended by the vanguard; now it is held aloft by the power groups, many of whom are in no way involved in any commitment to the Christian faith." Gutiérrez therefore admonishes his readers: "Let us not be deceived. Their purposes are very different. Let us not unwittingly aid the opponent." Fortunately, he continues, "contemporary theological reflection has also eroded the model of the distinction of planes."[39]

The debilitating effects of such a dualist worldview are most clearly discernible in the traditional dichotomous view of body and soul. In shifting to a more holistic view of our life in the world, Gutiérrez deals with the ideas of body and soul within the context of Christian "spirituality." He argues that body "designates the [whole] human being in its external aspect." It is "the field on which the flesh as death-dealing power operates, but where at the same time the Spirit, the power that gives life, is also active." These biblical teachings confront us with a deeply religious choice:

We have to decide between death and life—that is, between flesh and spirit. The choice is not between body and soul; nothing could be further from the thinking of Paul who establishes instead a religious (and not a philosophical) opposition between flesh and spirit. He is always dealing with the human person as a whole. It is the whole person who must know how to choose the Spirit and life.[40]

The attempt within liberation movements to recover a more holistic way of life also comes to expression in the following biblical-theological emphases.

Community. The liberation movement is rearticulating the biblical teaching that people are created to live in community/communities. It is therefore critical of the individualist views of society that have resulted from long-standing Western domination of Latin America. Concretely, it rejects individualism in the form of the absolute right of large private-property holdings by the oligarchy. It also repudiates collectivism in the form of state absolutism. Instead, it advocates a communitarian view of our life together in God's world. This is clear from its strong emphasis on the ideas of "peoplehood," "the people of God," "the church of the poor," and "popular organizations."[41] The beginnings of such a communitarian vision have already been incorporated into the liberation movement in the form of Christian base communities, cooperatives, movements for land reform, and other popular organizations. To the extent that such communal ways of structuring life relationships take hold in Central America, giving shape to a pluralist view of society, we can lay to rest the misleading notion that this regional crisis is at bottom an East-West confrontation.

Knowledge, Faith, and Truth. Breaking with scholastic systems with their rationalist notions of knowledge, faith, and truth, liberation theologians are discovering anew biblical insights in answer to the perennial questions: What is knowledge? What is faith? What is truth? For these issues, too, bear directly upon the harsh realities that define their daily experience. Appealing to the Word, they are discovering, as José Míguez Bonino puts it, that

> the faith of Israel is consistently portrayed, not as a *gnosis,* but as a *way,* a practical way of acting. . . . This background . . . may explain Jesus' use of the word *way* to refer to himself. . . . Faith is a way of "walking" . . . [of] "doing the truth." . . . Only he who *does* the Word will know the doctrine.[42]

Biblically based knowledge, faith, and truth are not static, abstract concepts, but dynamic realities that give hope to poor and powerless people.

Theory in the Service of Christian Practice. Liberation theology arises from the practical faith experiences of Christian base communities. It draws its strength from a simple "walking in the truth" on the part of thousands of common believers—with all the risks that such a venture involves in places like Central America. Such theoretical reflection is therefore rooted in the beans-and-tortillas realities of everyday living. In the words of Míguez Bonino, "true knowledge can only be acquired starting from the concrete actions of men." On this, he says, Christians and Marxists are agreed, but with an important difference.

> For both Christians and Marxists, knowledge is not a theoretical contemplation of abstract truths but a concrete engagement, an active relationship with reality. For the Marxist, this is a specific revolutionary action; for the Christian, historical praxis takes place in the context and under the demands of a covenant relationship which God himself has opened and defined for us. But in both cases neutral, purely objective, . . . uncommitted knowledge is an impossibility.[43]

Thus liberation theologians play a significant servant role in practical kingdom living on the part of the Christian community.

Church and Kingdom. For centuries a form of Christianity reduced largely to "churchianity" prevailed in Central America. The institutional church, epitomized in the hierarchy, was seen as representing the fullness of Christian living. The biblical reality of the kingdom suffered near total eclipse.

Now, with a rediscovery of "the church as people of God," localized in "the church of the poor," and with "the conversion of the church to the world," liberation theology is helping to open up a more full-orbed vision of kingdom living. The church as institute is called to serve as a means to that end. In keeping with this high view of the kingdom as "the original, all-encompassing message" of the Scriptures, Mortimer Arias, rector of the Biblical Seminary in San José, Costa Rica, warns against various ways of eclipsing "the subversive memory of Jesus." Most common among them is that "we have reduced the kingdom to the institutionalized and visible kingdom of the church."[44] The old guard in Central America still clings to this ideal. But wherever the traditional church fails to equip believers for celebrating jubilee, there grass-roots Christian communities are springing up, with the support of liberation theologians, to offer "a new way of being church" in the service of the coming kingdom.

Appendix 1: Guidelines for Reformational Approaches to the Central American Crisis

Consistent with the overall thrust of this book, the CCCS team offers the following guidelines for addressing the crisis in Central America.

For North American Policymakers

1. **Accept the perspective of the poor**—i.e., orient national policy toward the greater good of the majority of Central American peoples.

    1.1. Support participatory democracy from below rather than formal democracy imposed from above.

    1.2. Develop economic policies that effectively help the many poor.

    1.3. Give equal opportunity to Central American products in North American markets.

    1.4. Work together toward a long-range reordering of the relationship between North America and Central America.

    1.5. Remember that what is best for the majority of Central Americans is ultimately best for the people and nations of North America.

2. **Allow Central Americans the freedom to shape their own socio-economic and political future.**

    2.1. Assume that people who live in Central America know more about the local situation than do North American policymakers.

    2.2. Encourage transnational dialogue, without foreign imposition, in Central American relations.

    2.3. Require that our ambassadors relate as closely with the common people, and in particular with the poor, as they do with the elite of Central America.

    2.4. Cooperate actively in the attainment of Central American goals.

    2.5. Allow Central Americans to set up tariff barriers to protect their products—just as England, the United States, and Canada did during their industrial revolutions—without in-kind penalties.

2.6. Encourage cooperative Latin American initiatives that aim at solving Central American problems—e.g., the Contadora peace initiative, the Arias Peace Plan, a common market, joint governing bodies, etc.

3. See problems holistically.

3.1. Accept the rule of international law, as defined by the International Court, the United Nations, and the Organization of American States.

3.2. Find ways of reducing the onerous burden of international debt.

3.3. Participate more actively, and nonmanipulatively, in international forums aimed at defining a more just international economic order.

3.4. Give due weight to the voice of Latin America in these forums.

3.5. Avoid reducing the Central American crisis to an East-West confrontation.

3.6. Take the North-South crisis seriously, lest we reach a point of no return.

4. Seek negotiated rather than military solutions.

4.1. Work on the basis of trust, not fear (e.g., the National Security Doctrine), in seeking viable solutions for the Central American crisis.

4.2. Avoid unilateralism by making decisions in concert with a community of nations.

4.3. Accept the full right of Central Americans to negotiate solutions to their own problems (e.g., the Arias Peace Plan).

4.4. Learn the lessons of justice and peace from past U.S. interventions in Central America.

4.5. Remember that a policy of life will gain more than all the machines of death.

For North American Christians

1. **Get to know the situation.** Get firsthand information whenever possible. Do not rely upon hearsay, opinions, or unsubstantiated press reports.

1.1. Pray for sensitivity to the needs of the people of Central America.

1.2. Read extensively (see our recommended bibliography).

1.3. Consult with people who have been to Central America.

1.4. Listen to different points of view.

1.5. Visit Central America or send a representative from your group.

1.6. Consider becoming involved in short-term study or service projects in Central America. Many church groups conduct regular tours or offer special opportunities for service and study in Central America.

2. Share your concerns and questions with others.

2.1. Create discussion groups. Get the help of knowledgeable people or use study guides.

2.2. Invite advocacy groups and Central American visitors to your discussions.

2.3. Express your concerns to friends, neighbors, and fellow church members.

3. Make a decision.

3.1. Clarify the options from a Christian perspective. Avoid secondary issues and a black-and-white mentality.

3.2. In the spirit of Christ, consider the needs of others— peoples and nations—before your own.

3.3. Try to make group decisions, however tentative.

3.4. Don't be afraid to take risks. Be a prophet.

4. Act upon your decision: Decide what steps to take.

4.1. Become personally involved whenever possible.

4.2. Share your new awareness with fellow Christians.

4.3. Sensitize your church to Central American issues.

4.4. Make your views known to public officials.

4.5. Join an advocacy group.

For North American Relief (Diaconal) Agencies

1. Reaffirm your commitment to reformational principles of Christian service.

1.1. God is the Lord of history. His will for humanity has priority over every other project.

1.2. God's will is for human beings to have abundant life through Jesus Christ.

1.3. The office of believers is to love God and to actively promote his kingdom.

1.4. To love God is to do justice to our neighbor, for in doing this all of the commandments are fulfilled.

1.5. To worship and serve the true God is to oppose the false idols that seek to have dominion over people.

1.6. To follow our Lord is to identify with the poor and oppressed.

2. **Evaluate your present programs in the light of this transformational worldview.**

2.1. Are you communicating a holistic gospel?

2.2. Does your ministry aim at transforming people and structures, or are you merely applying Band-Aids?

2.3. Does your program engender additional long-term dependency? How does it overcome present dependency?

2.4. Who are the responsible agents in policy decisions? Nationals or North Americans? Or are the decisions made jointly?

3. **Promote projects that respond to needs as defined by Central American Christians.**

3.1. Facilitate the communication of Central American concerns to North American agencies—e.g., by inviting Central Americans to serve on North American boards.

3.2. Orient your objectives to life-promoting programs— those focusing on supplying food, health, education, housing, etc.

3.3. Remember that in the Two Thirds World, small is beautiful.

3.4. Give priority to labor-intensive projects.

3.5. Prioritize your peace-building initiatives in Central America as well as through North American public policy.

4. **Work in cooperation with other churches and agencies.**

4.1. Give priority to national agencies that work ecumenically in their own countries.

4.2. Practice cooperation in North America as an example to non-cooperative agencies in Central America.

4.3. Create joint councils and task forces for action on special issues.

4.4. Require responsible stewardship of available resources at all times.

For North American Church-related Workers Living in Central America

1. **Trust Central Americans.** Keep the following in mind:

1.1. The indwelling Holy Spirit and the presence of the Word require that we respect all our sisters and brothers, without exception.

1.2. Shared responsibility promotes mutual trust.

1.3. Central American Christians have the same right to learn by trial and error as we do.

1.4. Christian communities are more effectively born where paternalism is absent.

2. Act for justice and righteousness.

2.1. Incarnate these gospel principles:

a. The right of creation—the right to be fully human within one's own culture, race, gender, and age group—must be respected.

b. Life has priority over death, always, even though some are called to give up their lives that others may live (e.g., Oscar Romero).

c. Christians must not hurt or deprive others for personal benefit or in order to avoid risk to themselves. This applies at every level of human relationships.

d. Ministry by word and ministry by deed are inseparably linked in the communication of the gospel.

2.2. Evaluate goals in the light of these principles. Then bring actions in line with the desired ends.

2.3. True missionaries (evangelistic, pastoral, diaconal), no matter what social class they work with, are guided by their identity with the poor. By their lifestyle and actions they invite the rich to join them in that option. Such a gospel is big enough to encompass both rich and poor.

2.4. Be willing to sacrifice—even your life, if need be— for the cause of Christ and of people who unjustly suffer.

3. Be a bridge between the people of Central America and your sponsoring agency.

3.1. Tell the whole truth in love, both the good and the bad.

3.2. Propose new avenues of service that respond more adequately to Central American needs.

3.3. Point out, with gospel freedom, the errors of those programs that do not promote life.

3.4. Be constructive: accentuate the positive, eliminate the negative.

4. Communicate Central American concerns to the North American public.

4.1. Look for innovative ways of communicating your concerns to North American church and community groups.

4.2. Challenge the uncritical acceptance of civil religion.

4.3. Interpret what is happening in Central America through letters and articles.

4.4. Keep government officials informed. Be true to the facts.

4.5. Clarify the options: our policies can mean life or death in Central America.

For Central American Christians, Agencies, and Officials

1. Try to understand the situation of North American Christians. Remember:

1.1. North Americans find it difficult to relate personally to Central American issues.

1.2. Media coverage on Central America is largely inadequate and often distorted.

1.3. Representative democracy does not give North American citizens direct power.

1.4. Even when concerned citizens are in the majority, the government can make foreign policy decisions over which citizens have very little control.

1.5. Ongoing Central American concerns are usually overwhelmed during election periods by local issues or by headline-grabbing crises in other parts of the world.

2. Forgive us our debts, especially the following:

2.1. Our provincialisms and our indifference to your needs.

2.2. Our past interventions, mostly for our own ends.

2.3. Our greater interest in what Central America can do for us than in what we can do for you.

2.4. Our maiming and killing of innocent citizens, which is being done largely with our arms and bullets—made in our factories and sent by our government.

2.5. Being more concerned about the fate of one U.S. adventurer in Nicaragua than for the fates of thousands of innocent peasants.

2.6. Making our national security more important than your lives.

3. Interpret Central American reality to us.

3.1. Make your feelings and judgments known to us with patience. God is not finished with us yet.

3.2. Challenge North American mission and diaconal agencies and individual citizens to open themselves up to dialogue with you.

3.3. Search for ways to communicate with North American citizens who are engaged in mission, social-service, business, diplomatic, and military agencies.

3.4. Help us to rediscover our historical roots and to relate what we learn to your history in Central America.

3.5. Speak to us in ways that we can understand: avoid slogan-eering and complex socio-economic jargon. Base your appeal upon our shared biblical heritage.

4. Propose concrete ways in which North American Christians can help you.

4.1. Recommend the economic policies that are needed and point out forthrightly which of our policies are hurting you.

4.2. Insist that agencies, businesses, churches, and governments discuss their policies with you and subject them to your review.

4.3. Demand adequate space for independent national action at all levels.

4.4. Suggest ways in which we can help interpret your concerns to our church and national leaders.

For North American and Central American Media People and Agencies

1. Give priority time and space to ordinary people.

2. Take all the factors into account. Go for the whole truth. Do not sensationalize.

3. Depend more upon direct Central American sources than on North American politically oriented releases.

4. Get the whole picture. Spend time in Central America talking to people in every walk of life.

5. Resist editorial repackaging and reinterpretation to fit what the public wants to hear.

Appendix 2: Statistics of the Central American Research Trip

The following is a sketchy tabulation of the meetings, interviews, and consultations held by the CCCS team during our January-February 1987 study tour through the five main countries of Central America, plus Belize and Panama.

POPULAR SECTOR
Displaced persons and refugees	7
Political prisoners	1
CEBs: leaders and groups	8
Labor unions	6
Campesinos (cooperatives, agrarian reform movements, etc.)	6
Education and culture groups	15
People in poverty-stricken areas	3

GOVERNMENT OFFICIALS
Political party leaders	8
Legislators	3
Cabinet ministers	4
Presidents and ex-presidents	5
Military leaders	3

INSURGENTS   6

NEWS MEDIA   3

BUSINESS AND MULTINATIONALS   4

CHURCH AND PARACHURCH LEADERS
Roman Catholic	12
Bishops	5
Archbishops	2
Protestant	26

HUMAN RIGHTS ORGANIZATIONS   10

CONTADORA	**2**
U.S. EMBASSIES/BASES/AGENCIES	**11**
MISSION AGENCIES AND PERSONNEL	**9**
RELIEF AND SOCIAL SERVICE AGENCIES	**24**
PROJECT CONSULTANTS, STUDY CENTERS, PROFESSORS	**16**

WORSHIP SERVICES: On Sundays we formed subteams, attending worship services in many different churches. We covered a wide ecclesiastical spectrum, including base communities, Assemblies of God, and traditional Roman Catholic, Presbyterian, Christian Reformed, Baptist, Lutheran, Mennonite, Charismatic Catholic, and Pentecostal groups.

Notes

1. The God of Life or the Idols of Death

1. Penny Lernoux, "The Long Path to Puebla," in *Puebla and Beyond,* ed. John Eagleson and Philip Scharper (Maryknoll, N.Y.: Orbis Books, 1979), p. 11; cf. also sections 328, 437, 1032, and 1269 in the Puebla document.

2. Plácido Erdozain, *Archbishop Romero: Martyr of Salvador,* trans. John McFadden and Ruth Warner (Maryknoll, N.Y.: Orbis Books, 1981), p. 3.

3. Although the concept "from below" can be read as referring to the "lower class" in a conventional, strictly economic sense, we view the poverty of the lower class as embracing not only economic privation but also social, political, and educational privation—i.e., cultural privation in the broad sense of the term, including illiteracy and lack of adequate health care. Therefore, though we shall continue to use the phrase "from below," together with its equivalents such as "from the bottom up" and "from the underside of history," we do so as a kind of shorthand for poverty in the full sense of the word.

4. Cf. Ignacio Martin-Bara, "Oscar Romero: Voice of the Downtrodden," in Romero's *Voice of the Voiceless: The Four Pastoral Letters and Other Statements,* trans. Michael J. Walsh (Maryknoll, N.Y.: Orbis Books, 1985), pp. 1-21.

5. *Witnesses of Hope: The Persecution of Christians in Latin America,* ed. Martin Lange and Reinhold Iblacker, trans. William E. Jerman (Maryknoll, N.Y.: Orbis Books, 1981), pp. 24-25.

6. Erdozain, *Martyr of Salvador,* p. 1.

7. Erdozain, *Martyr of Salvador,* pp. 13-17.

8. Erdozain, *Martyr of Salvador,* pp. 18-20, 43-48, 52-53, 60-64, 84.

9. *A Martyr's Message of Hope: Six Homilies by Archbishop Oscar Romero* (Kansas City: Celebration Books, 1981), p. 161. Subsequent references to this book will be made parenthetically in the text.

10. Cited in *Voice of the Voiceless,* pp. 50-51. Subsequent references to this book will be made parenthetically in the text.

11. "Intercessors for Peace and Freedom," Washington: Evangelicals for Social Action, Apr. 1987.

12. In addition to works already cited, note the following works: James R. Brockman, *The Word Remains: A Life of Oscar Romero* (Maryknoll, N.Y.: Orbis Books, 1982); and *The Church Is All of You: Thoughts of Archbishop Oscar Romero,* ed. James R. Brockman (Minneapolis, Minn.: Winston Press, 1984). Subsequent references to the latter book will be made parenthetically in the text.

13. Upon the successful conclusion of the Nicaraguan revolution, Romero said he welcomed "the dawn of liberation in our brother country." The Salvadoran church rejoiced in "the satisfaction of having been in solidarity with the Nicaraguan church." For "we feel very close to the Nicaraguan church, and share in its joys and responsibilities—responsibilities ranging from prayer to enlightening people by the spread of the gospel." For decades the anguished cries of the Nicaraguan people had gone unheard. So finally "it had to come to this bloodbath, the result of the absolutization of power. Deified power! A tyrant thinks he is indispensable; it does not matter to him that the whole nation dies" (*A Martyr's Message of Hope,* pp. 55-56).

14. *The Church in the Present-Day Transformation of Latin America in the Light of the Council,* ed. Louis Michael Colonnese (Bogotá, Col.: General Secretariat of CELAM, 1973), p. 34.

15. *Transformation,* pp. 39-40.

16. *Transformation,* p. 41.

17. *Transformation,* p. 56.

18. *Transformation,* p. 37.

19. Cited in *Voice of the Voiceless,* p. 67. See also pp. 39-40 and p. 172 for a further elaboration of Romero's views on holistic evangelization within a kingdom perspective.

20. Cf. Richard Shaull, *Heralds of a New Reformation: The Poor of South and North America* (Maryknoll, N.Y.: Orbis Books, 1984).

2. Profitable Death or Rich Life

1. Lawrence Goodwyn, *The Populist Moment: A Short History of the Agrarian Revolt in America* (New York: Oxford University Press, 1978), pp. 168-69; Gary B. Nash and Julie Roy Jeffrey, *The American People: Creating a Nation and a Society* (San Francisco: Harper & Row, 1986), p. 590.

2. James Dekker, "Conversion and Oppression: A Case Study on Guatemalan Indians," *Transformation* 2 (1985): 12-13.

3. Quoted in Jim Handy, *Gift of the Devil: A History of Guatemala* (Boston: South End Press, 1984), p. 24.

4. Quoted by William L. Sherman in *Forced Native Labor in Sixteenth-Century Central America* (Lincoln: University of Nebraska Press, 1979), p. 195.

5. Murdo J. MacLeod, *Spanish Central America: A Socio-Economic History, 1520-1720* (Berkeley and Los Angeles: University of California Press, 1973), pp. 224-25.

6. *Popol Vuh: The Sacred Book of the Ancient Quiché Maya,* English version by Delia Goetz and Sylvanus G. Morley, from the translation of Adrian Recinos (Norman: University of Oklahoma Press, 1950), p. 167.

7. "Land of the Few," in *Guatemala,* ed. Susanne Jonas and David Tobis (New York: NACLA, 1974), p. 17.

8. John Leddy Phelan, *The Millennial Kingdom of the Franciscans in the New World,* 2nd rev. ed. (Berkeley and Los Angeles: University of California Press, 1970), pp. 61, 63. This analogy presaged the title of a well-known book on Latin American-U.S. relations, *The Shark and the Sardines* (New York: Lyle Stuart, 1963), written by Juan José Arévalo, a former president of Guatemala.

9. Quoted in Handy, *Gift of the Devil,* p. 23.

10. Nancy M. Farriss, *Maya Society under Colonial Rule: The Collective Enterprise of Survival* (Princeton: Princeton University Press, 1984), pp. 91-94.

11. *Popol Vuh,* pp. 77, 79-80.

12. Phelan, *The Millennial Kingdom of the Franciscans in the New World,* pp. 65, 49; and Enrique D. Dussel, *Desintegración de la Cristiandad Colonial y Liberación: Perspectiva Latino-americana* (Salamanca: Ediciones Sígueme, 1978), pp. 55-56.

13. Quoted in Adriaan C. Van Oss, *Catholic Colonialism: A Parish History of Guatemala, 1524-1821* (New York: Cambridge University Press, 1986), p. 136.

14. Quoted in Robert F. Berkhofer, Jr., *Salvation and the Savage: An Analysis of Protestant Missions and American Indian Response, 1787-1862* (Lexington: University of Kentucky Press, 1965), pp. 168-69.

15. MacLeod, *Spanish Central America,* pp. 121-25, 134.

16. *Guatemala,* p. 30.

17. Farriss, *Maya Society under Colonial Rule,* pp. 312-18; and Victoria Reifler Bricker, *The Indian Christ, the Indian King: The Historical Substrate of Maya Myth and Ritual* (Austin: University of Texas Press, 1981), p. 179.

18. Handy, *Gift of the Devil,* p. 167.

19. Quoted in *Guatemala in Rebellion: Unfinished History,* ed. Jonathan Fried et al. (New York: Grove Press, 1983), p. 25.

20. Alain Y. Dessaint, "Effects of the Hacienda and Plantation Systems on Guatemala's Indians," *América Indígena* 22 (1962): 323-54; and Handy, *Gift of the Devil,* p. 67.

21. Dessaint, "Effects of the Hacienda and Plantation Systems on Guatemala's Indians," p. 331.

22. Dessaint, "Effects of the Hacienda and Plantation Systems on

Guatemala's Indians," pp. 331-32; and Ralph Lee Woodward, Jr., *Central America: A Nation Divided*, 2nd ed. (New York: Oxford University Press, 1985), p. 217.

23. Quoted in Dessaint, "Effects of the Hacienda and Plantation Systems on Guatemala's Indians," pp. 338-39.

24. Dessaint, "Effects of the Hacienda and Plantation Systems on Guatemala's Indians," pp. 338-40.

25. Dessaint, "Effects of the Hacienda and Plantation Systems on Guatemala's Indians," pp. 348-49.

26. Quoted by Robert F. Berkhofer, Jr., in *The White Man's Indian: Images of the American Indian from Columbus to the Present* (New York: Vintage Books, 1979), p. 173.

27. Dessaint, "Effects of the Hacienda and Plantation Systems on Guatemala's Indians," pp. 342-43.

28. Quoted by Robert Blauner in "International Colonialism and Ghetto Revolt," in *Crisis in American Institutions*, ed. Jerome H. Skolnick and Elliott Currie (Boston: Little, Brown, 1970), pp. 112-13.

29. Dussel, *Desintegración de la Cristiandad Colonial y Liberación*, p. 52.

3. Development Strategies: Success Consumed by Failure

1. Robert Williams, *Export Agriculture and the Crisis in Central America* (Chapel Hill, N.C.: University of North Carolina Press, 1986), pp. 118-21.

2. Williams, *Export Agriculture and the Crisis in Central America*, pp. 122-24.

3. Williams, *Export Agriculture and the Crisis in Central America*, pp. 126-34.

4. Tom Barry, *Roots of Rebellion: Land and Hunger in Central America* (Boston: South End Press, 1987), p. 140.

5. For additional contextual accounts, see the Stanford Central America Action Network, *Revolution in Central America* (Boulder, Colo.: Westview Press, 1983), pp. 72-74, 307-14; and Guillermo Molino Chocano, "Honduras," in *América Latina: Historia de Medio Siglo*, vol. 2: *Centroamérica, México y el Caribe* (Mexico: Siglo Veintiuno Editores, 1981), pp. 254-55.

6. Three transnational giants dominate the banana and pineapple business in Central America. United Fruit (UFCO), which became United Brands in 1969, ranks second in bananas and third in beef in the U.S. business world; it handles numerous other products as well. Castle and Cooke has Standard Fruit as its subsidiary, carries Dole as its brand name, and is the largest banana and pineapple company in the United States. R. J. Rey-

nolds, the biggest U.S. tobacco company, has the Del Monte subsidiary, which is the most important U.S. producer of canned fruits and vegetables. Its purchase of Nabisco in 1985 makes it the largest food and consumer-products corporation in the United States (Barry, *Roots of Rebellion,* p. 72). See also Ralph Lee Woodward, Jr., *Central America: A Nation Divided* (New York: Oxford University Press, 1985), pp. 177-83.

7. Woodward, *Central America,* p. 181.

8. *Honduras: Pieza Clave de la Política de Estados Unidos en Centro América,* ed. Victor Meza (Tegucigalpa, Hond.: CODEH, 1986), pp. 57-59.

9. Chocano, "Honduras," pp. 146-47.

10. During the 1950s the combined work force of the banana companies was about 70,000; today only half as many workers remain (Barry, *Roots of Rebellion,* p. 73).

11. *Honduras,* p. 58.

12. *Raíces y Perspectivas de la Crisis Economica,* Para Entender Centroamérica, vol. 4, ed. Edelberto Torres-Rivas and Gabriel Aguilera Peralta (San José, Costa Rica: Instituto Centroamericano de Documentación e Investigación Social [ICADIS], 1986), p. 13.

13. *Tugurios* is variously denominated throughout Latin America—*vecindades* in Mexico, *callampos* in Chile, *favelas* in Brazil, *pueblos nuevos* in Peru, and *villas de miseria* in Argentina.

14. Elizabeth Ferris, "The Politics of Asylum" in *Journal of Interamerican Studies and World Affairs* 26 (1984): 357-84.

15. María Eugenia Gallardo and José Roberto López, *Centroamérica: La Crisis en Cifras* (San José, Costa Rica: IICA y FLACSO, 1986), p. 240. Other sources estimate that there are as many as 250,000 refugees in Mexico, 50,000 Salvadorans and Guatemalans in transit to the United States and 100,000 living in Mexican cities, and 100,000 Guatemalan peasants (95 percent Indian), mostly families, near the Mexican-Guatemalan border (Ferris, "The Politics of Asylum," p. 357ff.).

16. The numbers granted political asylum are small: two Salvadorans in 1981, seventy-four in 1982. The immigration policy for Latin American people is restrictive. The president proposed the following numbers for 1983: 64,000—East Asia; 15,000—Soviet Union and East Europe; 3,000—Africa; and 2,000—Latin America. In 1982 congressional testimony claimed that the INS (Immigration and Naturalization Service) was sending back between two and three hundred people daily. All this despite the declaration by the UNHCR in May 1982 that all Salvadorans should be eligible for protection as refugees, since they face personal danger upon returning to their country (P. Weiss Fagen, "Latin American Refugees: Problems of Mass Migration and Mass Asylum," in *From Gunboats to Diplomacy: New U.S. Policies for Latin America,* ed. Richard Newfarmer [Baltimore: Johns Hopkins University Press, 1984], pp. 231-35).

17. For the last few years U.S. administration officials have been warning of a possible flood of refugees if we do not suppress the guerrillas in El Salvador by military force and support the Contras. The statistics cited in the previous note confirm that the flood is already within our gates, though the immigrants are mainly victims of military persecution and economic hardship under the current "democratic" governments of El Salvador and Guatemala.

18. The paragraphs on cotton and cattle-raising and exports use data from the excellent study by Robert Williams entitled *Export Agriculture and the Crisis in Central America,* pp. 31-35, 113-14, 197-98, 204-6.

19. Williams, *Export Agriculture and the Crisis in Central America,* pp. 61-63, 70-73.

20. This description is traceable to Edelberto Torres Rivas, cited in *Revolution and Counter-revolution in Central America and the Caribbean,* ed. Donald E. Schulz and Douglas H. Graham (Boulder, Colo.: Westview Press, 1984), p. 5.

21. Paddock, *We Don't Know How: An Independent Audit of What They Call Success in Foreign Assistance* (Ames, Iowa: Iowa State University Press, 1973), p. 107.

22. William H. Durham, *Scarcity and Survival in Central America: Ecological Origins of the Soccer War* (Stanford: Stanford University Press, 1979), pp. 21, 47.

23. Gallardo and López, *Centroamérica,* pp. 158, 160. See also Barry, *Roots of Rebellion,* pp. 201-5.

24. Woodward, *Central America,* pp. 224-69.

25. Gary W. Wynia, *The Politics of Latin American Development,* 2nd ed. (New York: Cambridge University Press, 1984), pp. 63-70.

26. Torres-Rivas, *América Latina: Historia de Medio Siglo,* p. 162.

27. See Wynia, *The Politics of Latin American Development,* pp. 110-21, for a concise discussion of progressive and conservative versions of modernization. There have been extensive discussions on the various post–World War II "development models." Rather than seeking to cover the entire body of literature, we have selected the work of several authors, including *Promise of Development: Theories of Change in Latin America,* ed. Peter Klaren and Thomas J. Bossert (Boulder, Colo.: Westview Press, 1986); Andre Gunder Frank, *Latin America: Underdevelopment or Revolution* (New York: Monthly Review, 1969); and Howard J. Wiarda and Harvey F. Kline, *Latin American Politics and Development* (Boulder, Colo.: Westview Press, 1979).

28. *Honduras,* pp. 63, 126. The statistical data on the following two pages come from this source.

29. The economic pressures of cheaper goods from the Orient (cars, electronic products, domestic artifacts) have stimulated much the same process in this decade. American workers and their unions are alarmed by

the prospect of U.S. industry relocating in foreign lands in order to take advantage of cheap labor and services.

30. Wiarda and Kline, *Latin American Politics and Development,* pp. 60, 69, 70, 84, 98, 102, 581. See especially p. 501 regarding Costa Rica, p. 514 regarding Nicaragua during the Somoza era, and p. 566 regarding Honduras.

31. Confirmatory figures are given by Barry in *Roots of Rebellion:* "In 1960 . . . the income from the sale of a ton of sugar bought 6.3 tons of oil, and the income from a ton of coffee bought 37.3 tons of fertilizer. By 1982, a ton of sugar bought only 0.7 tons of oil, and a ton of coffee bought only 1.6 tons of fertilizer" (p. 40).

32. Gallardo and López, *Centroamérica,* p. 125.

33. "No 'Instant Solution' to Debt Problem," *Christian Science Monitor,* 19 Mar. 1987, p. 5.

34. Cited in *The External Debt of Latin America* (Washington: Inter-American Development Bank, 1984), p. 3.

35. Wynia, *The Politics of Latin American Development,* pp. 126-31.

36. Frank, *Latin America,* pp. 3-17. The quoted phrase is the title of the first chapter of this book.

37. "An Alternative Policy for Central America and the Caribbean," in *Cuadernos de Pensamiento Propio,* ed. Jabier Gorostiaga (Managua: INIES and CRIES, 1983), pp. 36ff.; and *Raíces y Perspectivas de la Crisis Economica,* pp. 243ff.

38. *Raíces y Perspectivas de la Crisis Economica,* p. 246.

39. *Raíces y Perspectivas de la Crisis Economica,* pp. 36-55.

4. "The Cubans Are Coming! . . . The Cubans Are Coming!"

1. T. D. Allman, *Unmanifest Destiny: American Nationalism in the Third World* (Garden City, N.Y.: Dial Press, 1984), p. 11.

2. Quoted in Allman, *Unmanifest Destiny,* p. 12.

3. Quoted in Raymond Bonner, *Weakness and Deceit: U.S. Policy and El Salvador* (New York: Times Books, 1984), p. 74.

4. An excellent summary of U.S. policy toward Chile at this time is Richard Fagen's "The United States and Chile: Roots and Branches," *Foreign Affairs* 53 (1975): 297-313.

5. Irene O'Malley, "Play It Again, Ron," in *Nicaragua: Unfinished Revolution,* ed. Peter Rosset and John Vandermeer (New York: Grove Press, 1986), p. 155.

6. John A. Booth, *The End and the Beginning: The Nicaraguan Revolution* (Boulder, Colo.: Westview Press, 1982), p. 37.

7. Booth, *The End and the Beginning*, p. 38.

8. Booth, *The End and the Beginning*, p. 39. See also Cole Blasier, *The Hovering Giant: U.S. Responses to Revolutionary Change in Latin America* (Pittsburgh: University of Pittsburgh Press, 1976), p. 320.

9. Montgomery, *Revolution in El Salvador: Origins and Evolution* (Boulder, Colo.: Westview Press, 1982), pp. 48-49.

10. Montgomery, *Revolution in El Salvador*, p. 50.

11. Montgomery, *Revolution in El Salvador*, p. 52.

12. Enrique Baloyra, *El Salvador in Transition* (Chapel Hill: University of North Carolina Press, 1982), pp. 11-12.

13. Gunther, quoted in Allman, *Unmanifest Destiny*, p. 27.

14. Allman, *Unmanifest Destiny*, p. 29; Baloyra, *El Salvador in Transition*, p. 14.

15. Solon L. Barraclough and Arthur L. Domike, "Agrarian Structure in Seven Latin American Countries," in *Agrarian Problems and Peasant Movements in Latin America*, ed. Rodolfo Stavenhagen (Garden City, N.Y.: Doubleday-Anchor, 1970), p. 48.

16. Richard H. Immerman, *The CIA in Guatemala: The Foreign Policy of Intervention* (Austin: University of Texas Press, 1982), pp. 71, 80.

17. Immerman, *The CIA in Guatemala*, p. 88.

18. The formal code name given to the project by the CIA was PBSUCCESS. See Immerman, *The CIA in Guatemala*, p. 138.

19. Immerman, *The CIA in Guatemala*, p. 162. Immerman's account of U.S. intervention in 1954 shows a striking similarity between those events and U.S. actions in Central America today. An important difference, however, is the much broader and more effective opposition to unilateral intervention by Washington throughout the Americas in the 1980s. Anastasio Somoza, whose regime owed so much to U.S. support, was eager to help out with the plan to overthrow Arbenz. Eventually Nicaraguan territory was also used as a place to train the invasion army and as a base from which U.S. pilots could fly the aircraft of Castillo Armas's air force. In this respect Honduras and Nicaragua played the same role in U.S. efforts to overthrow a Guatemalan government in the 1950s that Honduras plays again today with respect to Nicaragua.

20. Brian H. Smith, "U.S.–Latin American Military Relations since World War II: Implications for Human Rights," in *Human Rights and Basic Needs in the Americas*, ed. Margaret E. Crahan (Washington: Georgetown University Press, 1982), p. 266.

21. *The Report of the President's National Bipartisan Commission on Central America* (New York: Macmillan, 1984), p. 11.

22. Smith, "U.S.–Latin American Military Relations since World War II," p. 269.

23. Quoted by James Chase in "Deeper into the Mire," *New York Review of Books*, 1 Mar. 1984, p. 45.

24. Harold Molineu, *U.S. Policy toward Latin America: From Regionalism to Globalism* (Boulder, Colo.: Westview Press, 1986), pp. 15-18.

25. Walter LaFeber, *Inevitable Revolutions: The United States in Central America* (New York: W. W. Norton, 1984), pp. 28-31; and Allman, *Unmanifest Destiny,* pp. 108-44, 270-87.

26. LaFeber, *Inevitable Revolutions,* p. 271.

27. Quoted by Molineu in *U.S. Policy toward Latin America,* p. 40.

28. Fagen, "The United States and Chile," pp. 297-98.

29. Quoted by LaFeber in *Inevitable Revolutions,* p. 271.

30. Quoted by LaFeber in *Inevitable Revolutions,* p. 274.

31. The Santa Fe Document was published by the Council for Inter-American Security based in Washington, D.C. It was authored by L. Francis Bouchey, executive vice-president of the council; Roger Fontaine, a professor at Georgetown University; David C. Jordan, a professor at the University of Virginia; Lt. General Gordon Sumner, Jr. (USA-Ret.); and Lewis Tambs, a professor at Arizona State University.

32. L. Francis Bouchey et al., "A New Inter-American Policy for the Eighties" (Washington: Council for Inter-American Security, 1980), pp. 3, 5.

33. Quoted by Eldon Kenworthy in "Why the United States Is in Central America," *Bulletin of the Atomic Scientist,* Oct. 1983, p. 15.

34. *Report of the President's National Bipartisan Commission on Central America,* p. 12.

35. *Report of the President's National Bipartisan Commission on Central America,* p. 12.

36. *Report of the President's National Bipartisan Commission on Central America,* p. 14.

37. *Report of the President's National Bipartisan Commission on Central America,* p. 26.

38. *Report of the President's National Bipartisan Commission on Central America,* pp. 28-29.

39. *Report of the President's National Bipartisan Commission on Central America,* p. 29.

40. *Report of the President's National Bipartisan Commission on Central America,* p. 26.

41. Quoted by George Black et al., *Garrison Guatemala* (London: Zed Books, 1984), p. 48.

42. For a detailed account of the Contra attack on Ocotal, see "Bitter Witness: Nicaraguans and the 'Covert' War," Witness for Peace Documentation Project (Santa Cruz, Calif.: Oct. 1984), pp. 155-60. One member of the CCCS team visited Ocotal, witnessed the devastation, and heard firsthand accounts of these events about three weeks after the attack occurred.

5. Expanding War and the Search for Peace

1. Compare two headlines in Tegucigalpa newspapers of 6 February 1987: "Contras amplain control de territorio hondureno" (*La Tribuna*, p. 9: "Contras Extend Their Control of Honduran Territory") and "12 comunidades bajo control de 'contras'" (*Tiempo*, p. 15: "Twelve Communities under Control of 'Contras'").

2. *Peace and Justice in Central America*, the report to the 1987 Presbyterian General Assembly by its Task Force on Central America, states, "The contra presence has led to the exodus and internal exile of 15,000 Hondurans from Paraiso Province" (par. 12.546). Honduran journalist Manuel Torres and some others put the number at 10,000.

3. "'Contras' siembran terror en la frontera" (*Tiempo*, 8 Jan. 1987, p. 10: "'Contras' Spread Terror on the Frontier"—i.e., in Paraiso province).

4. *Christian Science Monitor*, 13 May 1987, p. 8.

5. Honduran officials, newspapers, and citizens regularly complain that the United States favors El Salvador at the expense of Honduras.

6. Several members of the CCCS team knew Noel Vargas personally and have spoken with survivors of the attack. The attack itself is described at length in "Bitter Witness: Nicaraguans and the 'Covert' War," Witness for Peace Documentation Project (Santa Cruz, Calif.: Oct. 1984), pp. 66-100.

7. John F. Kennedy, "Foreign Aid Message," quoted by Willard F. Barber and C. Neal Ronning in *Internal Security and Military Power: Counterinsurgency and Civil Action in Latin America* (Columbus: Ohio State University Press, 1966), p. 31. The speech is also discussed by Michael McClintock in *The American Connection*, vol. 1: *State Terror and Popular Resistance in El Salvador* (London: Zed Books, 1985), p. 13; and by Richard Alan White in *The Morass: United States Intervention in Central America* (San Francisco: Harper & Row, 1984), p. 14.

8. *A Compilation of Materials Relating to United States Defense Policies in 1961*, quoted by Barber and Ronning in *Internal Security and Military Power*, p. 180. It should be added that one of the political and psychological activities consists of "civic action" projects; at Palmerola, the CCCS team heard an impressive account of the medical and dental services given at the military base to a group of local residents. Another psychological and ideological activity—the surveillance of religious groups and trends—has recently become increasingly important.

9. Quoted by McClintock in *The American Connection*, vol. 1, p. 14.

10. See, for example, Peter H. Smith, "Origins of the Crisis," in *Confronting Revolution: Security through Diplomacy in Central America*, ed. Morris J. Blachman, William M. LeoGrande, and Kenneth Sharpe (New York: Pantheon, 1986), pp. 13-17; Thomas P. Anderson, "The Roots of Revolution in Central America," in *Rift and Revolution: The Central American*

Imbroglio, ed. Howard J. Wiarda (Washington: American Enterprise Institute for Public Policy Research, 1984), p. 110; Walter LaFeber, *Inevitable Revolutions: The United States in Central America* (New York: W.W. Norton, 1984), pp. 106-26, 201-4; and Edelberto Torres-Rivas, *Interpretación del Desarrollo Social Centroamericano,* 7th ed. (San José, Costa Rica: EDUCA, 1981), pp. 149-230.

11. Millett, "Praetorians or Patriots? The Central American Military," in *Central America: Anatomy of Conflict,* ed. Robert S. Leiken (New York: Pergamon Press, 1984), p. 70.

12. Johnson, *The Military and Society in Latin America* (Stanford: Stanford University Press, 1964), p. 37.

13. Johnson, quoted by Ron Seckinger in "The Central American Militaries: A Survey of the Literature," *Latin American Research Review* 16 (1981): 249. Cf. Jim Handy, "Resurgent Democracy and the Guatemalan Military," *Journal of Latin American Studies,* Nov. 1986, pp. 383-408.

14. Millett, "Praetorians or Patriots?" p. 77.

15. Anderson, "The Roots of Revolution in Central America," p. 110.

16. For more details on the consequences of militarism in such countries as Guatemala, see Daniel L. Presso, "Political Assassination in Guatemala: A Case of Institutionalized Terror," *Journal of Inter-American Studies and World Affairs,* Nov. 1981, pp. 429-56; "Guatemala: A Government Program of Political Murder," *Amnesty International,* Feb. 1981; and "Guatemala: The Roots of Revolution," *Special Update,* Washington Office on Latin America, Feb. 1983.

17. LaFeber, *Inevitable Revolutions,* p. 99.

18. LaFeber, *Inevitable Revolutions,* p. 99.

19. Given the historical background just sketched, describing Costa Rica as a successful model of "democratic capitalism," as Michael Novak and others do, hardly seems to fit the reality of the Costa Rican experience.

20. Col. John D. Waghelstein, "Post-Vietnam Counterinsurgency Doctrine," *Military Review,* May 1985, pp. 42-49.

21. A definitive article is "Low-Intensity Conflict: An Operational Perspective" by Maj. Gen. Donald R. Morelli and Maj. Michael M. Ferguson, *Military Review,* Nov. 1984, pp. 2-15. A six-month study by civilian and military experts produced a 1,000-page-long *Joint Low-Intensity Conflict Project/Final Report.*

22. Miles, "The Real War: Low Intensity Conflict in Central America," *NACLA Report on the Americas,* Apr./May 1986, p. 25.

23. Waghelstein, "Post-Vietnam Counterinsurgency Doctrine," p. 42.

24. Waghelstein, "Post-Vietnam Counterinsurgency Doctrine," p. 42.

25. Sarkesian, "Low-Intensity Conflict: Concepts, Principles, and Policy Guidelines," *Air University Review,* Jan./Feb. 1985, pp. 7, 9.

26. Morelli and Ferguson, "Low-Intensity Conflict," p. 7.

27. Col. James B. Motley, "A Perspective on Low-Intensity Conflict," *Military Review,* Jan. 1985, p. 7.

28. Machiavelli et al., *The Prince and the Discourses,* trans. Luigi Ricci (New York: Random House, 1950), p. 45.

29. Dickey, *With the Contras: A Reporter in the Wilds of Nicaragua* (New York: Touchstone Books, 1987), p. 12.

30. White, *The Morass,* p. 35.

31. Kelly, in *Special Operations in U.S. Strategy,* ed. Frank R. Barnett et al. (Washington: National Defense University Press, 1984), p. 223.

32. Sarkesian, "Low-Intensity Conflict," p. 21.

33. Machiavelli, *The Prince,* p. 65.

34. *The Imposition of Economic Sanctions and a Trade Embargo against Nicaragua* (Washington: U.S. Government Printing Office, 1985), p. 97.

35. Smith, "Dateline Havana," *Foreign Policy,* Fall 1982, p. 161. A retired U.S. career diplomat, Smith served in Cuba from 1958 to 1961, was director of the State Department's Office of Cuban Affairs from 1977 to 1979, and was chief of the U.S. interests section in Havana from 1979 to 1982.

36. Peter Kornbluh, "The Covert War," in *Reagan versus the Sandinistas: The Undeclared War on Nicaragua,* ed. Thomas W. Walker (Boulder, Colo.: Westview Press, 1987), p. 24.

37. Smith, "Dateline Havana," p. 161.

38. Edgar Chamorro, testimony submitted to the International Court of Justice, 5 Sept. 1985. Cf. also Edgar Chamorro and Jefferson Morley, "Confessions of a 'Contra,'" *New Republic,* 5 Aug. 1985, pp. 18-23; and E. Bradford Burns, *At War in Nicaragua: The Reagan Doctrine and the Politics of Nostalgia* (San Francisco: Harper & Row, 1987), p. 53.

39. Markey, quoted by Burns in *At War in Nicaragua,* p. 38.

40. Borge, quoted by Wayne S. Smith in "Lies about Nicaragua," *Foreign Policy,* Summer 1987, p. 89. Smith says the State Department white paper "shamelessly misrepresents what Borge said." A forceful statement of the Reagan administration's view can be found in Nestor Sanchez's "The Communist Threat," *Foreign Policy,* Fall 1983, pp. 43-50. Sanchez quotes a statement of the House Permanent Select Committee on Intelligence dated 13 May 1983. However, no evidence is offered to back up the statement.

41. See the fascinating account provided by Cole Blasier in *The Hovering Giant: U.S. Responses to Revolutionary Change in Latin America* (Pittsburgh: University of Pittsburgh Press, 1976), pp. 90-100, 177-210.

42. William M. LeoGrande, "Rollback or Containment: The United States, Nicaragua, and the Search for Peace in Central America," *International Security,* Fall 1986, p. 95.

43. "Contadora: A Text for Peace," *International Policy Report* (Washington: Center for International Policy, Nov. 1984), p. 1.

44. For an excellent review of U.S. concerns, see Nina M. Serrafino, "The Contadora Initiative: Implications for Congress," Congressional Research Service Issue Brief, 28 Oct. 1986, pp. 3-4.

45. Shultz, quoted by William Goodfellow in "The Diplomatic Front," in *Reagan versus the Sandinistas,* p. 149.

46. Betancur, quoted by Burns in *At War,* p. 105.

47. LeoGrande, "Rollback or Containment," p. 114.

48. Jim Morrell and William Goodfellow, "Contadora: Under the Gun," *International Policy Report* (Washington: Center for International Policy, May 1986), p. 5.

49. Bob Levin, "Sabotage and Failure," *Maclean's,* 23 Feb. 1987, p. 25.

50. "Getting to the Table: The Arias Plan and the Central American Summit," *Central American Historical Institute Update,* 31 July 1987, p. 6.

51. Shultz, quoted by Susan Bennett in "$270 Million to Be Requested for Contras, Shultz Testifies," *Fort Worth Star Telegram,* 16 Sept. 1987.

6. They Cry "Democracy, Democracy!" But There Is No Democracy

1. *Department of State Bulletin,* Apr. 1986, p. 65.

2. All of the information in this paragraph is taken from an extended briefing given on 19 Jan. 1987 by Prof. Edelberto Torres-Rivas, a CCCS project consultant, and his staff at the Latin American Faculty of Social Sciences (FLACSO) in San José, Costa Rica.

3. The Latin American Catholic Church is not a unified whole. It is fractured both vertically and horizontally by theological and ideological fissures. One can find at least four strands within Latin American Catholicism: the hierarchical church, the charismatic movement, popular religiosity, and the so-called "church of the poor." Although these four strands are not mutually exclusive, they are distinct enough to require careful nuancing when one is referring to the Catholic Church.

4. *The Documents of Vatican II,* ed. Walter M. Abbott (New York: Association Press, 1966), p. 285; see also pp. 233, 272.

5. Second General Conference of Latin American Bishops, *The Church in the Present-Day Transformation of Latin America in the Light of the Council,* ed. Louis Michael Colonnese (Bogotá, Col.: General Secretariat of CELAM, 1973), sec. 2, par. 14.

6. *The Church in the Present-Day Transformation of Latin America in the Light of the Council,* sec. 14, par. 9.

7. *The Church in the Present-Day Transformation of Latin America in the Light of the Council,* sec. 15, par. 10.

8. *Puebla and Beyond,* ed. John Eagleson and Philip Scharper (Maryknoll, N.Y.: Orbis Books, 1979), par. 641.

9. *Puebla and Beyond,* pars. 1160-63.

10. The first-known CEBs appeared in Brazil in 1956. According to information that we gleaned in our interviews and have gathered from mimeographed publications, the CEBs started in Panama City in 1963, in Managua in 1966, and in San Salvador in 1968. Cf. Pablo Richard, "The Church of the Poor in Nicaragua" (San José, Costa Rica: DEI, July 1979); and the Oct.-Dec. 1986 issue of *Informaciones* (published by Honduran Delegates of the Word) entitled "III Asamblea de Comunidades Eclesiales de Base de la Arquidiocesis de San Salvador." See also the article by José Marins in *International Review of Mission,* vol. 68, no. 271, pp. 237-38.

11. For a more complete treatment of this phenomenon, see Pablo Richard, *The Church Born by the Force of God in Central America* (New York: Circus Publications, 1985), pp. 18-25.

12. Montgomery, "Christianity as a Subversive Activity in Central America," in *Central America: Anatomy of Conflict,* ed. Robert S. Leiken (New York: Pergamon Press, 1983), pp. 139-77.

13. "Final Document: III Assembly of CEBs in the Archdiocese of San Salvador." Cf. also Mons. Luis Alfonso Santos, Bishop of Santa Rosa de Copan, Honduras, "La celebracion de la Palabra de Dios y la proyección social de la iglesia católica hondureña," from a 21 Nov. 1986 radio address in *Informaciones,* Oct.-Dec. 1986, p. 9.

14. Marcello de C. Azevedo, "Basic Ecclesial Communities: A Meeting Point of Ecclesiologies," *Theological Studies,* no. 46, 1985, pp. 612-13.

15. Montgomery, "Christianity as a Subversive Activity in Central America," pp. 139-77.

16. Romero, *Voice of the Voiceless: The Four Pastoral Letters and Other Statements,* trans. Michael J. Walsh (Maryknoll, N.Y.: Orbis Books, 1985), pp. 90, 91.

17. T. S. Montgomery, *Revolution in El Salvador: Origins and Evolution* (Boulder, Colo.: Westview Press, 1982), pp. 130-42.

18. Luis Serra, "The Sandinista Mass Organizations," in *Nicaragua in Revolution,* ed. Thomas W. Walker (New York: Praeger, 1982), pp. 95-113; and *The Nicaragua Reader: Documents of a Revolution under Fire,* ed. Peter Rosset and John Vandermeer (New York: Grove Press, 1983), especially Part IV.

19. Shaull, *Heralds of a New Reformation: The Poor of South and North America* (Maryknoll, N.Y.: Orbis Books, 1984).

20. Leonardo Boff, *Ecclesiogenesis: The Base Communities Reinvent the Church,* trans. Robert Barr (Maryknoll, N.Y.: Orbis Books, 1986). See

also Pablo Richard, *The Church Born by the Force of God in Central America.*

21. "Religion and Revolution: A Protestant Voice," in *Guatemala in Rebellion: Unfinished History,* ed. Jonathan L. Fried and Marvin Gettlemen (New York: Grove Press, 1983), pp. 230-31.

22. Constantinianism is a name for the ideology that upholds Christendom, the religious system that gave cohesion to church and society during the Middle Ages. It developed after the recognition of Christianity by Constantine the Great and his successors in the fourth and fifth centuries. Constantinianism is a powerful "top-down" and absolutist religious and political worldview that dominated the West until well into the twentieth century. The militant religion of the Spanish *conquistadores* mirrored earlier expressions of Constantinianism (during the last centuries of the Roman Empire and on into the Middle Ages). Its instruments were the cross and the sword. Wherever the Constantinian mind-set has deluded Christian movements, it continues to be authoritarian—an ideology of death. During a millennium and a half, countless dissident sects vigorously protested this radical distortion of Christianity and were branded heretical, driven underground, and often destroyed—until the very eve of the Reformation. For a treatment of Constantinianism in relation to North and Latin America, see Shaull, *Heralds of a New Reformation,* pp. 58-75. For a discussion of the ideological components of Constantinianism, see also Alistair Kee, *Constantine versus Christ: The Triumph of Ideology* (London: SCM Press, 1982).

23. For more information on the dissident Protestant groups in the sixteenth and seventeenth centuries, see the following sources: F. H. Littell, *The Origins of Sectarian Protestantism* (New York: Macmillan, 1964); Leonard Verduin, *The Reformers and Their Stepchildren* (Grand Rapids: Eerdmans, 1964); and G. H. Williams, *The Radical Reformation* (Philadelphia: Westminster Press, 1962).

24. The formal expression of this principle is *ecclesia reformata semper reformanda est,* "the church reformed is always being reformed."

25. John Dillenberger and Claude Welch, *Protestant Christianity—Interpreted through Its Development* (New York: Scribner's, 1954), pp. 313-14.

26. Dillenberger and Welch, *Protestant Christianity,* pp. 325-26.

27. For further information on the Protestant movement during the English Revolution, see Christopher Hill, *The World Turned Upside Down: Radical Ideas during the English Revolution* (New York: Penguin Books, 1972); and Michael Walzer, *The Revolution of the Saints: A Study in the Origins of Radical Politics* (New York: Atheneum, 1976).

28. Writing on the subject of the place of every Christian in the body of Christ, John Calvin says, "None of the brethren can be injured, despised, rejected, abused, or in any way offended by us, without at the same time,

injuring, despising, and abusing Christ by the wrongs we do; that we cannot disagree with our brethren without at the same time disagreeing with Christ; that we cannot love Christ without loving him in the brethren; that we ought to take the same care of our brethren's bodies as we take of our own, for they are members of our body; and that, as no part of our body is touched by any feeling of pain which is not spread among all the rest, so we ought not to allow a brother to be affected by any evil, without being touched with compassion for him" (*Institutes of the Christian Religion*, 4.17.38).

29. Azevedo, "Basic Ecclesial Communities," p. 613.

7. When Jubilee and Kingdom Embrace

1. Cf. Thomas Hanks, *For God So Loved the Third World* (Maryknoll, N.Y.: Orbis Books, 1983), esp. pp. 97-105.

2. Mesters, "The Use of the Bible in Christian Communities of the Common People," in *The Challenge of Basic Christian Communities*, ed. Sergio Torres and John Eagleson (Maryknoll, N.Y.: Orbis Books, 1981), p. 203. The quotation should not be read as if it intended to deny the historical reality of the biblical narrative ("Abraham is us") or the necessity and validity of careful biblical exegesis.

3. The story of the Solentiname community has often been told. See, for example, Phillip Berryman, *The Religious Roots of Rebellion: Christians in Central American Revolutions* (Maryknoll, N.Y.: Orbis Books, 1984), pp. 7-24. These tape-recorded Bible studies are collected in four volumes entitled *The Gospel in Solentiname*, ed. Ernesto Cardenal, trans. Donald Walsh (Maryknoll, N.Y.: Orbis Books, 1976-82).

4. *The Gospel in Solentiname*, 1:147ff.

5. *The Gospel in Solentiname*, 1:61; 2:6; 4:229; 1:77-79.

6. *The Gospel in Solentiname*, 1:196.

7. Cf. Guillermo Cook, *The Expectation of the Poor: Latin American Base Ecclesial Communities in Protestant Perspective* (Maryknoll, N.Y.: Orbis Books, 1985), p. 71.

8. The terms "evangelical" and "Protestant" are used here interchangeably. In Central America all Protestants are called *evangelicos*, whatever their theological beliefs and church affiliation. It is important to keep in mind that although Central American and North American evangelicals have much in common, they are not identical.

9. Following are the percentage of Protestants per total population: Guatemala, 29.6 percent; Costa Rica, 17 percent; El Salvador, 9.7 percent; Nicaragua, 17.2 percent; Honduras, 11 percent (source: IMDELA, San José, Costa Rica). Projecting the present rate of growth into the future, it is estimated that by the year 2020, 60 percent of Central America, including Belize and Panama, will be Protestant.

10. The first Protestants to land on Central American soil were

marooned pirates. They were tried, and the more fortunate were deported by the Holy Inquisition. Protestants most of them, "they looked upon the plundering of the Spanish [galleons] as almost a Holy War," notes Wilton Nelson in *Protestantism in Central America* (Grand Rapids: Eerdmans, 1984), p. 21. The author quotes an Anglican priest who chronicled the early history of the Caribbean coast of Central America. See also Virgilio Zapata, *Historia de la iglesia evangelica en Guatemala* (Guatemala City: Genesis Publicidad, 1982), pp. 25-42.

11. Cited by John Stam in "Missions and U.S. Foreign Policy: A Case Study from the 1920s," *Evangelical Missions Quarterly,* Oct. 1979, pp. 170, 172.

12. Cited by John Stam in "Missions and U.S. Foreign Policy," pp. 173-74.

13. Irene Foulkes, "Protestant Churches and Social Change in Central America," unpublished paper, Latin American Biblical Seminary, San José, Costa Rica, 1987, p. 10.

14. Foulkes, "Protestant Churches and Social Change in Central America," p. 9.

15. Assmann, *La Iglesia Electronica y su Impacto en America Latina* (San José, Costa Rica: DEI, 1987), pp. 128-29.

16. Cook, *The Expectation of the Poor,* pp. 148-54.

17. Foulkes, "Protestant Churches and Social Change in Central America," pp. 10-11.

18. Although there are some profound contradictions in his personal philosophy, Rios-Montt followed it with remarkable consistency during his sixteen months in office. An estimated 17,000 persons were tortured and killed or disappeared. Pastors and missionaries were picked up by plain-clothesmen or fled into exile. Rios-Montt instituted special tribunals for subversives and refused to grant clemency even to a young evangelical leader; he was instead executed by a firing squad. But Rios-Montt also affirmed the spiritual in his weekly TV homilies. Spiritual values are in fact primary, he insisted.

19. Assmann, *La Iglesia Electronica y su Impacto en America Latina.* See also "El Evangelio y la Religion Electronica," ed. Plutardo Bonilla, *Pastoralia,* July 1987, pp. 39-54, 139-61.

20. This information was given to us by a Protestant Indian pastor who works with evangelical and ecumenical base communities in Guatemala.

21. "Religion and Revolution: A Protestant Voice," in *Guatemala in Rebellion: Unfinished History,* ed. Jonathan L. Fried and Marvin Gettleman (New York: Grove Press, 1983), pp. 230-31.

22. "Religion and Revolution: A Protestant Voice," p. 231.

23. Hill, *The World Turned Upside Down: Radical Ideas during the English Revolution* (New York: Penguin Books, 1972), pp. 386-87.

24. Note the updating on the topic of "spirituality" that takes place as Gustavo Gutiérrez moves from his earlier work, *A Theology of Liberation* (1973), to his later work, *We Drink from Our Own Wells: The Spiritual Journey of a People* (1984).

25. Bonhoeffer, *Letters and Papers from Prison*, ed. Eberhard Bethge (New York: Macmillan, 1971), p. 17.

26. Richard, "The Church of the Poor within the Popular Movement *(Movimiento Popular)*," pp. 13-14, in *La Iglesia Popular: Between Fear and Hope*, ed. Leonardo Boff and Virgil Elizondo (Edinburgh: T. & T. Clark, 1984).

27. Tamez, *Bible of the Oppressed*, trans. Matthew J. O'Connell (Maryknoll, N.Y.: Orbis Books, 1982), pp. 73, 1-2, 74. For a similar study, see Thomas Hanks, *For God So Loved the Third World* (Maryknoll, N.Y.: Orbis Books, 1983).

28. Tamez, *Bible of the Oppressed*, p. 37.

29. Cf. Ronald Wallace, *Calvin's Doctrine of the Christian Life* (Grand Rapids: Eerdmans, 1959), pp. 148-52.

30. Kuyper, *Christianity and the Class Struggle* (Grand Rapids: Piet Hein, 1950), pp. 27-28.

31. *Church Dogmatics,* 2/1:386.

32. Sobrino, "Poverty Means Death to the Poor," *Cross Currents,* vol. 36, no. 3, pp. 267-69. Commenting on the biblical view of creation, Sobrino adds, "We are interested in eschatology, but our problem is not eschatology—it's *protology.* Do you know what that means? What is at the beginning. Of course we hope and work for the new creation. But our problem is creation itself. Is this type of life and death God's creation?" (p. 268).

33. Sobrino, "Poverty Means Death to the Poor," p. 268.

34. Sobrino and Pico, "Bearing with One Another in Faith" / "Solidarity with the Poor and the Unity of the Church," in *Theology of Christian Solidarity* (Maryknoll, N.Y.: Orbis Books, 1985), p. 96.

35. Núñez, *Liberation Theology* (Chicago: Moody Press, 1985), p. 140.

36. Among the troublesome points in liberation theology are the following. First, there is the acceptance of an evolutionary, dialectical view of reality in which an ultimate antithesis is pushed back into the very fabric of creation from the beginning. Good and evil then become necessary and essential components of all world history (cf. Juan Luis Segundo, *Evolution and Guilt,* trans. John Drury [Maryknoll, N.Y.: Orbis Books, 1974]). Life then remains unredeemable, and the cause of liberation becomes a vain hope. Second, there is another view, closely related to the first, that regards creation as the first act of salvation (cf. Gustavo Gutiérrez, *A Theology of Liberation* [Maryknoll, N.Y.: Orbis Books, 1973], pp. 154ff.). Although God reveals himself in Scripture as both Creator and Redeemer, this does not warrant departing from the biblical story-line of creation, fall, and re-

demption as ongoing turning points in world history. For departing from this view also casts a heavy cloud of uncertainty over the possibilities for real liberation. Both of these positions obscure the blessings that come with the biblical doctrine of the good creation, and with it, the realistic hope for the restoration of justice, liberation, and peace. Third, there is the tendency to allow history to serve as a second source of revelation. Analysis of the so-cial-economic-political situation begins to assume the role of a second canonical "text," alongside the "text" of Scripture. Exegesis then becomes an oscillating movement between these two "texts"—the Bible and praxis (cf. Segundo, *Evolution and Guilt,* pp. 6-10). Scripture must indeed be read within our historical context. But history itself is never normative. For other-wise the spectre arises of some form of historical determinism, which also paralyzes all serious efforts at true liberation.

37. Archbishop Oscar Romero, *Voice of the Voiceless: The Four Pastoral Letters and Other Statements,* trans. Michael J. Walsh (Maryknoll, N.Y.: Orbis Books, 1985), p. 181.

38. Brown, "Liberation Theology: Paralyzing Threat or Creative Challenge?" in *Liberation Theologies in North America and Europe,* Mission Trends no. 4, ed. Gerald H. Anderson and Thomas F. Stransky (Grand Rapids: Eerdmans, 1979), p. 11.

39. Gutiérrez, *A Theology of Liberation,* pp. 63-72.

40. Gutiérrez, *We Drink from Our Own Wells,* trans. Matthew J. O'Connell (Maryknoll, N.Y.: Orbis Books, 1984), pp. 65-71. The view of man set forth by Gutiérrez is strongly reminiscent of G. C. Berkouwer's view in "The Whole Man," chap. 6 of *Man: The Image of God* (Grand Rapids: Eerdmans, 1958).

41. Cf. the essays in *La Iglesia Popular.*

42. Míguez Bonino, *Doing Theology in a Revolutionary Situation* (Philadelphia: Fortress Press, 1975), pp. 86-104.

43. Míguez Bonino, *Christians and Marxists: The Mutual Challenge to Revolution* (Grand Rapids: Eerdmans, 1976), pp. 93, 118-19.

44. Arias, *Announcing the Reign of God: Evangelization and the Subversive Memory of Jesus* (Philadelphia: Fortress Press, 1984), p. 66.

Selected Book List
for Further Reading

History and Society

Barry, Tom. *Roots of Rebellion: Land and Hunger in Central America*. Boston: South End Press, 1987.

Berryman, Phillip. *Inside Central America*. New York: Pantheon Books, 1985.

Burns, E. Bradford. *At War in Nicaragua: The Reagan Doctrine and the Politics of Nostalgia*. San Francisco: Harper & Row, 1987.

Child, Jack, ed. *Conflict in Central America: Approaches to Peace and Security*. London: C. Hurst, 1986.

Dilling, Yvonne, with Ingrid Rogers. *In Search of Refuge*. Scottdale, Pa.: Herald Press, 1984.

Kinzer, Stephen, and Stephen Schlesinger. *Bitter Fruit: The Untold Story of the American Coup in Guatemala*. London: Sinclair Brown, 1982.

LaFeber, Walter. *Inevitable Revolutions: The United States in Central America*. New York: W. W. Norton, 1984.

Millett, Richard. *Guardians of the Dynasty: A History of the U.S. Created Guardia Nacional De Nicaragua and the Somoza Family*. Maryknoll, N.Y.: Orbis Books, 1977.

Nelson-Pallmeyer, Jack. *The Politics of Compassion: A Biblical Perspective on World Hunger, the Arms Race and U.S. Policy in Central America*. Maryknoll, N.Y.: Orbis Books, 1986.

Woodward, Ralph Lee, Jr. *Central America: A Nation Divided*. 2nd ed. New York: Oxford University Press, 1985.

Church and Theology

Arias, Mortimer. *Announcing the Reign of God: Evangelization and the Subversive Memory of Jesus*. Philadelphia: Fortress Press, 1984.

Belli, Humberto. *Breaking Faith: The Sandinista Revolution and Its Impact on Freedom and the Christian Faith in Nicaragua.* Westchester, Ill.: Crossway Books, 1985.

Berryman, Phillip. *The Religious Roots of Rebellion: Christians in Central American Revolutions.* Maryknoll, N.Y.: Orbis Books, 1984.

Cleary, Edward. *Crisis and Change: The Church in Latin America Today.* Maryknoll, N.Y.: Orbis Books, 1984.

Gutiérrez, Gustavo. *We Drink from Our Own Wells: The Spiritual Journey of a People.* Trans. Matthew J. O'Connell. Maryknoll, N.Y.: Orbis Books, 1984.

Núñez, Emilio. *Liberation Theology.* Chicago: Moody Press, 1985.

Richard, Pablo. *The Church Born by the Force of God in Central America.* New York: Circus Publications, 1985.

Romero, Oscar. *A Martyr's Message of Hope: Six Homilies by Archbishop Oscar Romero.* Kansas City: Celebration Books, 1981.

Shaull, Richard. *Heralds of a New Reformation: The Poor of South and North America.* Maryknoll, N.Y.: Orbis Books, 1984.

Tamez, Elsa. *Bible of the Oppressed.* Trans. Matthew J. O'Connell. Maryknoll, N.Y.: Orbis Books, 1982.

Glossary of Terms

Alliance for Progress: an aid program for Latin America launched in 1961 by the Kennedy administration in response to the Cuban revolution

Arias Peace Plan: a proposal for a negotiated settlement of Central American conflicts initiated by President Oscar Arias of Costa Rica and signed by the presidents of all Central American countries in August 1987

Bolsheviks: a term used in the United States in the first half of the twentieth century to refer to movements and peoples allegedly influenced by or associated with Russian and Soviet communism

Campesinos: small-scale peasant farmers

Caudillismo: a highly personalist and often demagogic style of leadership, common to Central America's past history and typically associated with military figures

CEBs (Comunidades Eclesiales de Base or Ecclesial Base Communities): a movement of mostly Catholic grass-roots congregations among the poor in Latin America

Central American Common Market (CACM in English, MCCA in Spanish): an attempt made by the Central American nations in the 1960s to promote regional trade and economic cooperation, similar to the European Economic Community

Central American Labor Council (COCA): an organization spearheaded by the small Guatemalan Communist Party that from 1925 to 1930 promoted union organizing and communist propaganda

Central Intelligence Agency (CIA): an agency of the U.S. government that functions nominally under the oversight of the National Security Council, having as its principal functions spying, counterintelligence operations, and other clandestine activities

Christendom: a term describing the religious world of the nations of Europe and their colonies from the fourth century onward, after Rome made Christianity the official religion of the empire

Christian Democratic Party: a political party of Catholic inspiration that in recent years has elected candidates to the presidency of Guatemala and El Salvador

Church of the poor: a phrase attributed to Pope John XXIII that in Central America is used to encompass groups such as the CEBs, the Delegates of the Word, Christians involved in popular organizations, middle-class priests, sisters, and religious who identify with the struggles of the poor

Comadres: the Committee of Mothers working in El Salvador, the full name of which is the Committee of Mothers and Relatives of Prisoners, Disappeared, and Politically Assassinated.

Committee of Santa Fe: an informal group of advisors that prepared position papers on Latin America for the Republican Party's 1980 presidential campaign, papers that defined Latin America as an important East-West issue

Communism: a political, economic, and social view of society based on the public ownership of land and capital and centralized state administration. In common discourse the word refers to the system of government found in the Soviet Union and China.

Conquistadores: Spaniards who conquered Latin America in the name of the Spanish crown

Conservative Parties: political parties rooted primarily in the landed elites who forged strong alliances with the Catholic Church and resisted modernization

Contadora Peace Initiative: a peace process initiated in early 1983 by four Latin American countries—Mexico, Panama, Colombia, and Venezuela—aimed at creating conditions for a negotiated settlement of conflicts in Central America

Contras: an abbreviated term used throughout Central America to describe the array of Nicaraguan exiles fighting the Sandinista government. The Contras are an instrument of LIC warfare in Central America.

Delegates of the Word (Delegados de la Palabra): a widespread movement of lay leaders that parallels and supports the Ecclesial Base Communities in Central America

Economic Commission on Latin America (ECLA): a United Nations agency established in 1948 to analyze the economies of Latin America and to make policy recommendations from a Latin American regional perspective

Encomienda: an early Spanish institution in Central America whereby Spanish colonists appropriated Native American labor and tribute

Evangelization: a current full-orbed view of the mission of the church in Latin America, calling not only for personal conversion but also for the renewal of unjust social structures

FML-FDR (Farabundo Martí Liberation Front and Democratic Revolutionary Front): a complex of five military and political organizations of the moderate and extreme left in El Salvador

FSLN (Sandinista Front for National Liberation): the dominant party in Nicaragua

Good Neighbor Policy: a foreign policy toward Latin America initiated by President Franklin Roosevelt that foreswore direct U.S. intervention in Latin affairs

Inter-American Development Bank (IADB): a banking institution created largely by the United States in 1961 to administer U.S. development loans to Latin American countries and thereby foster internal economic and social reforms favored by the U.S. government

International Monetary Fund (IMF): a specialized agency of the United Nations that was established in the 1940s to promote international economic growth and stability, especially by granting loans to meet debt repayment schedules and to regulate international exchange rates

Liberal Parties: political movements in Central America that were originally anticlerical, favored free trade, and promoted modernization through foreign investment

Liberation: a Latin American concept that functions not as an Enlightenment idea expressing human autonomy or as an expression of Marxist ideologies but primarily as an equivalent of the biblically based ideas of salvation, redemption, and the restoration of God-given human rights

Liberation Theology: a theological movement emerging out of Latin America in the wake of Vatican II (1962-1965) and the Medellín Council (1968) oriented strongly to the reality of poverty in the Southern world

Low-Intensity Conflict: a doctrine of warfare applied primarily in Third World regions, such as Central America, where fighting is done by local proxy armies and the war is aimed at the entire grassroots population

Manifest Destiny: a doctrine used widely in the nineteenth and early twentieth centuries to justify U.S. expansion, first westward and later into the Third World

Marxism: a term associated historically with the thought and writings of Karl Marx, a German intellectual who lived in the nineteenth century. Marxism refers to a particular political ideology, a program for social revolution, and an analysis of societal relationships based on economic differentiations.

Matanza (literally "The Massacre"): the brutal repression of a peasant uprising in El Salvador in 1932, ending in the slaughter of up to 30,000 people, mainly Native Indians

Medellín: the Second Latin American Conference of Bishops, held in Medellín, Colombia, in 1968

Mestizo: the Spanish word for someone of mixed Amerindian and European—especially Spanish—heritage

Minifundia: a land-tenure pattern based largely on the ownership and use of small plots of land

Military Assistance Program (MAP): an arm of the U.S. foreign-aid program that was begun in the early 1950s in order to furnish military supplies and training to foreign governments, the Latin American MAP being designed to bolster hemispheric defense against outside attack and to strengthen internal security and counterinsurgency forces

Miskitos: a term referring to several minority groups living in eastern Nicaragua, especially the Miskitu, Sumu, and Rama Amerindians and Creoles of African and Amerindian descent, who together represent about 5 percent of the population of Nicaragua

Monroe Doctrine: a presidential declaration of 1823 warning European powers against further colonization in the New World, later used to justify frequent U.S. intervention in Latin America

National Bipartisan Commission on Central America: a commission created by President Reagan in the spring of 1983 to make recommendations on U.S. policy toward Central America

National Guard: a rural police force organized in El Salvador and Nicaragua, but later a major security force in El Salvador and the sole armed force in Nicaragua under Somoza rule

National Security States: regimes run directly or indirectly by the military that tend to emphasize national security at the expense of the freedoms of the citizenry, usually resulting in widespread violations of human rights

North Americans: a term that refers technically to residents of Mexico, Canada, and the United States, but is used in Central America almost exclusively to refer to citizens of the United States

Oligarchy: a form of government in which power is restricted to a few, referring in Central America to the small number of families that control large portions of land, wealth, and power

Operation Success: a name given to the CIA operation that led to the overthrow of the Arbenz government in Guatemala in 1954

Organization of American States (OAS): a regional treaty organization set up in 1948 to promote cooperation and security among the nations of the Western Hemisphere

Popular organizations: broadly based groups of peasant and labor unions, religious groups, and political parties representing the interests of the masses in Central America

Puebla: the Third Latin American Conference of Bishops, held in Puebla, Mexico, in 1979.

Reformational: a worldview based upon the societal principles of the Reformation held in common by Christians from various traditions

Second Vatican Council: the worldwide meeting of Roman Catholic bishops in Rome (1962-1965), convened by Pope John XXIII and continued under Pope Paul VI, dealing with church renewal, closer relations with non-Catholics, and the problems of the modern world

United Fruit Company (UFCO, now known as United Brands): a powerful U.S. multinational corporation, formed in 1899, that for most of the twentieth century used its dominance of Central American fruit exports, especially bananas, to exert considerable influence in internal Central American affairs

United States Agency for International Development (US-AID): a semi-independent agency within the State Department that directs economic and technical assistance programs, provides political advice to the president regarding foreign affairs, and assists foreign counterinsurgency policies through civic action projects and aid to local security forces

Voluntarism: a movement arising out of the Reformation, granting people the right to free choice in their religious and other affiliations